More Praise for Jessica Maxwell's

Roll Around Heaven

"After you've been there and done that, it's time to figure out what it all means. Jessica Maxwell applies her deceptively light touch to the idea of spiritual seeking. Highly recommended."

—**TIM CAHILL**, author of *Hold the Enlightenment* and *Lost in My Own Backyard*

"Seasoned travel and adventure writer Maxwell has penned an irresistible combination memoir, travelogue, and soul-searching odyssey. Readers who enjoyed *Eat, Pray, Love* will hop aboard and enjoy every minute of this rollicking spiritual ride. An inspirational feast for the faithful and enlightening food for thought for the more cynical."

—**MARGARET FLANAGAN**, *Booklist*

"Successful magazine travel writer Maxwell didn't intend to write a book about spirituality. The author of books on golf, fishing and other nature adventures claimed an "allergy to religion," yet spirituality seemed to find her anyway. After stumbling upon a lovable pig farmer/spiritual teacher, the self-proclaimed spiritual klutz finds herself wading through adventures with auras, demons, psychics, and Jesus. In this book, Maxwell catalogues sixteen years of spiritual experiences. The reader is taken through her quest for peace and understanding as she discovers that, regardless of the path, all religions call for loving others. Her training as a nature writer allows her to see an experience from the outside in a way inward-looking spiritual writers often cannot. Her cheeky-to-chaste style is both conversational and controlled. Readers will enjoy watching this "former spiritual dodo-brain" discover beauty beyond nature."

—*Publishers Weekly*

ROLL AROUND HEAVEN

an all-true
accidental spiritual
adventure

jessica maxwell

ATRIA PAPERBACK
New York London Toronto Sydney

BEYOND WORDS
Hillsboro, Oregon

ATRIA PAPERBACK
A Division of Simon & Schuster, Inc.
1230 Avenue of the Americas
New York, NY 10020

BEYOND WORDS
20827 N.W. Cornell Road, Suite 500
Hillsboro, Oregon 97124-9808
503-531-8700 / 503-531-8773 fax
www.beyondword.com

The Blue Grosbeak ©2008 Ridgefield, by Mark Catesby, page 55
Exquisite Corpse ©2004 Scott Dalgarno, page 89

Managing editor: Lindsay S. Brown
Editor: Marie Hix
Copyeditor: Meadowlark Publishing Services
Interior design: Devon Smith
Composition: William H. Brunson Typography Services

First Atria Books/Beyond Words trade paperback edition July 2010

ATRIA PAPERBACK and colophon are trademarks of Simon & Schuster, Inc.
Beyond Words Publishing is a division of Simon & Schuster, Inc.

For more information about special discounts for bulk purchases, please contact Simon & Schuster Special Sales at 1-866-506-1949 or business@simonandschuster.com.

The Simon & Schuster Speakers Bureau can bring authors to your live event.
For more information or to book an event, contact the Simon & Schuster Speakers Bureau at 1-866-248-3049 or visit our website at www.simonspeakers.com.

Manufactured in the United States of America

10 9 8 7 6 5 4 3 2 1

The Library of Congress has cataloged the hardcover as follows:

Maxwell, Jessica,
   Roll around heaven : an all-true accidental spiritual adventure / Jessica Maxwell.
     p. cm.
1. Maxwell, Jessica. 2. Spiritual biography. I. Title.
BL73.M387A3 2009
204.092—dc22
[B]

             2009015043

ISBN: 978-1-58270-236-0 (hc)
ISBN: 978-1-58270-237-7 (pbk)
ISBN: 978-1-43914-975-1 (ebook)

The corporate mission of Beyond Words Publishing, Inc.: *Inspire to Integrity*

For Rande, who knew from the beginning,
and for Tom, the rock around which my heaven rolls

With special gratitude to Her Majesty Queen Elizabeth II for her tireless
efforts to honor the world's great faiths and celebrate the thread of
goodness that binds them all.

Except ye see signs and wonders,
ye will not believe.

JOHN 4:48

Many Thanks
to Rose Garden
for your very
important god work!
your fan,
Deirdra McDell

Contents

An Invitation

First, my father's face appeared in the sky three days after he died. Then the Holy Pig Farmer showed up. Next thing I knew, I was having lunch with Deepak Chopra, dancing with Stephen Hawking, reading the auras of big league pitchers, seeing Celtic visions on the Isle of Iona, and discussing war, peace, and woman presidents with the daughters of Islam.

This was not the adventure I had bargained for. I am an adventure writer by trade and training, and my goals were stubbornly earthbound, if a little exotic, and usually involved going fishing or wildlife watching somewhere far, far away. That's what I thought adventure was ... until my life turned into a supernatural circus.

I had never asked for a spiritual journey—or a spiritual teacher, especially one who moonlights as a pig farmer! I didn't know enough about spirituality to request such things. Or even to be a cynic—a glimpse of a Himalayan partridge would have been more than enough for me. But there I was, a total nonbeliever, regularly having the sort of authentic mystical experiences any seeker would sell her soul for. Well, maybe not her soul, but I know one desperate pilgrim who sold his house so he could take a trip around the world to look for God. He's probably meditating in southern India right now, begging Krishna or Buddha or Moses or Christ or Mohammed ... anyone with bona fide credentials to give him at least a shred of evidence that God really does exist beneath the painful veneer of this messed-up world, and that good things verily will be given unto him thanks to all his hard upper-chakra work.

Which begs the question: why are so many of us so drawn to spirituality these days? Why do we collect books by the Dalai Lama, or Anne Lamott, or any number of spiritual writers? Why have millions of us quietly worked all manner of spiritual practices into our daily lives? Buddhist chanting, Hindu meditation, Native American sage smudging, old-fashioned praying to Jesus. You name it, someone's doing it.

Our personal spiritual ardor has rubbed off on the general culture too. Spas once concerned only with the very physical now offer "energy work," hotels from Thailand to Wales regularly hold "spiritual retreat weekends" that book up a year in advance, and you're likely to read about the power of prayer in *Parade Magazine.* Time and again, polls show that more people are likely to identify themselves as "spiritual" than "religious"—and that some 80 percent of us believe in God, or a "Higher Power."

Unfortunately, this means that spirituality is dangerously close to becoming another commodity, like yoga lessons and God Is My Copilot bumper stickers. And once commercialized, the peerlessly noble pursuit of the Divine risks doing a belly flop onto our to-do lists, right up there with "lose ten pounds" and "drink more water." If my own unexpected spiritual marathon has taught me anything, it's this: if we think we can buy—or trivialize—our way into the kingdom of heaven, we are in serious trouble.

And that is why I've written this book, which is nothing less than the unlikely testimony of a former spiritual dodo-brain, humbly offered up to both cynics and wind-blown seekers alike, that (a) the spiritual realm is real, (b) it is accessible to all, and (c) nothing is more important than doing something about (a) and (b). Because when even the most jaded among us bears witness to the exquisitely weird presence of God, I don't see how he or she can help but suspect—despite tsunamis of evidence to the contrary—that the superglue of the universe is not competition or power or money or, God forbid, bland indifference, but simply love ... just as the prophets and the Beatles and every saint worth her prayer beads always tried to pound into our moronic heads.

"God," of course, is a supremely loaded word, fraught with daunting definition snafus, gender issues, unhappy historic implications, and rather severe scientific challenges. As a big fan of scientific studies, I love the fact that research steadily reports connections between science and spirituality. Neuroscientists at the University of Oregon have found that meditation not only lowers blood pressure and reduces anxiety, but it actually rewires the brain to feel more compassion. Talk about the spirit-body connection! And University of Pennsylvania neuroscientist Andrew Newberg suspects that "spiritual capacity" is just another human ability, like being naturally good at math, or at making alarm clocks stop blinking "12:00! 12:00!" So if some of us are born able to perceive spiritual dimensions others can't quite yet, does it really make sense to kick the dog for hearing the dog whistle?

Religious history is filled with prophets and seers, visionaries and those who "hear the voice of God." But as for modern-day religious stereotypes, what's an intelligent person to think? Here we are, still staring down the sore throat of the "Christian Right," which couldn't be more wrong about everything Christ tried to teach us, principles that many mainstream churches practice with quiet unsung devotion year after year. The media, of course, take conflict like a vitamin and feed us endless misconceptions about nearly every spiritual tradition. One can only hope that fear-wracked control-freak us-against-them extremists of *all* faiths come to their senses and recognize the truly radical promise of peace that is at the heart of every one of the world's great religions. And that the only leaders we will take seriously are those who champion international cooperation and personal tolerance with all their hearts.

Lucky for me, I'd never given God or Jesus or any holy anybody a second thought until He/She/It grabbed me by the ear, marched me into the divine principal's office, and told me in no uncertain terms to stop goofing off and start paying attention. When I did, *Roll Around Heaven* is what happened.

The most important point of sharing my story is to prove that "God experiences" are not the territory of the lucky or the spiritually gifted or the superreligious—they are the birthright of us all. As mysterious beings on this most mystifying of planets, so pretty and fertile and spinning as it does in a universe with no center and no end, personal communion with the Divine is as natural to us as wondering what's for dinner. We should be hungry for it. We need its soulful sustenance as much as we need calcium and sunlight and clear, clean water. When Jesus met the Samaritan woman at the well and told her only "living water" (spiritual nourishment) would quench her thirst forever, he meant it. When she left her empty water jar behind and followed him, she meant it. And when Oprah said she wanted to "sit in God's palm too," she really meant it. So did Buddha when he made the startling suggestion that we "become lamps unto ourselves."

Each and every one of us carries deep within our consciousness a treasure map pointing to our own personal secret passageway back to our own godhead. Or rather, back to the awareness of our own godhead, since it's always there waiting for us like the most devoted of friends. Yet we're the ones who continually deny its existence and run around feeling unimportant, abandoned, and alone. "The winds of grace are always blowing," says India's beloved nineteenth-century master Ramakrishna, "but you have to raise a sail."

"Remembering that we are holy children of God is the reason we're here," echoes my friend and mentor, Lory Misel, whom I affectionately call the Holy Pig Farmer. Recognizing this fact is just the beginning. Whether you hunt it down like a starving person or accidentally crash land on it as I did, hitting the spiritual trail is a journey like none other. "It will beat the hell out of you," the Holy Pig Farmer warns. This is because your ego will sense its own impending doom and basically go nuts, throwing every possible obstacle in your path. Even the Masters had to deal with this: Buddha meditated under the Bodhi Tree while his mind dredged up all Seven Deadly Sins—greed, lust, just one more cookie—as the biggest distractions to enlightenment it could muster. And Jesus had to fend off the devil in the desert, who kept offering him some very serious real estate in exchange for his soul.

So, the spiritual path ain't for sissies. You can count on it being a very rocky road, and most likely find yourself in the arms of full-frontal bliss one moment and wrestling in the mental mud the next. Your inner yo-yo will drive you completely crazy—which will send you back to your spiritual practices over and over and over again.

The good news is that nothing on earth is more thrilling than finding your way back to God. The more your ego fights your holiness, the more your holiness comes back at you with more compelling evidence: a serendipitous meeting, a symbolic dream, a coincidence that defies all odds, a sweet bouquet of signs and wonders designed just for you with more supernatural plot twists than you can shake a TV reality show at.

For the record, *Roll Around Heaven* is 100 percent nonfiction. It is not "based on a true story." It is one. I've chronicled everything just the way it happened. But unlike stalking giant salmon in Outer Mongolia or tracking monster grouse in Norway or any of my other adventures that have been published in relentlessly down-to-earth magazines for two decades, *Roll Around Heaven* was not my idea ... or my idea of a good time. My best friend Rande refers to the whole business as "Lucille Ball Trips Over God." And if a total spiritual klutz can end up rolling around heaven right here on Earth, anyone can!

My highest hope for this story is that it will do for you what it has done for me: serve as a body of evidence you can return to whenever you find yourself staring into the dark ditch of despair, reminding you that there are far more joyful dimensions to dwell in than reality-as-usual, and many time-tested ways to get from here to there with a very willing personal support staff waiting in the cosmic wings to assist you. All you have to do is ask ... and sometimes you don't even have to do that.

So come along with me on this adventure of adventures. And if it starts getting a little too wild for you, do this: ask yourself where you are. You'll probably answer that you are on your lunch break in city X or in your bedroom in state Y. No, you are not. You are sitting on a rock in outer space reading a book—and it doesn't get any weirder than that.

My mother certainly believed in the healing power of *Roll Around Heaven*. Just before she died, she told me that on the day I was born she fell into a kind of trance and found herself flying through stacks and stacks of books piled up many stories high. "I kept flying down and down and down," she said, "until I got to the last page of the last chapter of the last book, and there was God, and He was laughing."

Jessica Maxwell
January 20, 2009
Oregon

Part I

The Holy Pig Farmer

You are here to bless the world.

LORY MISEL, THE HOLY PIG FARMER

1

THE FACE IN THE SKY

May 1992

"G uido!" I wailed. "My Green-Butted Skunk looks like a Blood-Sucking Leech!"

"A green butt is a green butt," he muttered, and hung up the phone.

Guido Reinhardt Rahr III was my fishing coach. My exasperating, aristocratic, demonically demanding Darth Vader-in-waders fly-fishing coach. If he didn't look like Brad Pitt I never would have put up with his abuse. We'd met two years earlier in the summer of 1990 on the first Western fishing expedition to Outer Mongolia. A fellow Northwesterner, Guido was scouting for *National Geographic*, and I was on assignment for *Esquire* magazine. I'd been writing for magazines for nearly ten years, and editors were finally letting me—a girl!—write international adventure stories.

I love adventure stories. I love the movement and surprise of them, their lively characters, far-away settings, built-in narratives, and, done right, their nineteenth-century explorer élan, something that suits my near-pathological fondness for missions just fine. Personally, I'd happily trade every modern relationship novel for the aerial prose of Beryl Markham's *West with the Night*: "I have lifted my plane from the Nairobi airport for perhaps a thousand flights," she writes, "and I have never felt her wheels glide from the earth into the air without knowing the uncertainty and the exhilaration of firstborn adventure." Like Markham, always, I wanted to witness something, see it, hear it, taste it, smell it, be part of it, and in rare instances—like golf or yodeling—try to master it (if I ever get a hole in one I'm sure I'll finally master yodeling).

So when Guido agreed to teach me to fly-fish there beneath the turquoise Mongolian sky, my mind reeled with joy. Once we were back home, every few months I'd leave my little log cabin on Vashon Island just off West Seattle and drive south to Portland, Oregon, where Guido lived. From there we'd head out to some pretty river and he'd give me a two-minute fishing lesson before going off somewhere to fish by himself, which is why it was taking me forever to develop a decent cast. And now he wanted me to learn to tie my own flies.

Tying flies looked like a magic trick when Guido did it. In my hands it felt like trying to organize dandelion fluff. Feathers would float away before I could whipstitch them to the hook, and I often tied my fingers to the vise. An early springtime zephyr blew through my open window, scattering chicken hackle in all directions.

"Darn him!" I said.

The phone rang again.

"Guido, I can't do this! … Oh, *Zelna!* Hi!"

I started to apologize, but my stepmother's voice was quaking.

"Scotty's in the hospital," she interrupted. "The doctors say it's serious this time. You'd better get down here, honey."

It sounds disrespectful, I know, but the truth is that this news annoyed me no end. My father was a smoker. Slowly, he was succumbing to the ravages of emphysema, and he had been in and out of the hospital for the last eight years. It was always "serious," but he was still here. And still smoking. I was sick of it.

I gathered up my fly-tying materials and mashed them into the old tackle box. The square of sky outside my study window glowed as blue as Mongolia's. All I wanted to do was learn to fly-fish. And get fishing assignments all over the world. But I had to have a decent cast first, and, apparently, I had to know how to tie a decent fly, and I couldn't do either yet and now my dad was sick again.

"Well, I'm not going," I said out loud. Tillie, my faithful corgi, stared at me.

"Don't look at me that way. I'm NOT going!"

I stomped into my bathroom, violently stripped off my clothes, and stepped into the shower. Then I heard it. The Voice.

"THIS IS IT. GO."

For a moment I just stood there, wondering what to do. Then I started to shake. Tears came and mixed with the shower water and I knew it was true. My father was dying.

I grabbed a towel and ran to the phone. There was one seat left on the next flight to Los Angeles. I called my husband at work. Sweet, but emotionally disconnected as usual, he agreed I should go. As usual, he didn't offer to go with me. I hadn't felt married for years.

My sister, Valerie, met my flight. Her husband and son were waiting for us in their minivan at the curb. Valerie, Scott, my beloved five-year-old nephew Jesse. My family. It felt so normal.

"How bad is he?"

"Bad," Valerie said, and started to cry.

Jesse showed me his new reptile book. My little nature buddy.

Everything was in slow motion and everything felt sped up. Moments stretched out to infinity and piled on top of each other. It seemed like seconds between hearing Zelna's voice on the phone and being at my father's bedside. By then I couldn't breathe much better than he could.

"Jeck," he said, and took my hand in his. It was so warm. He looked so healthy. His face was so tan. His cheeks so pink. Was he dying or wasn't he?

Daddy adjusted the tubing in his nostrils. He spoke like someone who had just finished a marathon.

"I'm......glad...you're...................here."

"Me, too," I said, patting his hand.

A nurse arrived to straighten his sheets. His legs! There was nothing left of them. They looked like the legs of someone starving in Africa.

So it was true.

I searched my father's eyes. Was he scared?

"Daddy, I brought ..."

"All right, Scotty, doctor's here to see you."

Another nurse shuttled us all to the other side of the curtain. Jesse announced that he was hungry.

"We'd better go," Valerie said. Zelna nodded. She said she'd stay. She'd been married to my father for twenty-five years; his and my mother's rocky marriage had lasted four. Valerie told Zelna we'd be back in the morning. She nodded again. She looked terrible. Of course she did. This was it.

We saw Daddy on and off during the next two days. I tried to think of questions only he could answer, answers I'd want to know when I couldn't ask him anymore.

"Did your mother really meet your father on a streetcar in Hawaii, or was it a bus?"

How lame was that.

I couldn't think of anything important. I asked nothing. Mostly, like everyone else does in this situation, I just told him I loved him.

But I also wanted to read him something from a little book my friend Debra Ryll had given me called *Thus Saith the Lord: Giddyap!* For some reason, people had always tried to get me interested in spirituality. Girlfriends, boyfriends, perfect strangers. Here, read this! An Indian swami is coming to town—wanna go? You've gotta see this new reincarnation movie. It was weird. Especially since I was only interested in the most earthbound things. I was an aspiring adventure writer, for chrissake!

But I liked this little book. *Thus Saith the Lord: Giddyap!* wasn't Buddhist and it wasn't Christian or Hindu; it honored all faiths, and it was funny. That's what bothered me most about "spiritual" people—they were so serious. Didn't Jesus rise again? Didn't Buddha find the way to end human suffering? Wasn't Nirvana all about bliss? And wasn't happiness, like, the goal? So why were spiritual people so miserable? But this book was different. It even quoted physicists. As far as I'm concerned, what happened in physics during the last hundred years should be required reading for everyone. Want to lighten up? Read quantum physics!

I brought the book with me because I was afraid my father was afraid. Afraid to die. Afraid to leave us. Afraid of what might—or might not—happen to him after death. And I wanted somehow to reassure him and thought maybe physicist David Bohm could. At least he had scientific credentials.

But during those last few days I was never alone with my father. Zelna was always there, naturally. Or Valerie. Or Valerie and Jesse. Or Valerie, Jesse, and Scott. Or Scott and Jesse, or Valerie and Scott. And if they weren't, then a nurse or doctor was. It felt like a conspiracy. Maybe I wasn't supposed to read this stuff to my dad?

But his mind did seem to be on spiritual matters, albeit expressed as the rote platitudes of his holy-roller English mother who had done the rather un-Christian deed of dumping her only child in an orphanage so she could go do the Lord's work in South Africa. This is just the sort of hypocrisy that made my mother, at age ten, refuse to return to the French Catholic church in East Texas where she was raised and where the nuns beat her little sister Katy for not being able to remember her catechism. How Christian of them. This is why I was staunchly antireligion, and especially anti-Christian. But there was my father on his death bed, his eyes closed, his head lolling back and forth on the pillow, chanting between wheezes: "Jesusdiedtotakeaway . . . oursins. Jesusdiedto. . . . .saveus."

I had no idea what to say to that. Finally, at the end of what turned out to be my father's last day, I found myself alone with him. I don't know how it happened. I don't know where everyone went. But there we were.

"Daddy," I said. "I want to read something to you."

He nodded and fiddled with his bedding. I felt silly.

"Okay. Well, this is what this physicist David Bohm says about . . . uh . . . the real nature of . . . Oh, I'll just read it, okay? Okay:

'As I have pointed out, the consciousness of mankind is one and not truly divisible. When you are experiencing persons, places and things, however wonderful, you are really only communing with the one Mind appearing in a form and a language you can understand . . . then you have translated matter back into its godly origin and you are enjoying the one, spiritual universe in the highest form!'

My father's eyes popped open. He pointed an index finger heavenward.

"That's it!" he said. He almost sounded normal.

I was shocked.

"You know?"

"I didn't know you knew," he replied. "That is the truth, Jeck. We're all part of ... a great whole, and that's ... all we are. That's it."

We talked about the illusion of solid matter and how physicists proved that all objects—the hospital bed, the window, our bodies—are really nothing more than empty space with energy flying through it. We talked about everything being linked to everything by that strange, intelligent energy. We talked about God. We didn't talk about Jesus.

"So, you're not afraid?" I said finally.

"No," my father replied, adjusting his oxygen tubes. "Just ... uncomfortable."

We both laughed.

At that moment Zelna walked in and Daddy took her hand.

"Jeck and I just ... had a ... conversation I wish we'd had twenty years ago!" he declared.

"No, no!" I protested. "What's important is that we had it now!"

Daddy smiled.

My father's body wound down like an old machine the following evening, and I flew home. The next two days were a blur. I wasn't grieving. Maybe I was in shock. I couldn't seem to do anything. I just wasn't there. Then, on the third morning, I woke up unnaturally early—and I'd never felt more there, more awake, more alive. It was embarrassing, given that my father had just died. I had so much energy I didn't know what to do with myself, so I reinstated an Alaskan salmon fishing assignment I'd canceled. Everything fell into place. Once again, there was one seat left on the plane I needed, the next flight to Alaska. I packed without a trace of my usual last-minute panic and left the house at 12:30 p.m., heading for the 12:50 ferry.

It was a big, polished spring day in late May. I drove north beneath a cloudless blue sky. I don't know what made me look up. But when I did, I saw it: my father's face. Filling the entire sky above me. It was gigantic, pulsing across that perfect plane of blue like an image projected in a movie theater. It seemed to be some sort of Technicolor holograph, translucent but absolutely bright. The image was made of every color of light, as if it was carved out of rainbows. The expression on my father's face was radiant with a kind of transcendent joy that simply is not human. This was not the father I knew: on earth Daddy had been the ever-anxious sort, and never the happiest of campers.

As I stared in wonder, his face seemed to quicken, its colors deepening as I watched. Then I realized this was a perfect confirmation of our last conversation—I really was "communing with the one Mind appearing in a form I could understand": my father's face! And I knew then that even from the silent bell of death, my father—or someone or something—was providing irrefutable evidence that reality truly is what scientists say it is: a blissful play of congealed light. David Bohm was right! Even after the death of the body, human consciousness really is indestructible, because there was my father, or some part of him, right there, right in front of my eyes, right then.

Many people report seeing the spirit of a departed loved one— maybe in a dream, or waving from a doorway. However, with the possible exception of Woody Allen, most of us aren't treated to such dramatic postmortem contact as seeing a parent's visage filling up the entire sky. But this resurrection of my father was no joke. It was some sort of heavenly gift, teaching me in no uncertain terms that both Daddy and dying were perfectly all right. Death's misery is reserved for the living. Of course, I wasn't about to share this confirmed wisdom with anyone. What would people think!

But then that evening my sister Valerie called me in Alaska.

"This is the most incredible day of my life!" she breathed. "I saw Daddy in a vision."

"Wait!" I said, wanting to be scientific. "Did you see his face in the sky?"

She gasped. Sure enough, at 3:30 that afternoon, exactly three hours after I saw it, my sister had seen Daddy's face in the sky. She was heading back to work after picking Jesse up at preschool, driving by herself just as I had been. She looked up and saw our father's face shimmering in the sky above the little Southern California beach town where we grew up and she still lives.

"He was so happy!" she told me. "He was just beaming and his face filled the whole sky right above me. It was sort of see-through but more vivid than anything around it—all these beautiful colors! He was so ecstatic! I had to make a turn so I waved and said, 'Bye, Daddy! Bye!,' but after I turned, there he was in that part of the sky too! He was everywhere I looked, like he was up there and all around me all at the same time."

We agreed we had just shared a very private miracle that would, we knew, help us handle the loss of our father—and anyone else we loved—from then on. What I couldn't have imagined was that this experience amounted to an initiation into a strange new spiritual world of such stunning originality and power that even those who have experienced it firsthand can scarcely believe it themselves.

2

Holy Pig Farmer

November 1994

The ring of the phone cut the air like a temple bell. In fact, I had been thinking about temples because I'd been trying to find a Buddhist monk to speak to the writing class I was teaching at the University of Washington. It was the last class of the year, and I wanted to bring in an inspirational guest speaker.

I'd just seen a film, *The Little Buddha*, about a boy from Seattle who was thought to be the reincarnation of a famous Tibetan lama. In the movie, the child's father challenges a Tibetan monk on the idea of reincarnation. The monk serves the man tea and proceeds to smash his own teacup, sending tea flying all over the place. The monk then explains that the teacup is like the body and the tea is like consciousness, and when the body dies, consciousness continues to exist, just in a different form—a variation on Einstein's energy-is-indestructible theory, and certainly conceptual support for seeing one's dear departed father's face in the sky. I desperately wanted someone to demonstrate this idea to my students so they could internalize the concept of egoless writing, wherein self-consciousness represented by the limited teacup—and preconceived notions—are banished and the ecstatic freed energy of true inspiration rushes in.

My plan wasn't working very well.

So far, I'd had a *Twilight Zone* talk with a monk who didn't speak a word of English at the Tibetan Buddhist monastery in downtown Seattle.

And another with what a friend refers to as a "white chick Buddhist" who answered the phone at the monastery the next time I called and assured me that the monks would never agree to speak to a university class. Instead she gave me the number of an American Buddhist scholar who taught in the Asian Studies Department.

"But is he Tibetan?"

He wasn't. He was another white guy Buddha-wannabe. Worse, he spoke in annoying, affected sentences whose pitch began artificially high as if he were chanting, then dropped off into a phonic abyss so you never quite got his point because you couldn't hear it. What I did manage to understand was surprisingly adversarial. First he took issue with the idea that jettisoning ego makes for better writing. "There are many very successful writers with huge egos that mumble-mumble-mumble." When I replied that I don't always tell my students exactly what I'm doing and often "ambush them with new ideas," he informed me that he considered ambush a "very violent word" and "seriously took issue with mumble-mumble-mumble."

As my Texas cousins like to say, nobody likes a shithead. But a Buddhist shithead is insufferable. I politely informed Mr. More-Buddhist-Than-Thou that this conversation was over.

By then it was Monday. My class was on Wednesday. I had just about given up on the inspirational speaker idea altogether when the phone rang.

"Having trouble finding your Buddhist monk ...?" the voice began.

It was my pal Jim Stewart, founder of Starbucks' forerunner, Seattle's Best Coffee. Jim's roasterie was on Vashon Island back then, and he had agreed to give my class a coffee-tasting demonstration as an exercise in describing tastes and smells with words.

"Who are you, the Psychic Coffee Guy?" I asked. "I can't find anybody!"

"Well, my leadership trainer volunteered to talk to your class."

His leadership trainer?

"What on earth is a leadership trainer?" I asked him.

It turned out that Jim had described the class to his counselor—how I spoiled my students with tea and treats and aromatherapy oils and fresh flowers and music because I've found that students always work hardest when they're well nurtured, something there seems to be a shortage of these days. "Kindergarten for adults," they called my class. Jim's counselor had surprised him by offering to be a guest lecturer. My adventure-girl curiosity kicked in, and since I was out of ideas anyway, I agreed, though with some trepidation because I had no idea what the guy would say.

But when Lory Misel walked into my classroom, some sort of holy electricity walked in with him.

It wasn't his looks—he was an utterly normal, somewhat tweedy fellow, tall, maybe in his late fifties, a little portly, bespectacled, wearing a nice wool jacket with leather elbow patches. But there was this light around him. Pure kindness seemed to radiate from his very being and he smelled like clean towels. Clearly, Lory was no everyday counselor. He was, I soon learned, a pig farmer with a small farm at the foot of Mt. Rainier, southeast of downtown Seattle. Despite his insistence that he was really "a family counselor who also raises pigs," (Lory never called himself a pig farmer before I did!) he was a spiritual teacher of the highest caliber—no ego, no ego trips, no sign-here-and-join-my-church missionary zeal, and no, thank God, high-pitched flaky faux-Buddha affectation. Lory didn't even charge us a speaker's fee. He spoke in a voice that cast a spell, both soothing and transportive, at once fully here-and-now and also able to take his listeners somewhere else, an auditory magic carpet to a place of great peace.

He said some wild things that night. That my students had "made a contract with God long ago" to meet together in my class (they *were* an exceptional group). He said they would be guided toward exactly what God wanted them to write, and that they were intellectually and emotionally incapable of underestimating their true worth in God's eyes. That they were, in fact, "holy children of God" who had been born only to "bless the world." Three hours later, most of my twenty-five students were dazzled. Many had tears running down their cheeks, and all were very pleased with this enlightening, if unexpected, end-of-term offering—with the exception of my one atheist student who resented the fact that I'd brought in a spiritual speaker at all ... "But, I forgive you, my child," she said, and made an exaggerated sign of the cross.

And I was on fire. Every cell in my body was vibrating at warp speed. Who is this guy?

The next morning I called Lory to find out.

Breathlessly, I thanked him again for speaking to my class.

"Oh, I was told I would meet you ten years ago," he said offhandedly.

I was stunned.

"You were 'told' you'd meet me?"

"Yes," he said. "I was told I would meet a redheaded writer and that we are going to write some very important spiritual books together."

I'd heard enough the night before to know that Lory meant he had received some sort of otherworldly guidance about this.

"But I . . . I," I stammered, "I'm an adventure writer! Are you sure I'm the . . . the one they meant?" (*Whoever "they" are*, I thought.)

"Oh, yes," Lory answered. "When Jim described you and your class, I knew it was you."

By the time I got off the phone we had decided to meet at Lory's farm and talk about the spiritual state of the world—and, I feared, my own.

3

The Last Supper

December 1994

I was finishing up a magazine assignment about snorkeling with hump-back whales in Hawaii—wanna feel like a human xylophone? Go snorkeling with a hormone-crazed male whale singing torch songs thirty yards beneath you. My friend Bonnie called to invite me to a welcomed post-deadline social event: the grand opening of the newly renovated St. James Cathedral in downtown Seattle ... just in time for Christmas. Her architect husband was the project's director, and the renewed church, I'd heard, was quite beautiful. Foregoing my usual allergy to religion in favor of a lifelong love of architecture, I said I'd love to go.

We arrived early, so Bonnie gave me a little tour, which included a visit to a small chamber just off the now refreshingly open center of the cathedral.

"What a sweet little room," I said.

"It's a chapel, really," Bonnie replied.

A chapel? Inside a church? I pondered this conundrum, thinking how goofy religion was, when my eye caught an exquisite bas-relief sculpture set into the chapel wall. It was a familiar scene even to a nonchurch person like me: the Last Supper with Jesus sitting at the traditional long table, flanked by his disciples. But this time when I looked at it, something strange happened. I felt a sudden wave of pain that was very nearly physical, like a hammer to the heart. Then I began to weep.

"Bonnie," I whispered, "What was the Last Supper exactly?"

As dumb as it sounds, I didn't really know what the Last Supper was all about. For all I knew, Jesus and his friends had just run out of food. Quietly, my friend, who had been raised Scottish Presbyterian, told me the real story. And as it turned out, her own husband was personally responsible for saving the little sculpture from being jettisoned during the remodel. While I was gazing at that lovingly restored monument to the religion that had so hurt my father, my mother, and my aunt, something shifted. An old door opened, and my heart rejoined something I had no tools to decipher. All I could do was sit in confused wonder as the evening's performance unfolded, my head filling with the operatic notes of old sacred music as they rang out from singers perched on high platforms very close to the ceiling of the sort of house of worship I'd avoided my whole life.

4

EVERYBODY'S SECRET

January 1995

O n the last stretch of the drive to Lory's farm, the massive pink triangle of Mt. Rainier filled my windshield like a vision. The sensation was one of being drawn in, rather than heading toward, and the resulting intimacy was daunting, especially compared to seeing the old volcano pierce Western Washington's eastern skyline from an impersonal distance the way most Seattleites do.

When I arrived I found Lory in a pigpen next to his house. It was January and, as usual, it had been raining. Lory waved and walked over to me through the mud, his rubber boots making squashed-tomato sounds with each step. Soon we were sipping tea in his study, where he sees private clients when he's not working at his office in downtown Seattle: a nice town-and-country balance, I thought. Thus began what I now think of as our Holy Weeks.

Lory's study was a comforting place. More than the overstuffed sofa and the soft pale walls, the place emanated the same feeling of peace that radiates from Lory himself. I couldn't help but wonder if his counseling tactic was designed to make people feel safe enough to handle having their circuits blown.

Right away, Lory began talking the way he did in my class, as if he were on some kind of automatic pilot. His soothing voice seemed to come from the center of the universe, if it had one.

17

"When did your spiritual life begin?" he asked me. It's the first question he asks everyone he counsels.

It hadn't, I told him. Really, I said, I'm just a down-to-earth adventure girl who spends her time out chasing moose or salmon, sometimes with a rifle or a fishing rod.

"I'm the most nonreligious person you ever met!"

"Everyone has a religion," Lory countered softly. "I was talking to a man who said he's an atheist and believes God doesn't exist. 'You're one of the most religious people I know,' I told him. 'Science is your religion—you read it, you believe in it.' Yet he's one of the most compassionate, community-oriented persons. Some of the most spiritual people I've ever met are atheists. Often people are living a profoundly spiritual life even though they don't even believe in God. Belief in God isn't required."

"You see," he said, "all people are holy. Whether they recognize it or not is not important. Whether you recognize it in them, that's very important. When you see every person as innocent and holy you change yourself and you change the world."

Lory looked at me intensely.

"You've had very spiritual experiences," he said suddenly. "Tell me about those."

Instantly, the image of my father's face in the sky flooded my mind. The euphoria of the experience descended once more as I told Lory about it. He nodded.

"He wanted to contact you," he said. "And he wanted you to know that he loved you. It was a way of saying 'I'm here, I'm okay. There is no death, there is no distance between us.'"

"Does people's emotional damage dissipate when they die?" I asked him. "Because Daddy was such a mess from all his childhood traumas. But his face was so ... happy. Beyond happy."

It felt ridiculous to even be talking about seeing a face in the sky. I squirmed in my comfortable seat.

"He was with God," Lory continued. "He'll still have things to work out in his next life."

Resisting my inclination to ask for proof that any of us has more than the life we're living, I went—I thought, anyway—to the heart of the matter.

"Have you ever heard of such a thing before?" I asked. "Seeing the image of a dead person's face in the sky?"

Lory nodded. "I know a woman, a psychologist—and an atheist—who drove down to Lake Washington one night, turned off the motor, and looked at the sky. And the whole sky filled up with Jesus's face."

"Whoa! I bet she believed in God after that!" I replied, realizing the chilling implication of what I'd just said: that now I did.

"No," Lory said flatly, "she didn't. Some people can grow from their spiritual experiences and some just can't deal with them. But everybody has them. I don't really label them as spiritual because they're so natural."

I couldn't help laughing.

"Well, if they're so natural, why do people think they're so weird?"

"Because they're afraid of what other people will think of them," Lory replied somberly. "That's the big resistance. 'What will people think of me if they know that I have these experiences?'"

"I know," I said. "That's why I wasn't going to tell anyone about seeing my dad's face … until my sister told me she saw it too. At least then I had a witness!"

"See, I do a spiritual history on people," Lory went on as he often did, not directly responding to what I had just said, as if something were coming through him from somewhere else. "I ask them that question about their spiritual experiences. You can tell more about people by their spiritual experiences than by their psychological experiences."

"Does anyone ever say they've never had any?"

"Yes, they do."

"Then what do you say?"

"Well, I know they've had them, but they've forgotten them. They're usually people who are very concrete."

"So, spiritual experiences are, like, everybody's secret?"

"Yeah," Lory said quietly. "Another interesting thing is that the most spiritual people I've met are women who have had incredibly abusive childhoods. Most people are born into spiritual kindergarten, then they grow up; these people are born into spiritual graduate school."

"But," I ventured, "I thought abused kids turn out to be, you know, damaged."

"They've had to use all of their senses to survive," Lory replied. "Especially their intuition, which is, essentially, the spiritual sense."

"Intuition is spiritual?" I asked Lory.

"Yes. It is the divine working through you."

How the heck could he be so sure? Not that I had a better explanation for intuition myself. I mean, if you think about it, intuition is completely bizarre. You just "know" something . . . and it turns out to be true? Hello???

"So is the pain of abused people sort of . . . their intuition teacher?"

"I don't know the real connection other than that their abuse was an advanced learning for them."

One thing I realized early on about Lory, he *doesn't* pretend to have all the answers. His wisdom seems to come to him, or through him, and if it doesn't, then he says so. Not exactly like the Bible-thumping know-it-alls on TV. His honesty certainly was refreshing.

"Do they seem more compassionate than most people, these abused women?"

Lory nodded. "They're very compassionate, very tender, very used to using all of their senses. They're comfortable with them all—in order to live a spiritual life, you have to be a multisensory person."

Lory looked at me for a long moment and finally said, "So when, really, did your spiritual life begin?"

5

The Knife Man Cometh

February 1995

B ut I told you, I don't *have* a spiritual life."

Lory asked me to tell him about "my spiritual life" every time we met, and his insistence that I had one was becoming annoying.

"I have an *adventurous* life!" I went on. "I just wrote about swimming with whales ... and I just finished a story about Caddy, the Canadian sea monster—a REAL sea monster ... and I ... and ... I'm going moose tracking next month in Montana ... for *Audubon* magazine!"

"You could be a master," Lory replied flatly. The words burned into my mind like a hot branding iron.

We stared at each other for a small eternity. Finally I erupted.

"Oh, *how* could you even *think* that, Lory?! I don't know *any*thing about this stuff! I never even went to church!"

His eyebrows lifted.

"Church has nothing to do with it," he said quietly. "And I can't explain how I know, I just know. It's like watching a kid throw a baseball and you can tell by watching him that he's a natural, that the potential is there. You're a natural. A spiritual natural. I just know. So, what was your very first 'otherworldly' experience?" he asked again. "Before seeing your father's face in the sky?"

He was impossible. Like Tomás de Torquemada disguised as a Holy Pig Farmer conducting some kind of Spiritual Inquisition. Well, that wasn't exactly fair since Lory Misel happens to be the nicest person on earth. But his questions really were getting on my nerves.

"Just think a moment," he offered gently, "and it will come to you."

I was about to say, "'*it*' what?" when I remembered: The Voice.

The drama of my father's aerial visitation had eclipsed the fact that I'd actually heard a voice, coming from *no one*, telling me that he really was dying and bidding me to go tell my father good-bye. And I remembered that I'd heard The Voice before.

It had been part of an all-too-real event I rarely spoke about. I was living in Santa Barbara, California, at the time, where I'd moved soon after college, and I was sharing a garret apartment with my closest college friend, Lauri Doyle. We'd just left a movie theater where we'd met after work, having driven there in our separate cars. I assumed she was driving home right behind me, so I left our front door unlocked, then drew myself a hot bath.

Soon I heard the front door squeak.

"Lauri?" I called out.

Moments later the bathroom door flew open and in flew a man with a knife.

"Get out," he commanded.

He was wearing a woman's wig and long black motorcycle gloves, and he had a red bandana tied around his face. All I could see were his eyes, green and crazy, but the moment I looked into them I heard these words as clearly as if someone standing next to me was saying them:

"He Will Not Hurt You."

When you're lying naked in a bathtub and a stranger is threatening you with a knife, it's pretty hard to believe you're not in danger. Nonetheless, I calmly rose, wrapped a towel around myself, and stepped out of the tub. The man immediately stepped behind me, grabbed me around the neck with one arm, and put the knife to my back with the other.

"I'll use it," he growled.

To my amazement, I heard myself say in a voice like clear water: "I believe you."

Thus began a series of statements, requests, and even endearments issuing forth from my mouth so unhurried and serene that the words seemed to have a life of their own. They must have, because I myself had no plan whatsoever. I wasn't thinking at all and cannot take the slightest bit of credit for what I said—had anyone asked me what I would do in this sort of situation, I would have replied, "Scream!" But the soothing words just came: "Let's talk, dear. Let's talk, darling. Let's talk."

Over and over I heard myself say kind things to this maniac. The effect was profound: he stopped manhandling me. Apparently, this was not at all what he was expecting, and frankly, I don't think he knew what to do with me. He appeared to be hoping for a fight. But all he got from me was: "Let's talk, dear. Let's talk, darling. We need to talk."

Finally, in desperation he threw me on Lauri's bed, then straddled my stomach. When I looked up, his wig was askew, his bandana was falling off his nose, and his shirt was riding up on his belly. It was all so ridiculous, so surreal, I almost laughed, but I was having trouble breathing under his weight.

"Move," I heard myself say. "I can't breathe."

"No," he replied roughly. "You'll run."

"I'm not going to run," I shot back. "I don't have any clothes on." I had had enough of this. "You have to move," I repeated. "I had asthma when I was little and I can't stand not to be able to breathe ... now MOVE!"

To my amazement, he did. In a heartbeat, the balance of power did a 180 from him to me and we both knew it was over. I sat up and took the knife out of his hand, and he jumped up and ran down the stairs and out the door, slamming it behind him so hard its glass windows shattered.

And so did my unnatural composure. Now shaking badly, I called 911. When the police officer arrived and heard my story, he stared at me hard.

"No one reacts like you did," he said. "That's what we tell people to do, but no one ever does it."

I wanted to insist I had nothing at all to do with my reaction, but just then Lauri arrived and as soon as I saw her I broke down.

Despite my winning *in situ* performance, I couldn't be alone in a room for weeks, and I couldn't take a bath without a phone and a locked door for years. Nonetheless, something or someone clearly had guided me through mortal danger and may have saved my life.

Two weeks after this incident, a friend of mine called. His girlfriend had been attacked in her home by someone who sounded a lot like the man who had attacked me, and she wanted to come over and talk with me about it. When she got out of the car, she was holding her bandaged right hand up over her head. We soon agreed that the same man must have assaulted us. But this woman's reaction made more sense.

"I fought him from one end of the house to the other," she said proudly. "There was blood everywhere!"

I thought for a moment, and then something came to me.

"Did he cut you on purpose?" I asked.

"No," she replied, "I just got in the way of the knife."

Lory nodded and rose to get us more tea.

"I think we have a life work to do together," he said.

"A what?"

"A life work. Everyone has a life work. I think our life works are joined. A life work is everything you do, really," he explained. "Once I was fasting and praying about what my life work is . . . asking over and over. It was my mantra. And I finally heard this voice as clear as yours that said 'Would you please stop asking that question!'"

Lory laughed his wonderful belly laugh.

"You see, every person's life is a curriculum designed for learning. And the reasons we keep repeating things is that we fail to learn the lesson. It's God's way of saying: 'Dear child, choose again.'"

"But what are we supposed to . . . choose?" I asked.

"Well, it's really simple. We choose another opportunity for forgiveness, another opportunity to be kind, another opportunity to choose hope and happiness. So every person's life, every encounter they have, is part of a divine curriculum. The most horrendous experience—like that man attacking you—is an opportunity for peace, for compassion.

"See, the thing that we're here to remember is that there is a place of great holiness and love inside us. And we get distracted by problems, by money issues, illness, the world—it's all just a distraction. Jesus said, 'Seek ye first the kingdom of heaven, and all else will be added unto you.' So that means that we're here to seek the holy child of God inside of us *first*.

"Every person is God's holy child," he continued, "filled with truth and grace, love, just like our Father in heaven."

Lory paused.

"I say 'Father' because it is comfortable for me to say. Others say 'Mother' or 'God,' and a tribe in Africa refers to God as 'Whew!'—a big sigh. But God has no preference as long as we wish to join with Him or Her or Whew!"

"Whew!" I replied.

"Every person is here to remember who they are," Lory continued. "We have angels and guides and the Holy Spirit and Jesus to assist us. We have all the help available that we need. So what is my life's work? To remember that I'm God's holy child, and that you are too. Every person is. We are literally brothers and sisters. You tapped into the energy of oneness when you treated your attacker so kindly. That's what Jesus meant by 'Love thy enemy.'"

I closed my eyes. Lory was talking about Jesus again, just as he had done in my classroom, just as he always did. My Tammy Faye Bakker phobia raised its heavily made-up face.

"I hope you're not going to tell me it was Jesus who saved me from that crazy guy."

"Don't know. Maybe."

"But, Lory, how could a dead person help a live person? I mean, you talk as if Jesus is still alive or something."

Lory smiled what I had secretly begun to call his Jesus Smile.

"He is."

That was the moment I realized Lory really believed this to be true. I stared at his open, grandfatherly face.

"Okay, okay," I said at last, "so tell me who you think Jesus was ... is?"

And how on earth, I wanted to add, can so many people still believe in him when the world has only gotten more insane over the last two thousand years?

Lory smiled again.

"Who is Jesus? Jesus is my teacher. I don't 'believe' in Him—I know Him, because I've had the direct, personal experience of Him. You don't need to believe it's hot when you're standing out in hundred-degree weather, you just need to experience it. Jesus is my friend. He's my elder brother. He adores me and I cherish Him. He's available to anyone who has but a little willingness; He doesn't require a great willingness. Who is Jesus? He's the ultimate, consummate, eternal personal friend. To know Him is to know God, because there is no separation between Him and God. He's the same. They're one."

"So," I began, "you're saying that people believe in him because they ... they actually experience him as real?"

"Many do. Many are just giving lip service to Him, playing a 'Christian' role. But many people do know Him."

"But Lory," I pleaded. "All that stuff about Jesus being the *only* son of God and the *only* way to salvation ... I just can't believe that Jesus is the world's only real path to God, the only real spiritual teacher. What about the four bazillion Buddhists in Asia, for instance—who, by the way, are a heck of a lot nicer than weirdo conservative Christians!!"

"He isn't," Lory replied sweetly. "There have been, and will continue to be, many advanced teachers of God. These are called the teachers of teachers, because God never leaves His children comfortless. Teachers have existed throughout time. Men and women. In all cultures. They teach the unity of life and the love of God. But Jesus ..."

Lory's voice trailed off and his mouth settled into his Jesus Smile and I saw that there were fresh tears on his cheeks.

6

Hibiscus Swami

March 1995

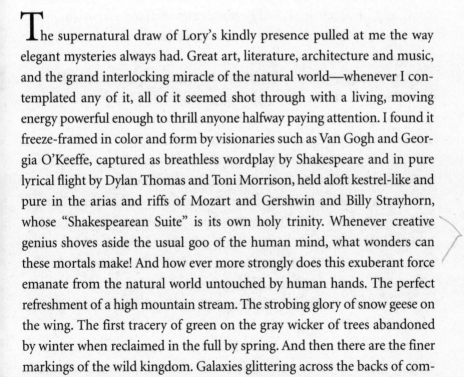

The supernatural draw of Lory's kindly presence pulled at me the way elegant mysteries always had. Great art, literature, architecture and music, and the grand interlocking miracle of the natural world—whenever I contemplated any of it, all of it seemed shot through with a living, moving energy powerful enough to thrill anyone halfway paying attention. I found it freeze-framed in color and form by visionaries such as Van Gogh and Georgia O'Keeffe, captured as breathless wordplay by Shakespeare and in pure lyrical flight by Dylan Thomas and Toni Morrison, held aloft kestrel-like and pure in the arias and riffs of Mozart and Gershwin and Billy Strayhorn, whose "Shakespearean Suite" is its own holy trinity. Whenever creative genius shoves aside the usual goo of the human mind, what wonders can these mortals make! And how ever more strongly does this exuberant force emanate from the natural world untouched by human hands. The perfect refreshment of a high mountain stream. The strobing glory of snow geese on the wing. The first tracery of green on the gray wicker of trees abandoned by winter when reclaimed in the full by spring. And then there are the finer markings of the wild kingdom. Galaxies glittering across the backs of common rainbow trout. The fragrant freckles of the vanilla orchid. Copper and opal aflame in mallard feathers. The piebald geometry of panda, wood duck, lunar moth, giraffe.

The infinite invention of nature alone had kept me enraptured for years. But the idea that the creative force of nature was *spiritual*? This was news. And the fact that the Holy Pig Farmer seemed to radiate spiritual creativity from his very being was the most compelling mystery of all ... even if it was forcing me into an embarrassing reevaluation of Jesus and Christianity. Darn it all!

Soon I began to look forward to my Tuesdays with Lory like Christmas morning. His quiet lessons seemed to resonate in the everyday fabric of my life for the rest of the week, their generous reverberations somehow having an influence on everything I did or tried to do or even thought about. I began to waltz through my days instead of "living like you're killing snakes," as my best friend Rande Anderson once put it.

"A pig farmer?" she asked. Her beautiful laugh bounded past the china-and-silver music of the Fairmont Empress Hotel's tea room in Victoria, British Columbia, where we'd escaped for one of our Girlfriends Getaways.

"A *holy* pig farmer," I said. "Can you imagine *me* studying with a spiritual master? Isn't that just completely weird!"

I thought Rande would find the concept hilarious, but a new expression crossed her face. She set her teacup down carefully.

"Actually, I don't think it's weird at all," she said. "I think this is your real work. You've just been messing around until now."

Coming from anyone else, this would have sounded patronizing at best. Coming from Rande it demanded serious attention. She had arrived in this world with part of her mind still resting in heaven ... wherever that was. As a very small child, Rande used to rock in the family rocker for hours with an open-mouthed smile on her face.

"My mother thought I was autistic," she says. "But I was really just being with God."

A natural clairvoyant, Rande has always known things she had no "logical" way of knowing, and is prone to prophetic dreams. Mostly, though, she radiates joy. She's a high school art teacher whose students tell her that her room "feels different" from other classrooms—they love to be there. Perfect strangers are so comfortable in her presence they often end up pouring out their life stories to her (whether she wants them to or not). And she has always been what she calls "a ghost magnet."

"They know they can communicate with me," she once told me wearily, "so they keep me up all night like I'm an all-night diner! And they always want to confess some horrible thing they did when they were alive and beg *me* for forgiveness until I want to scream: 'You got yourself into this mess, you get yourself out of it! I CAN'T HELP YOU!!!'"

If Rande is to get any sleep at all when we travel together, we have to avoid old hotels, yet that's exactly where we met. We were college students and had both managed to win *Mademoiselle* magazine's annual Guest Editorship contest, which included staying at the historic Barbizon Hotel in New York for a month. Rande always says that the moment she laid eyes on me there in Sylvia Plath's old haunt, she knew we were, as she puts it, "split souls."

As usual, I was clueless.

But our similarities really are striking. Fair-skinned Celtic girls of French/Scottish heritage, we both grew up in Southern California on opposite ends of Santa Monica Bay and suffered terribly under the tyranny of the über-tan surfer girls who seemed to win the heart of every boy we ever had a crush on. We have two sisters apiece, artistic mothers, and emotionally distant fathers who flew Air Force bombing missions during World War II. Creative romantics by nature, our shared passions cut a wide and idiosyncratic berth: Chopin, *I Love Lucy*, old Japan, French Expressionism, 1940s fashion, natural medicine, cats, and marzipan. We even share odd constitutional glitches: touchy digestive systems and an extreme reactivity to alcoholic beverages that turns us into Lucy and Ethel in no time. And we both have an odd kind of directional dyslexia that ends up working out just fine: if Rande is driving and I say, "Turn right," when I meant to say, "Turn left," inevitably Rande will turn left anyway so we always get there. I was Rande's maid of honor when she married Glen Anderson, the man of her dreams (I introduced them), and in the reception line so many of her friends from work whom I'd never met said "Oh, you must be Rande's sister!" that the exasperated flower girl standing beside me finally whispered, "Just say you are!" Perhaps, then, it shouldn't have been a surprise that I had finally found myself linked to the ethereal realm that has been Rande's private world for as long as she can remember. So if she thought I was onto something serious with this new venture into the spiritual, then she knew there was something to it. I did, too, but I wasn't nearly as comfortable with it as she was.

Rande's eyes suddenly filled with little-kid glee. "Of course," she added, "if you were going to have a spiritual teacher, it would *have* to be a pig farmer!"

April 1995

"You know," I told Lory, "my best friend thinks this is my real work."

"It is," he replied.

"Well," I stammered, feeling light years away from my comfort zone, "she also thinks I may have met a teacher of teachers when I lived in Santa Barbara."

Lory nodded. I could almost hear him thinking, "See, you *have* had many spiritual experiences."

I explained that my parents had been so horrified at the assault by the man with the knife that they insisted I move to a safer neighborhood where they would help out with the rent. So I found a charming bungalow on the protected premises of a vintage hillside hotel called El Encanto— "The Enchanted."

Around that time I had decided to finally make good on my love of the natural healing arts, and I enrolled in the Santa Barbara College of Acupuncture. I adored every minute of it. I sailed through my classes. And found that I could locate meridian points—energy entryways—with my fingers without looking at the diagrams.

My new career plans didn't last long. Out of the blue, I was asked to apply for one of the most coveted literary grants in the country, a National Endowment for the Arts Creative Writing Fellowship. A man who somehow had managed to capture the most unlikely of prizes— a grant to help writers get grants—called and invited me to a meeting with an NEA representative who was coming to town. I demurred. I was just a lapsed magazine writer; NEA grants were for "real" writers. He persisted. Very reluctantly, I attended the meeting. Over my further protests, the NEA rep insisted that I apply for a grant, which, inexplicably, months later I ended up winning.

"Like I've always told you," Rande told me when she heard, "you're supposed to stick with writing."

So I dropped out of acupuncture college. But not before meeting an interesting young professor there. Not only was he well versed in Oriental medicine's mysterious energy circuitry, but he had an Indian guru. For years he had been a devotee of a fellow known as Swami Satchidananda, and had even lived in one of the Swami's ashrams. The professor and I began dating, and soon he wanted to teach me to meditate.

The point, he told me, is to clear your own thoughts from what he called the "Small Mind" so that something called "Divine Mind" could reveal itself to you. Then he launched into a description of "the spiritual path," and how the real game here on earth is to dissolve our Small Mind so it can merge with Divine Mind, "which," he said, "is what people call God."

I found it all very confusing. I only had one mind that I was aware of, and it seemed to flit around like a caged bird.

"That's the nature of the Small Mind," my new boyfriend assured me. "Divine Mind is like a still lake."

He walked outside and returned with a yellow hibiscus from El Encanto's enchanting gardens. Then he had me sit cross-legged on my living room floor, and he set the flower in front of me.

"Just look at it and try not to think of anything else."

Moments later I gasped.

"What's wrong?" he asked.

"I ... I don't know," I stammered. "... I was just staring at the flower and all of a sudden I couldn't tell if I was the flower or the flower was me!"

His eyes clouded.

"You can't be that advanced!" he practically spat.

He seemed angry. But I had no idea why because I had no idea what I was doing.

"But I really did lose myself in that flower," I told Lory, "and it felt so creepy I never wanted to meditate again."

As usual, we waited in a comfortable silence for Lory to speak.

"You know, Jesus said you have to lose yourself to find yourself," he offered finally.

"Jesus did? What on earth did he mean by that?"

"He meant that you have to lose the Little Me that you have made up as your adaptation to the world. These roles we play, these names we call ourselves, you have to let those go to find your Christ Self, and your Christ Self knows you're one with everything. That's what you experienced when you looked at the flower.

"Now, that terrified your Little Me. In Buddhism they ask you to meditate upon the question, Who am I. I'm a wife, I'm a tall person, I'm a daughter, I'm a husband. If you look closely at all these things, those are just roles we play—it's not who we are. But you, as God created you, can never be overestimated ... you are only capable of underestimating your worth—that's how grand you are, that's how grand each of us is. Each one of us is God's holy child."

Lory looked out the window at the rain falling on his pastures, then he looked back directly at me.

"Now, what happens is that when you're confronted with your Big Me, your Little Me—which is your ego—panics. That's what happened. You began to experience the Christ You who is one with all creation, including the hibiscus, and your ego panicked."

"Is that because your ego threatens your, um, Christ Self?" Even saying the word "Christ" still made me squirm.

"No, it's the other way around. The ego's big threat to you is: 'If you discover your holiness you'll die.' What it really means is that if you discover your holiness *it* will die, because your ego is not who you are. But we forget that."

"We forget what?"

"That our ego is not who we are."

"But ... isn't it, like, part of who we are? I mean, you are a pig farmer, and I am, you know, half-Scottish."

Lory tilted his head like a curious crow.

"At the heart of each of us, at our essence, beneath the labels and the roles and our genetics, all we are, all we really are, is holy. That's what we forget."

"And," I ventured, "you want to remind us?"

Lory sat quietly for a moment, then said, "yeah."

I told Lory that Swami Satchidananda had tried to remind my boyfriend of his own holiness—or, at least, his Out There-ness—too. When he was living in the swami's ashram, he had had a peculiar experience while helping the swami work on one of the old cars he collected; apparently Swami Satchidananda had been a car repairman before his Small Mind graduated to the machinations of the cosmos. The swami had suddenly looked at my boyfriend and reality as he knew it "just went away." All he could see were lights and stars and galaxies on end, and any sense of himself vanished completely.

"It was," he told me, "a little taste of cosmic consciousness. And it was terrifying."

Sensing his panic, the swami brought his student's mind back to Earth, then turned around and continued to rebuild a carburetor.

"I asked my boyfriend what the heck cosmic consciousness was," I told Lory, "and he told me to read a book called *Autobiography of a Yogi* because it has the best description of cosmic consciousness in it he'd ever read."

"Did you?" Lory asked.

"I tried to," I said. "Twice. The first time I just couldn't get into it. The second time I left it on a train in France!"

Lory laughed. "You weren't ready," he said. "You will be someday."

"So, do you think my Santa Barbara boyfriend was a teacher of teachers?" I asked him.

Lory shook his head.

"No. He wasn't. But his teacher was. You met him, right?"

"Swami Satchidananda? Yes, actually, I did."

A few months after my disastrous attempt at meditation, we learned that the swami was giving a New Year's Eve talk at a nearby monastery. My boyfriend wanted to go, but I wasn't sure I wanted to exchange a festive

New Year's Eve party for a night with some Indian guru guy. Why would anyone be interested in someone from India, anyway? India doesn't even have sanitation! Finally, as usual, curiosity got the better of me and I agreed to go.

The swami's talk was held in a small chapel on the monastery's lovely cloistered grounds. The place was packed. *How do all these people even know about this guy?* I wondered.

At the front of the chapel, young Americans in white robes and silly-looking turbans fussed over what looked like a throne fitted with tacky lime-green cushions—my worst aesthetic nightmare. Soon, one of the swami's smiling female devotees passed around a large tray of fruit-and-nut balls rolled in coconut—my favorite! I gladly accepted one and took a bite. And immediately felt giddy.

"What's in this stuff?" I demanded, suspecting drugs.

My boyfriend laughed and told me it was called "*prashad*," meaning that the swami had personally blessed it, infusing it with "*shakti*," the "spark of higher consciousness."

I took another bite. And felt another wave of ecstatic joy. I finished the weird little treat, then asked if I could have another one. My boyfriend shook his head.

"We can only handle a little taste of cosmic bliss at a time," he warned.

I told Lory that I didn't remember much of the swami's talk that night, but I continued to feel strangely elated. In fact, whenever I think of that chapel, I see it in my mind's eye as being filled with pink light, as if the atmosphere there had some kind of special charge to it.

"Also, the swami appeared to me in a dream that night," I recalled. "My parents, my sisters, my boyfriend, and I were all sleeping on cots in this plain, big room, waiting for someone. Outdoors was a brightly lit courtyard with white pillars. Finally, Swami Satchidananda showed up and we all raced out of the room, running toward him like children. But before we reached him he vanished, then immediately reappeared somewhere else. And we all gleefully ran to his new location, only to have him disappear and remanifest somewhere else, and off we'd go, playing our joyful supernatural game of hide-and-seek.

"He only spoke to us once," I said. "He stopped and looked at my little sister Heather and said: 'I don't want you walking around alone at night anymore.' Then he reached his hand into her heart—it went right into her body!—and made some kind of adjustment and waved her away as if to say, 'Okay, that's fixed.'"

I told Lory that I woke up very early the next morning lying on my back with my arms crossed mummy-like on my chest—not the way I sleep. Later that morning while I was washing the breakfast dishes, I began to weep with gratitude for being shown the existence of the spiritual path. And that there was a way out of this madhouse of a world. Just describing the experience had me weeping again.

"But, Lory," I said, "I'd forgotten all about this. How on earth could I have forgotten such an important thing?"

7

RABBI EYE MOVEMENT

April 1995

Lory waited a long time before he spoke.

"Jesus said He didn't come here to judge the world, He came here to save the world. This was His blessing to the world."

"Jesus?" I asked, startled.

"Yes, God sent Him into the world to bless the world. But you know what? God sends each one of us, His holy children, into the world to bless the world. Jesus is a mentor, helping us to fulfill our function of blessing the world."

"But ... what does Jesus have to do with the swami?"

"Jesus was fully awake," Lory replied. "The swami was trying to get you to wake up. In Genesis it says that Adam fell into a deep sleep; it never says he woke up. There's been no comprehensive awakening since. Jesus woke up. Buddha woke up. Krishna woke up. The swami gave you a little spark of awakening in the fruit candy, and you realized that waking up is possible. We're here to wake up. If you're a spiritual pilgrim, which you are, Jessica, you're on The Journey, because once you have a taste of waking up, you're hooked."

"You have to be kidding."

Lory looked at me with a new seriousness.

"No. I'm not. But the spiritual path is not an easy path. It just beats the hell out of you. Once you say to God, 'Okay, my life will be to serve and bless,' then everything is arranged. In the process, though, the ego begins digging into its arsenal of demons—greed, fear, jealousy, guilt … or just plain resistance. They all come roaring out, trying to divert us. But if we hold on to the willingness to bless, then we're able to get through them."

Lory smiled his Jesus Smile. Whenever he did that, I knew his spiritual radar had just picked up something new, and I was in for yet another lesson in the unexpected. *Do all spiritual teachers teach this way?* I wondered.

"I used to be a counselor at a California prison," he began. "The O. H. Close School for Boys in Stockton. There was a kid in there for violence, and we were talking about his mother in counseling one day and he got enraged and ran out. I told the other counselors to go get him and bring him back, but they said, 'No way—you go get him.'

"He was in the gymnasium, so I went over there. He was a big, muscley kid, six feet four. I slowly walked up to him and he pulled a rattail comb out of his pocket, sharpened into a weapon, and pushed me against the wall. At that moment I was completely overcome with compassion for him, and I said, 'Oh, Ron, you've had so much hurt in your life, you don't need to do this.' And he dropped the weapon and hugged me, crying like a small child."

Lory smiled again.

"When you said kind things to your attacker in your apartment, you helped heal something in him while you protected yourself. I think everyone comes here with gifts that can help others heal. That's a big message in the book you're going to write."

That mythic book again. Why on earth did Lory think I was going to write a spiritual book? Then, like a bright-colored bird arriving unannounced in a leafless winter tree, I suddenly remembered something else.

"Lory!" I breathed. "You know when I had that dream about Swami Satchidananda? Well, I'd forgotten all about this, too, but back then I had a wonderful friend named Noah benShea. He always reminded me of a young ancient rabbi, though he wasn't a rabbi. He was a philosopher—a real one!—who had given many talks to a broad community. Well, Noah was also very hip, and like you, very spiritual. One morning not long after that Swami dream, Noah called me out of the blue and told me in this big rich voice of his that sounds like God or something that he'd had a dream that I'd written a spiritual book. Lory, he said it was a very important book that helped many, many people."

"Yes," Lory replied. "That's the one. That's the book."

I didn't understand how I could have forgotten all this. Another wave of resistance washed over me. Actually, it was more of a tsunami.

"But this is so crazy!" I practically yelled. "How could I write a book on anything as . . . as chaotic as spirituality? I mean, it's here, it's gone, you're all happy and everything's perfect, you wake up and everything's a mess again. And everyone believes different things, and . . . and everyone's always fighting about what they believe, and people get completely be-true-to-your-school WEIRD, and make women wear veils or won't let anyone dance or . . . or would rather let kids die of AIDS than let them use condoms . . . in the name of *Christ the Healer*???? . . . it's all so dumb . . . it's TOO dumb . . . especially for someone who . . . who . . . who reads the *New Yorker!* And it's like . . . their way or the highway with all their meannie-yeannie little neenie-weenie RULES, as if following them is the only way to get to . . . to whatever they think their Oh So Holy Goal is . . . and if you yourself happen to, you know, actually LEARN something really holy, you end up totally forgetting what it was for, like, ten years, until a farmer, a PIG farmer for God's sake—no offense—shows up and makes you remember it and you suddenly feel all holy inside and then . . . then you completely freak out over . . . over a phone bill!! God, Lory, how on earth can anyone ever wake up??"

Lory, as always, had listened to my entire tirade with quiet respect. While I sat there panting, his serenity seemed to fill the room in concentric circles. From the deep middle of that holy vortex, he finally spoke.

"When you start on The Path, you meet with nonstop resistance."

That's all he said. If holy water could speak, it would have sounded like the Holy Pig Farmer did that day. And for some reason his peaceful tone made me furious. I actually stood up and stomped my foot.

"Lory, this is too hard. It's just not *worth* it!!"

For the first and only time, the Holy Pig Farmer wheeled on me, skewered me with a withering look, and in a voice like smoking steel said:

"There is nothing—*nothing*—more important than waking up to God."

8

THAT'S HIM

April 1995

I left Lory's farm in a blue rage. Miles of waterlogged farmland raced by as I fought the inevitable.

"He's trying to do it," I fumed. "He's trying to turn me into a ... a spiritual person! 'Just a LITTLE bit of willingness,'" I mimicked. "'That's ALL *He* needs ... just a little bit! Just a little bit! Just a little bit of blooming ... idiotic *willingness!*'

"OKAY!!" I hollered. "All right! I'm WILLING, you crazy Bozo-brain pig farmer ... I'm WILLING, okay? I have *willingness* ... all right?! I have one eensy-beensy teensy-weensy nanogram of WILLINGNESS to know *HIM*—*capital H!!!!* Mr. Holy Holy Holy his hokey-pokey Holy Self our Lord and Savior JESUS Christ ... Okay???!! ... but I will *never*, EVER read the Bible!"

"You don't need to," Lory's voice rang inside my head. "You just have to be willing to know Him. That's all He wants."

I was acting like a brat and I knew it, but I couldn't get embarrassing visions of jerks like Jerry Falwell out of my head. Him and all the other smarmy, hypocritical rip-off artist TV evangelists who get millions of trusting, ignorant people to send them bazillions of dollars that they spend on insane right-wing political imperatives ... and eye shadow! Really horrific things like taking away women's right to control our own

41

bodies and turning us back into property. Or starting faux wars to create markets for their buddies' dirty little arms manufacturing businesses.

"And in Jesus's name, no less! Jesus, the Prince of *Peace*? Ha!" My fury, it should be said, was also fueled by the powerful fear that I was teetering on the brink of Super Dorkiness.

"I *hate* this," I hissed as my Trooper made its way through the pretty countryside.

"This is *SO* uncool!"

Still furious, I turned onto Highway 18 heading west, and absently reached out and snapped on the radio. Immediately, the announcer said, "If you're heading west on Highway 18, you will want to find an exit as soon as possible. There's been an accident that will cause very long delays."

I looked up. A handy exit—the only one for miles—happened to be right there. As if my car had a mind of its own, it turned off the highway, slipping me out of harm's way. At that moment, I sensed it. A presence. The kindest, sweetest, most gentle thing I'd ever experienced in my life. I saw nothing, but I felt it, and it felt like being in love multiplied a million times. It felt very much like what the expression on my dad's face in the sky looked like: like heaven itself—true heaven, not some childish image of clouds and cherubs, but the pure, unstudied, nonintellectualized, unadulterated, non-denominational, real, live, living experience of being in a perfect state of perfect love. And the bearer of this preternatural state of being was right there in the car with me. Right *there*. *With* me.

"Oh, my God," I breathed. "It's true!"

As impossible and bizarre and, yes, uncool as it was, I knew this meant that Lory was right: Jesus—or his spirit—or something about him—was real. Very real: I had just experienced it.

Stunned to my bones, I drove home as if I were coasting on clouds. As soon as I walked in my front door, I called Lory and told him what had happened. And Lory's quiet, lake-like voice replied:

"That's Him."

9

THE AURAS OF
BIG LEAGUE PITCHERS

April 1995

The next morning I felt as though I'd slept on rose petals. I was absolutely, perfectly at peace. Everything felt right. Until I remembered what had happened on the drive home from Lory's the day before. Then I suffered a case of the shudders. Could it be true? Could I really have experienced the *living* spirit of Jesus? It was one thing to have seen my father's face after his death; at least I had visual evidence, and that of my sister as well. We were personally attuned to our father, of course. But to feel the presence of someone as storied and important . . . and distant, at least chronologically, as Jesus Christ? To have been in direct (if invisible) contact with him. "Or Him," I mentally corrected. And to have it verified by the Holy Pig Farmer too?

"Jesus!" I said out loud, then clapped my hand over my mouth. The day did seem to have an uncommonly cheery life of its own.

Things fell into place effortlessly, and my writing class prep work almost did itself—no hectic last-minute running around, no stress at all. Checks really did arrive in the mail. I even soared through my aerobics instructor's hard new dance routine. Unheard of.

A long phone call made me miss the early ferry off the island, but rather than end up in Seattle's famously bad rush-hour traffic, I drove as if I had a protective bubble around me. For the entire route from West Seattle through downtown and on to the University of Washington campus, there wasn't a car within twenty yards of me. Not one.

The youthful bravado of early spring seemed to echo my euphoria. The barelegged deciduous trees were knitting themselves new chartreuse lace undergarments, and even the evergreens were covered with points of soft fresh green. The air was so clean it almost smelled of mint. I'd planned to go without supper, but there was an open parking place in front of my favorite campus Thai restaurant. Never.

The pretty Thai hostess's eyes grew round with wonder when I walked in.

"Do I look that hungry?" I asked her, laughing.

"No," she said quietly. "You look like the Buddha."

Class that night was the best since Lory's visit four months earlier. Ideas flew from my mind with the greatest of ease, and the words to express them found themselves with uncommon grace. At our tea break one of my students who really can read auras told me that my own was bright turquoise and filled the entire room.

When I drove home late that night under an unusually starry sky, something my mother used to say came to me. She'd be rolling out dough for chicken-and-dumplings, trying, as always, to make her dumplings turn out as good as her mother's—a near-impossible mission that would vex my mother mercilessly if she let it. "You can either roll around heaven or roll around hell," she'd say with a laugh, "the choice is yours, honey." Under the Holy Pig Farmer's guidance, I had somehow chosen to roll around heaven! This, I realized, is what the term "heaven on earth" really means.

And I realized that waking up to grace, *really* waking up to it, experiencing peace beyond reason *as reality,* even for a moment, banishes the hell of everyday existence completely. I didn't understand it. I couldn't explain it. How could this possibly be? The whole thing made no sense according to "normal" logic: your dad dies, you see his face in the sky, the Holy Pig Farmer shows up, and then you meet Jesus on the freeway. Sure. Why not. Just another normal life on Planet Earth. But the deeper implications were not lost on me. Somehow, I'd been given the keys to a hidden doorway that leads to a parallel universe that's a perfect replica of this one, except ... perfect. There I was, in my same old car, driving on the same old roads, under the same old sky, but everything was glossy with perfection, and there was a distinct absence of ... what was it? Resistance? Yes, Lory was right—resistance. There was none anywhere. None from me to life, and more astonishing, none from life to me. No daily drama whatsoever, which, really, was the grandest drama of all. All was perfect peace, perfect delight, all was ease and beauty and purity of purpose, and none of it was my doing. I felt like a feather on the breath of God.

But how do you stay there?

October 1995

"Did you know sports teams have an energy field?" Lory asked suddenly.

"You mean, like, when the TV sports guys say a team is 'in the zone'?"

"Yeah," Lory said. "When a team's energy field is strong, players can do no wrong. They make no errors, hit one three-pointer, or home run, after another. You can feel the energy working."

I told him how the energy had been working for me since I'd met him, and that I wanted to live in The Zone forever.

"Do you ... do you think people can see, um, Zone energy?"

"Some can, yes."

"But I mean like reading auras ... only sports auras." And then I told him about something very odd that had happened the previous week.

At the time, Seattle had a bad case of Mariners Fever. My husband, a talented amateur left-handed first baseman and big baseball fan, was ecstatic. The Mariners were in a dogfight with the Anaheim Angels for the West Division title. When they won it in a single-game playoff, Seattle went crazy.

It seemed as though every Seattleite was hoarse for two weeks after that. The Mariners had moved into the American League division series playoffs, up against "the hated Yankees" in a five-game series. They held their own, then lost, then won again, much to the delight, terror, and palpable relief of sports-crazed Seattleites.

Then the moment of truth came: the decisive fifth game. Both teams had two wins. My husband had decided Game Five was going to be such a historic event that even a nonfan like me shouldn't miss it, so he put a

Mariners baseball cap on my head and included me in a carload of his sports buddies heading for the final big game. We drove to some out-of-the-way residential street to buy a $70 scalper ticket, and I soon found myself alone in the nosebleed section of the Seattle Kingdome. I was way up near the ceiling with a bird's-eye view of the field, wedged between a planet of a fan with the biggest tub of popcorn I'd ever seen and a guy listening to the game on a portable radio, which seemed rather redundant.

The yelling was so incessant I had to wear earplugs. Two hours later, the game became yet another tug-of-war that ended up in extra innings. This prompted the Mariners to call in starting pitcher Randy Johnson, who'd only had two days' rest. Johnson was supposed to "throw relief," a phrase I felt he'd only deserve if he could make everyone shut up even for five minutes.

The crowd went even crazier when Johnson took the mound. A tall, gangly fellow nicknamed "the Big Unit," Johnson began warming up. For some reason the Kingdome lighting crew decided to shine an icky lime-green light on him. Since I was practically sitting on the ceiling, I looked up to try to locate the source of the weird green light. Nothing. I searched everywhere, but I couldn't find the light anywhere. Where on earth was it coming from? Then the Big Unit took a step sideways—and the light moved with him. Not like a spotlight, but swaying with his whole body, as if it came from within him, not from without. Uh oh.

"Oh no!" I cried. "Now I'm seeing AURAS!"

My popcorn-gobbling neighbor eyed me sideways.

What else could it be? The light surrounded Johnson's body like a frog-colored force field and followed him like a shadow. It didn't seem fair. He wasn't exactly the most handsome guy on the planet; couldn't they have given him a nice golden light or something? Then I noticed another thing: the light actually reached from Randy Johnson's body almost to home plate.

Whoa, I thought. *It's, like, his … will, or something.*

The yucky green light laid down a pathway directly to the batter's box.

"He's gonna throw heat," I announced.

My neighbor stopped mid-gobble.

Sure enough, Johnson struck everyone out that inning. Then the Yankees came on the field. I wondered if I could see their pitcher's aura too.

There it was! But it was clear, not pond-slime green like Randy Johnson's. It moved the way heat waves do, and I could see that it reached only halfway down the pitcher's mound.

"He's got nothin'," I muttered.

My neighbor nodded.

The Yankee pitcher proceeded to walk everyone, much to the loud approval of every set of vocal cords in the Kingdome. When Randy Johnson returned to the field, the noise volume rose another impossible ten decibels, but I saw that the green light had weakened and now reached only just past the pitcher's mound. My neighbor hiked an eyebrow in my direction. I shook my head.

"He's done."

My neighbor offered me some popcorn.

About that time, my husband came over to check in with me. I tried to tell him that I was seeing pitchers' auras, but he had started to yell again and didn't hear me. Then Edgar Martinez saved the day in the bottom of the eleventh by hitting a double down the left field line that scored two Mariner runs and gave them a 6–5 win—and the series.

Pandemonium broke out. Everyone in the Kingdome was on his or her feet. Fans flooded onto the baseball field, and my auric connection with the pitcher's mound vanished in the happy chaos.

My husband dropped me off at the house that night and then went on to the local tavern for more celebrating. When he got home he told me he'd run into a guy on his softball team.

"And he said, 'When Johnson took the mound you could just feel his energy reaching all the way to home plate,'" my husband practically yelled.

I stared at him.

"Did you tell him what I saw?"

"Of course not!"

Then he took my baseball cap off my head. I thought I'd been kicked out of the Mariners Fan Club forever. Instead, he turned the cap over and lifted the ribbon lining. A tiny hill of orange dust fell out onto the table. My husband grinned.

"Pitcher's mound dirt," he said. "Bob and I stormed the field after the last game. I put some in all our hats for good luck!"

Lory laughed.

"That's a good one," he said. "The thing about spiritual experiences is that they're unpredictable, just like reading auras at a baseball game. They just show up, and they show up at the right time."

But spiritual experiences, he added, are not "a one-time deal."

"The thing everybody has to understand is that they happen all the time. And they should never be controlled—if you try to control them you get into egocentric mindless magic."

Spiritual experiences, he said, are always unfolding, and every time you go back to contemplate the experience, you can learn more.

"It's as if they're continuously trying to teach you. When you are ready to seek the mysteries of God, you want to go back to your spiritual experiences, just like you want to go back and read the Scriptures again and again, and every time you do they reveal more and more. They're gifts."

"Even seeing the auras of big-league pitchers? I mean, that was sort of bizarre."

Lory nodded.

"Spiritual experiences are to be honored. They should never make you afraid. If you are afraid of your spiritual experiences, you just ask the Holy Spirit: 'Teach me what you would have me learn from this.'"

Without laying it out in any recognizable form, especially for a non-church person like me, Lory continued to invoke basic religious terminology. Scripture. Jesus. The Bible. And now the Holy Spirit. I'd heard them all before, of course, but just as I didn't know what the Last Supper really was, I didn't know—and I really hadn't cared to know—about the rest.

"Lory, what the heck *is* the Holy Spirit?"

"The Holy Spirit is the energy and voice of God that exists in all of us," he answered immediately. "In Genesis it says that Adam fell into a deep sleep—it never said he woke up. The dream we're dreaming is that we're separate from God. But God never leaves his children comfortless—that's one of the things the Holy Spirit is called: the Comforter. It's also called The Holy Whisper—I like that one. The still, quiet voice within that always speaks of love and peace.

"So these are never-ending stories," he went on. "You go back again and again to your father's face in the sky, to the pitchers' auras, and ask to be taught, and you'll learn a great deal. The Holy Spirit will interpret the experience for you. In fact, the Holy Spirit will interpret every experience you have, whether it's mystical or not.

"As a child of God we have incredible power, we're a powerful holy child of God speaking to a powerful holy parent. And yet most people pray to God like Eddie Haskell."

"Eddie Haskell??"

"Yeah, you know, the creep on *Leave It to Beaver.* We pray like we're stuck-ups, filled with hatred and greed and fear and anger, and we don't tell God what's really going on. We try to hide the truth of our lives from God, but He already knows. And He sends us spiritual experiences when we're ready for them."

"But they, they just feel so strange. Like you're in a different dimension or something."

"And isn't it a beautiful feeling?"

I had to think about that one.

"Well, I guess so. They're kind of peaceful and sparkly at the same time. And they change how you see things—I mean, when you're having one everything seems, I don't know ... perfect. Like being on Earth is rolling around heaven ... instead of hell."

Lory laughed.

"Grace is perfect peace. It's the highest goal. There's nothing higher. Falling out of grace is like a fish falling out of the ocean. It's impossible. You can't fall out of grace because grace always is. Now, the big question is, What thoughts are you holding on to that disconnect you from experiencing the grace you're in?"

10

MUD AND WATER

November 1995

It didn't take long to realize that it's not only our thoughts that disconnect us from grace. Sometimes it really is the constant messages from our personal environment and the people in it. In one gin-clear moment, almost a year to the day after meeting the Holy Pig Farmer, I knew my marriage was over.

I was standing in my kitchen washing dishes when the realization hit me—it was time for me to go. The truth was, I was on some kind of spiritual fast track that my husband wasn't remotely interested in and didn't—or couldn't—understand. I really didn't understand it either, but the journey had begun like a runaway train. Or, more accurately, like a lightning bolt made out of rosebuds. And as eerie as it was, I wouldn't have stopped it if I could have—it was intoxicating! Talk about an adventure. I had no idea what supernatural event was going to happen next. Snorkeling with a lovesick whale is a cheap novel compared to the true romance of the spiritual path.

Still, like most people, I remained in a marital stall. A divorce is a kind of death, the destruction of a small civilization, someone once said, whose roads reach out to family and friends in all directions. Leaving a marriage, even when you need to, can be a very difficult thing to do. Someone else said that your spirit leaves a bad marriage years before your body does. In the end, what finally kicked me out the door was a book.

51

A magazine editor had called to offer me an assignment on a Southern California spa that specializes in mud treatments, my usual earthbound type of story. Thrilled at the thought of studying the natural healing properties of clay, I ordered a suite of books on geology from the library. The first one to arrive was titled *Mud and Water.*

But it was no science tome. It was, in fact, the spiritual teachings of a fourteenth-century Japanese Zen Buddhist master named Tokusho Bassui. What goofy good fortune! A fervent electricity ran through his words, even on the printed page.

"As the sun shines everywhere in a cloudless sky, how can you place limits on the power derived from seeing into your own nature? The words of this ragged monk cannot describe this supernatural power properly. It's like a spinning wheel which moves faster than a flash of lightning ... it destroys the power of evil demons, blows out the burning charcoal under boiling kettles of hell. All are equipped with this original nature. From the beginning everyone is complete and perfect."

Wasn't that another way of saying we are all holy children of God? Master Bassui sounded an awful lot like the Holy Pig Farmer. And when I read his words, flames seemed to leap up from them and burn holes in everyday reality ... nice light reading for the ferry ride to West Seattle.

"Listen to this," I said excitedly to my husband. "The substance of this Buddha nature is like a great burning fire. Life, death, and nirvana will be yesterday's dream.

"The countless worlds will be like foam on the sea. You will be like a log thrown into a fire, your whole body ablaze, without being aware of the heat!!" I was practically panting. But when I looked up, I saw that the man I had vowed to have dinner with for the rest of my life would have been just as intrigued by a new cure for lice.

"You're not interested in this at all, are you?" I asked. He gazed at me blankly and shook his head.

"But why *not*?" I implored him.

"I don't know," he replied, and I saw that he really didn't.

That night I escaped the deficiencies of my own marriage by observing the obvious sympatico between our host and hostess. We had gone to

Thanksgiving dinner at the home of newly married friends of ours. The man of the couple was recovering from lymphatic cancer and his doctors had just informed him that chemotherapy had rendered him permanently sterile: he would never be able to father a child. He and his wife were heartbroken. Musicians both, their very movements seemed to harmonize with one another, moment by moment. What a tragedy that a child couldn't come from such a union.

As I stood by their small stove helping them cook our supper and wondering about this injustice, without warning a little boy came running full-throttle through the kitchen. I saw him as clearly as I saw my own husband sitting in the corner reading the sports page. The child was so real I jumped out of his way, much to everyone's surprise. I looked at our friends and they looked at me and I put a hand on my hip and declared in no uncertain terms:

"I don't care *what* your doctors say, you guys are going to have a son."

Mud and Water

A COLLECTION OF TALKS
BY THE ZEN MASTER
BASSUI

Translated by Arthur Braverman

Part II

Flowering Bay

The Blue Grosbeak by Mark Catesby

May all be free from sorrow and the causes of sorrow;
May all never be separated from the sacred happiness which is sorrowless.

<small>FROM THE FOURTEENTH DALAI LAMA'S PRAYER</small>

11

LITTLE HOUSE IN THE BIG WOODS

February 1996

The property was an abandoned hazelnut farm when I found it, a glorious piece of McKenzie River waterfront just twenty-five miles east of Eugene. Perfect for a Duck, which I was at the time, being a student at the University of Oregon, home of the Ducks. My parents had asked me to look around for vacation property for them, and the moment I saw that little piece of the McKenzie River Valley, I knew it was theirs.

Sure enough, they flew up the next day, took one look, and bought the old orchardland on the spot. My parents loved the place so much they decided to move themselves and the family business there a few years later, turning what had begun as a summer home into their permanent residence.

In educational circles, my mother, Mary Meeker, was and remains a legend. A professor of educational psychology at the University of Southern California and former Harvard lecturer, she pioneered the first comprehensive diagnostic and remedial program for pinpointing and addressing common learning problems in children. Her work took off with the help of my stepfather's computer genius, and in 1969 they founded the Structure of Intellect Institute to market their groundbreaking tests and training materials. Her work earned her many honors, including being voted Education Leader of the Year in 1981 and being selected by the U.S. Office of Education as one of five social scientists "whose work holds promise for education in the twenty-first century."

But to us, Mother was always our mother first. I'm sure my sisters and I will never know the full extent of her and my stepfather's sacrifices to provide us with every opportunity and all possible support, none of which she received growing up, which made it all the more dear. "I have never found that words really expressed adequately my love for each of my daughters," she had written each of us four years earlier in cards she'd painted herself to accompany recordings of the Maori opera virtuoso Kiri Te Kanawa. "And so when I first heard Kiri sing Puccini's 'O Mio Babbino Caro,' I knew that the music and her voice were expressing for me the depths of my feelings for each of you. So listen, please, and understand that it says with music what I could never say. If children do choose their parents," she added, "then I am forever grateful that you chose me."

You can imagine, then, the unspoken comfort of being invited back home when I so needed a place to heal. Now, ten years after Mother and Bob had bought the property, there were flower gardens, raspberry patches, fruit trees, a pond with a little waterfall (and big frogs), even a croquet court, but they left most of it in woods. It was a kind of paradise, anchored in the quiet, deep love that radiated from my mother and stepfather at all times. When I had told them I was leaving my own less-than-perfect marriage, rather than try to talk me out of it, they offered me their small guesthouse next to the big woods. The little house even sidelined some of the best steelhead holding water on the McKenzie, an unexpected plus since I had just signed a contract to write a book about learning to fly-fish.

Only the peaceful image of my Little House in the Big Woods calmed the endless fireballs of guilt that scorched my mind every time I thought about leaving my sweet but hapless husband. I imagined myself snug in my new home, with rain tiptoeing on the roof and the call of the osprey to keep me company, my parents just across the roses for good measure. I would meditate in the woods every day (and become so holy, holy, holy). There would be steelhead and trout in the fall, wild truffles in the winter (Oregon does have them), the orchards in bloom in the spring, and pie berries all summer long. The new year lay out before me like the burning wheel of dharma Master Bassui wrote about: balanced, purifying, and spinning new life into the void of my current one. I said "I'm so sorry!" a thousand times in one direction while thinking "Get me outta here!" a thousand times in the other. Over and over I told my soon-to-be-ex that there was nothing wrong with him, we were just a mismatch and I knew he'd meet someone wonderful someday. "Someone who can give you children," I added, something we both wanted terribly and I'd failed at completely. Blinking back tears of genuine sorrow and authentic joy at the same time, I blindly packed up my trusty Isuzu Trooper, and then Tillie the Wonder Corgi and I left the island for the last time, arriving at my parents' little guesthouse just in time for Christmas. Tillie and I moved in, settled down, and started our new routine.

Five minutes later I was bored out of my mind.

How could this be? How could Perfect Peace be undone so quickly? I had seen my father's face in the sky! I had studied with the Holy Pig Farmer! I'd even been visited upon by the real live Living Christ, for Chrissake! And I *knew* that the realm of the Spirit was as real as the material world. Realer! But alone in my little house, that precious sacred knowledge ceased to mean much at all. I wanted playmates. Action. Someone to talk with. I wanted *people* to relate to and share all this peace with. The endless quiet was driving me insane. So much for instant enlightenment. Lory Misel's edgy benediction ricocheted in my head: "The spiritual path will beat the hell out of you." I should have listened. Instead, only two months into my much-anticipated new life on the river, in desperation, I called the only person I still knew in Eugene: Harrison Brandt.

Truth be told, Harrison was a former suitor I had ditched ten years earlier because he was just too weird. My mother had introduced us, thinking him excellent husband material: well-bred, wealthy, and handsome in a golfer sort of way. I quite agreed. At our first meeting—lunch with my mother—when we shook hands little electrical explosions had run up my arm. Yikes.

Regular postcards had followed, filled with praise and witty wordplay (be still my heart). It was like living in a modern Jane Austen novel, all foreshadowing and promise. Soon, Harrison began making the very long trek from Eugene to Seattle just to see me. Always the gentleman, he would take me out to dinner somewhere fabulous, we'd talk for hours, then he would escort me back to my apartment and go off to a hotel room he'd booked for himself—where, I never knew. Harrison Brandt had breasted his romantic cards like no leading man since Mr. Darcy. After a half dozen of these opaque visits he still hadn't even held my hand. Confused to the point of dizziness, I had ended up succumbing to the All American easy-to-read attentions of the man I did marry, the one I had just left. Now, here was Harrison again, returning my call with his usual ardor as if no time had passed at all when, in fact, so much had.

"Where are you?" Harrison asked softly, his voice slipping through the phone lines like gin and tonic.

"Upriver," I replied.

"For how long?"

"Well, actually . . . I live here now."

Pause.

"I want to see you."

He wants to see me? His voice rang with eighteenth-century urgency. I couldn't thwart a schoolgirl giggle. Mr. Brandt had been light-years away from my life's center for almost a decade—so, what was this sudden fire all about?

"Well, come out for lunch with Mother and me," I suggested. That seemed innocent enough.

Harrison's impending arrival threw me into rounds of fresh activity, much as awaited visits by city gentlemen must have titillated English country maids. Or, perhaps, as a rotten egg excites a starving person—something I might have considered but didn't.

The day bloomed cool as usual, and fair, one of the great secrets of Western Oregon: our darkest months are marked by a surprising number of vivid sunny days, the design, I'm sure, of a merciful God intent on keeping Northwesterners from jumping en masse into the Pacific each winter. Outsiders—Lewis and Clark, for instance—tend to miss these brilliant weather breaks and end up freighting their journals with desperado statements like Clark's on November 22, 1805: "O, how horriable [sic] is the day!"

Lunch was pleasant. We sat in the rose garden with our jackets on, Harrison's winter tan glowing like a neon sign screaming "Palm Springs! Palm Springs!"

"Golf," he explained, then asked me to show him the property.

"Looks like a lot of changes have happened around here in the last ten years."

I fought off a "duh" and settled on: "So, how are things at home?"

Mother had told me Harrison was married, I hoped more happily than I had been. His mouth made a tiny o.

"I'm separated," he said gravely.

I stifled a laugh. He sounded so eggular, as if his interior were divided in two, ála cookbook directions, or a recipe for disaster. My amusement skidded to a halt when Harrison suddenly reached out and put his hands on my shoulders.

"So, what is your version of what happened?" he asked as if we were standing in the wind on the moors.

For one awful moment I thought he thought I somehow had inside information on his marital troubles.

"Uh, what happened to *what*?" I ventured.

"To us."

I had to laugh that time.

"Oh, you know, Mother thought we were perfect for each other and was sure we'd get married ... but I didn't think you even liked me!"

Harrison looked as though I'd just hit him with a nine iron. Real tears welled in his eyes.

"I carried the torch for you ever since you ..." he said in a voice that dropped like heavy water, enriched and dangerous. "And the strangest part? I just threw out all your letters last month, figuring there was no hope. Now here you are. Maybe God is giving us a second chance."

I've spent years wondering why I didn't say: "Well, what happened to the first chance God gave us?" Or just run shrieking into the woods. My best guess is that it's just a little too romantic to hear someone so much like Mr. Darcy (well-bred, wealthy, handsome) admit he's been pining away for you for years. Regardless, instead of fleeing I stepped willingly into purgatory; I knew this guy was weird. It soon became clear that my own path to Deep Heaven ran, by necessity, directly through the fires of hell with Harrison. His family name should have been a clue. Brandt: "a farmer who lives on land cleared by burning."

12

GOD SPEED

April 1996

You're going salmon fishing in *Argentina*? Why don't you just fish in front of your own house?"

Rande always thought my adventures were more trouble than they were worth, and this from someone who thinks nothing of making eight pies for Thanksgiving. One woman's torte is another woman's torture.

"The Northwest doesn't have golden salmon," I explained.

Luckily, one of the prettiest regions in South America does, and an editor had agreed to send me there in pursuit of this rare trophy fish that looks as if it really is dipped in gold. Just the Holy Grail I needed to get me away from home. Or, more precisely, Harrison.

The more he had become a regular visitor to my riverside haven, the more I descended into perpetual discontent until it had bottomed out in a kind of chronic contamination, an unctuous blue glue from which I seemed incapable of escaping. Worse, whenever Harrison left my little house to drive back to town, I would be struck down by a grief so vicious my poor parents didn't know how to comfort me. It felt as though I was stuck in some kind of nonsensical tragic drama, playing Ophelia to Harrison's Othello. Rande could barely stand it.

"I liked you a lot better as Lucy," she sniffed.

So did I; hence my upcoming trip to South America—traveling always makes me happy. But that was still weeks away. I'd love to be able to say that my fun travel plans allowed me to put Harrison out of my mind and get back to being my goofy, if slightly bored-in-the-countryside, self, but they did not. I seemed to be under some sort of spell.

"I don't think your grief is from this lifetime," my mother said finally.

This untenable sorrow continued to shadow me like bad weather until, in the middle of yet another round of falling asleep clutched by the talons of this griefus absurdis, I was awakened by something not of this world.

When I opened my eyes that remarkable night, I saw that my alarm clock read 3:00 AM. I also saw that there was something in the room with me. It was big and it was red and it was hovering above the foot of my bed. It looked like some sort of red light, or, more accurately, a red light being. It was not human, but I sensed that it was both alive and intelligent, the way one senses the presence of a cat or a bird. I also somehow knew that it was feminine. And it radiated a kind of rapt benevolence, like a disembodied version of Cinderella's fairy godmother.

But this light-creature did not belong to any earthly zoological roster. A good four feet in diameter and shaped like a galaxy, it was a long oval blurred at its edges. And it was moving. For many minutes it remained suspended in midair in front of me, rotating clockwise very slowly, its pace deliberate and full of what can only be called grace. It reminded me of the way Lory Misel talked—that soft, calming cadence—and, oddly, of the deep sweet peace in the pace of the old song "In the Still of the Night."

The light being was so beautiful, its presence so soothing, that I wasn't afraid of it at all. Quite suddenly I realized that for the first time in months I was happy. Deeply, profoundly happy. Even happier than my old pre-Harrison happy self. I was ecstatically happy and completely at peace, much as I had always been after Tuesdays with Lory. It was as if the slow orbits of the strange red light moved, if you will, at the speed of God, its beneficent force field creating some kind of centrifugal dynamic that drew out and neutralized every single shard of negativity in my little corner of the universe.

I could hardly wait for morning so I could call Lory.

"I've had experience with orange light beings, but not red," Lory said as if color selection were the point. "Sometimes, when I'm doing group therapy, an orange ball of energy comes in and moves around the room."

"Really?"

"Yes."

"And does everyone feel ... really happy?"

"The energy of God is always cooperative; it's all assistance and love. When you wish to receive the energy of God, which exists only to love and bless, you're given all the assistance you need."

"But are we supposed to ... to see it?"

"Sometimes we see it and sometimes we don't. The energy of God is beyond our five senses. If everyone could see God's energy all the time, we wouldn't play this game, would we?"

I could hear the metal music of Lory's car keys.

"I've got to get to the feed store," he said. "I'll call you soon."

13

EVIL FURNITURE

March 1997

The Visitation of the Great Red Light Being had offered the same thing the Holy Pig Farmer did: spiritual assistance—that's what its presence felt like. And after two predictably glorious weeks in Argentina, my home front persona improved considerably. Nothing like catching golden salmon in a lagoon full of purple water lilies to cheer yourself up. Not to mention a super friendly ghost. In Washington I had a real, live spiritual teacher who happened to be a pig farmer; in Oregon I had one totally weird night light ... Okey-dokey!

But as the rest of the year rolled on, I felt as though I were a million miles away from the Holy Pig Farmer's healing presence. How could I have been stupid enough to leave not only my best friend, Rande, but spiritual assistance personified?

By 1997, Harrison had begun to work through his own divorce proceedings—mine were pretty much a fait accompli by then—and I had resolved to stay happy before and after his upriver visits, which is all we ever had because he still claimed not to be "ready" to be seen with me in public lest his wife see us and demand even more money. Not exactly the cherry on top of my self-esteem sundae.

I signed up for Zydeco dance lessons and a fly-tying class in town. At the latter, I made a wonderful new friend—Greg Tatman—who quickly

67

became, like Guido, the fishing brother I never had. Greg even looked like he could be my brother.

A tall, redheaded, slow-talking jokester, Greg was famous in the Pacific Northwest for founding Tatman Wooden Boats, a little company that built classic McKenzie River driftboats, the traditional fly-fishing vessel of the McKenzie Valley.

"Want to fish Redside Riffle with me this weekend?"

"Oh, darn ... I can't!" I wailed into the phone. "I have to finish my golden salmon story then get back to my fishing book and Tillie needs her nails clipped and I promised Mother I'd help her frame some paintings and then I'm meeting Rande in Portland ..."

"... and Bob's your uncle ..." Greg added.

Any Girlfriend Getaway with Rande, of course, was like hitching a ride on the Good Humor Ice Cream truck. So when Rande told me she had to attend an educational seminar only a two-hour drive away, I had jumped at the chance.

On a practical note, Rande could pick up the pretty antique vanity I'd been making payments on at a shop just north of Portland.

We had our usual wonderful time: a Dagwood sandwich of new discoveries (new must-read books, mascara that really doesn't clump), musings (only in super politically-correct Eugene would guys apologize for leading during dance lessons), rants (there were more unwed mothers at Rande's high school than ever), true confessions (I'm afraid the spiritual life isn't all it's cracked up to be; Rande can't get enough time alone with God), and, always, our creative progress reports: Rande on her latest ceramic designs, I on my fishing book. She was such a balm to Harrison's bomb—O, why didn't we live next door to each other! When we transferred my antique vanity from Rande's minivan to the Trooper and hugged good-bye, Rande whispered, "I hope you get rid of that guy soon."

The spider was the first sign of a problem with the vanity. There I was driving seventy miles an hour down Interstate 5 when the thing suddenly appeared on the driver's door inches from my elbow: the biggest, hairiest, most menacing orange-and-black spider I'd ever seen. In fact, I'd never seen anything like it. Normally, I'm the naturalist who escorts indoor spiders outdoors before someone else squashes them. But this one only inspired instant violence. I grabbed my purse and beat the thing to gooey smithereens . . . then burst into tears. I never kill innocent insects! What the heck was wrong with me? Of course, technically, spiders aren't insects, and this one sure didn't seem to be innocent.

Back at the guesthouse, my parents' property manager, Mike Treadway, helped me move the vanity to my upstairs bedroom loft. I'd collected antiques my entire adult life, and with my old Larkin writing table and Victorian bed, the ornate little vanity nicely completed my pretty bedroom trilogy. I hoped Harrison would like it. That night, before I turned out the lights, I glanced lovingly at my new acquisition. I could scarcely believe my eyes: the vanity was seething. A furious energy seemed to radiate from it in all directions. It looked possessed.

Oh, great, I thought, *yet another step on the path of spiritual insanity.*

I regarded my antique writing table; it was its sweet and peaceful self. I looked at my antique bed. Same thing. I glanced back at the vanity—it positively throbbed with rage.

"Well, I have finally lost it," I told myself, and turned off my reading lamp.

The tug-of-war between logic and intuition continued for about a week. Each time, logic won—the vanity stayed. But every morning I woke up with my back to the thing, sleeping on the opposite side from which I normally sleep.

Finally, a terrible dream woke me up in the middle of the night. It was really more like watching a horrifying home movie. A bloodied, naked man was kneeling on the floor beside my vanity, his right arm held up over his head, his wrist handcuffed to one of the vanity's winged wooden mirror brackets. Towering above him was another man dressed head to toe in black leather, like a Ku Klux Klansman from the Darker Side. This man was holding some kind of awful whip studded with metal, a modern cat-o'-nine-tails.

When he lifted it to beat the crouching naked man, I woke up gasping.

I glared at the vanity. "That's IT!" I yelled. "I have HAD it with evil furniture!!"

The next morning I asked Mike to come over and look at the vanity. A sensitive, God-loving fellow, he always makes a valiant attempt to treat everyone with patient kindness, and often repeats his favorite Bible mantra: "A soft word turneth away wrath—Proverbs 15:1," which, you have to admit, is a lot better than going around appeasing God with the pleasing odor of burnt female goat fat—Leviticus 4:28–31.

"Do you sense anything strange about this thing?" I asked Mike.

He put a hand on his chin and studied the vanity.

"You mean, like, 'I'm here and you're not?'" he replied.

"Exactly." Mike had read the vanity's there's-only-room-in-this-loft-for-one-of-us energy perfectly.

"It's outta here," he declared, and moved the vanity into the garage of The Building, our name for a big structure on the other side of the property that houses my parents' educational business.

Later that night, all the lights in The Building suddenly went on for no apparent reason. Sheepishly, I told my mother the truth.

"Oh, great, Jessica," she said. "Well, we'd better call Alan," meaning her favorite antique dealer.

When Alan arrived the next day, he took one look at the vanity and made the chilling announcement: "I know who'll buy this—one of the satanic cults in town." Then he let out such a loud hooting laugh I wasn't sure if he was joking or not.

The next time the Holy Pig Farmer called to check in on me, I told him about the vanity.

"Every object carries its history," he advised. "When the Indian mystic Sai Baba meets someone, he knows everything about their past and everything about their future. He sees it. We radiate energy. Everything does. And we leave our psychic imprints on objects."

Lory said that we're always reading the energy emanating from other people or things, that it's part of being the "multisensory beings" that we are, which explains why sometimes we want to turn around and run out of someone's house the moment we walk into it, and sometimes we want to stay at a new place forever.

"Psychics are able to read the subtler energy associated with an object," he said. "Many years ago, a woman was teaching me about energy. She gave me an object and told me to close my eyes and tell her what I saw. I saw a teacher in a room, a classroom, and I described this person perfectly. I knew that she only worked there part time. She was the person who had given the woman this item as a gift."

Lory paused for what felt like an eternity.

"See, everything is energy," he said at last. "That's what 'things' really are. That's what we are. The basis of all life is just glorious, mysterious, beautiful, intelligent energy, and that energy was around for billions of years before human beings came on the scene. All primitive people tried to dance with this energy, and then religion came in and taught us to stop interacting with it and start thinking about it. People who embrace the loving energy in life are dancing with the energy of the universe itself. And," he added, "people who are full of anger or fear are drawn to people filled with joy and love."

"But ... why?"

"Because they run on the energies of the ego, and the whole motivation of the ego is to get—to get whatever they can, from others, from nature, from anyone or anything. Since holy energies only want to give, ego-driven people are very drawn to holy people. They try very hard to make you dance with their negative energy, which is a sort of Death Dance ..."

Lory's voice slipped into the lower registers. I heard him inhale through his nose, like an opera singer or a tai chi master. Or a concerned spiritual coach.

"If you're going to be a holy woman, Jessica, you must only dance with joyful, creative, sensual, loving energy. Dance with anything else and you will lose your way."

Rande flew down to visit a few months later, and Harrison took us all out to dinner. When she and I were alone back in my little house afterward, I spilled the beans about how miserable I was with Harrison.

"It's like he's never fully with me, and I always end up feeling like one of those Victorian butterflies stuck in a glass case."

I didn't have to say much more. Rande already knew how bad it was. She looked at me with the laser-like eyes of a best friend and said: "He's trying to destroy you, Jess. You need to think of Harrison as the devil. If you marry him, I won't come to your wedding."

14

FLOWERING BAY

July 1997

Greg Tatman shook his head. His round glasses bounced on his nose. He looked like a mop-topped *Sesame Street* character disapproving of somebody's manners.

"No," he said. "Nope. Not hardly. No, this guy Harrison, he doesn't get it."

Greg had driven out to fish the tailwater in front of my parents' place with me, and I'd told him about The Trouble with Harrison on our walk to the river. Greg sighed when I told him I'd never been out in public with Harrison. At that, Greg stopped midstride and looked at me.

"Well, it's all about him, isn't it. He's a drinker, right?"

"Used to be," I replied.

"Uh huh. Alcoholics love happy people like you."

I cringed. My ex-husband drank too. What is it with these guys and me?

"Pardon my French, but alcoholics think they're the piece of shit the world rotates around. They just love someone who wants to take care of them. Harrison go to AA?"

"Yes."

"That's a start. My big brother's been in AA for years. Still fighting his demons. Some alcoholics get healed if they take the spiritual part of AA seriously. But for others …" he shook his head again. "See, it might be a personality type issue. Some people are just hardwired to see themselves—and not you—at the center of their universe. They make lousy partners for anyone."

Greg brightened.

"Hey, maybe Harrison could fall into an upholstery machine and come out fully recovered!"

Greg Tatman on the McKenzie River

We fished in front of my parents' place all afternoon, and as much fun as Greg was, even a day on the water with him didn't chase away the blues that had descended once more after Harrison's visit the day before. No matter how hard I tried, I just couldn't seem to stuff the corners of my life-beyond-Harrison with enough goodness to stay on spiritual true north while he was at the heart of things. Wasn't this why I had left my marriage? Being with Harrison was much worse. It did feel like . . . a Death Dance.

"The thing that keeps us from enlightenment is comfort."

Lory's voice seemed even richer with compassion than usual.

"We are all busting our tails to be comfortable, then we find ourselves in a position where everything we thought was good and right and true isn't. Jesus went into the desert. The Buddha sat under the Bodhi Tree. Native Americans went on vision quests and asked to be put into the dark night of the soul. Going there makes you realize you can't rely on yourself, you must rely on something greater. When you left the island, you began your Heroine's Journey."

"I did?" I had no idea I was on a girl's version of Joseph Campbell's renowned "Hero's Journey."

"Oh yes," Lory replied. "You are on it. You're living the dark night of the soul now. That's when epiphanies usually happen. Darkness, the deep dark places, those energies can be your best teachers. Yes, yes."

"But then why did that beautiful red light being show up?" I interrupted impatiently.

Silence.

I knew what the Holy Pig Farmer was thinking. To brush off an experience that has throttled your senses and backed you into an intellectual corner, desperate for both examination and clarity—that sort of spiritual marginalization is precisely what the ego would have us do. It's what poet Gerard Manley Hopkins meant when he instructed all of us standing on the "frightful, sheer, no-man-fathomed" cliffs of the mind to "hold them cheap." He was joking. He knew that to make light of the immutably deep, the wildly unanswerable, to clobber it with clichés, froth it into mindless "God Is My Copilot" soufflé ripe for logic's penknife (one would assume that, if anything, one is God's copilot), to beat it into a manageable pulp so one might smear it, mask-like, across one's mortified face in an attempt to hide one's mortification ... *that* is holding the unfathomable cheap.

Meaning it's too hot to handle otherwise. And that just would not do. Not for someone lucky enough to have seen the light. The *red* light.

Yes, I had seen a glorious red light. I had *seen* a glorious red light, a moving, healing, astonishing, feminine red light that had somehow brought me perfect peace when I had been in a complete psychic free fall, the mind's steepest no-man-fathomed cliffs whistling past me at impossible emotional velocities. I had seen a red light, and it, apparently, had seen me. It was real. And its existence proved the existence of such things. In real time. In one's waking state, not in "a dream." On earth, as it is in heaven. Genuine bodiless light beings that know you exist and, even more astonishingly, care about you and your—speaking globally—small, small problems ... at least care enough to pay you a friendly visit in the middle of the night and do something about them.

It is one thing to "see a ghost," a common spectral apparition in the form of, say, the deceased resident of a very old house—though, if you think about it, such an event speaks volumes about "reality." But it's quite another to be visited upon by a life form you've never heard of that is clearly in full possession of intelligence and intention and the will to use either and both for the highest good. *Your* highest good.

And didn't the very goodness of The Red One presuppose an actual *source* of goodness, as well as its willingness and ability to send in relief on its behalf? The more I gave the experience pause, the more I saw it as astoundingly irrefutable evidence of the very same source of goodness that turned C. S. Lewis toward the spiritual, toward *Christ* for goodness sake, in the first place.

The Holy Pig Farmer's voice echoed its usual message of hope into the phone yet again: "When you are ready to seek the mysteries of God, you want to go back to your spiritual experiences, just like you want to go back and read the Scriptures again and again, and every time you do they reveal more and more."

I was indeed visiting this particular spiritual experience anew. What I wanted to know this time was why the miraculous peace the red light being had brought me so many months ago didn't stick. And why had it been made visible to me in the first place? Why hadn't it just arrived on soundless wings and done its job, allowing me to wake up in the morning feeling like my jolly old self *and keep feeling that way*, allowing me to chalk it all up to good luck . . . or something I ate? That I was able to witness this thing at all was a completely different riddle: why me? Why on earth was I suddenly, for lack of a better term, seeing angels?

Harrison drove out for dinner again a few days later. Once again, my extreme grief returned after he left. But before I woke up the next morning I had a most unusual dream.

It was more of a flashback, really. In it, Harrison and I were standing on a vast piece of lush property. It was warm, maybe late spring. Somehow, I knew we were in the American Deep South, but where? I also knew this had taken place long, long ago. We were very young, and very much in love, and, I realized, we were engaged to be married. Harrison was showing me the land that soon would be our new home.

With a gallant wave of his arm, he described where we'd put the horse barns and the house. Then in soft, almost British tones, he started

identifying the wildflowers around us, an odd role reversal since in this
life I'm the informed nature lover, not he. He went on and on with a
schoolboy's pride, saying this is so-and-so and that is such-and-such.
The only name I remember is something I'd never heard of: "flowering
bay." In my dream the plant had fragrant, big white magnolia-like
blooms and strange bright red berries suspended from some sort of hard
brown seed pods hanging from slender threads. I awoke with Harrison's
words in my mind: "And this, my dear, is flowering bay." When I opened
my eyes, I was as full of fresh joy as I had been after the red light being
visited me.

Not a split second later the phone rang. It was Harrison.

"I just had the strangest experience," he said.

He had been doing his morning meditation, when, he said, all of a
sudden his mind opened up.

"It was like watching a movie," he told me. "First I saw a close-up of
these black leather shoes with big buckles. Then I saw some britches, and
one of those old-fashioned ruffled white shirts. And I realized I was wearing
these things. I was quite the strapping lad," he said, "living on a southern
plantation two hundred years ago. I'm pretty sure it was in Virginia. And
you were my wife."

Harrison told me I was standing on the porch of our plantation home,
waving at him as he walked in from the fields. I was, he said, wearing a
dress held wide by a hoopskirt, an item of horribly inconvenient feminine
apparel that, inexplicably, I've always loved. In fact, I own one.

"As I was walking up to the house," Harrison told me, "a young man
came riding up on horseback, full tilt. He jumped down and handed me an
important letter. Whatever it said—something political—I had to leave
immediately and was embarrassed that I didn't have time to change into
my city clothes."

It turned out that the Revolutionary War was beginning, and Harrison—or whoever he was back then—was involved in the complex politics
of the birthing of America. "The bottom line is that I went away to war,"
he said, "and I didn't come back. I was fine, of course, but you … you
were destroyed."

I rushed over to my parents' house to tell my mother what had happened. Her eyes widened with recognition.

"Well," she said, "I guess that explains things."

Some years later, when I Googled "flowering bay" on the Internet, a beautiful botanical print of a bird popped up. It was an etching of a blue grosbeak by the English naturalist Mark Catesby, who, in 1731, published the first guide to American flora and fauna, a two-book set widely hailed as the authority on New World plants and animals for nearly a century. Catesby began his research during a 1712 trip to America to visit his sister who lived in Virginia. In this particular print, the blue grosbeak is perched on a branch, eating bright red berries that hang on slender threads from hard brown seed pods among rich white blooms of *Magnolia Lauri folio*, Latin for "sweet flowering bay."

15

LET HIM GO

August 1997

 I n the near future, scientists are going to realize that there are parallel universes stacked up next to each other."

The Holy Pig Farmer was on his cell phone, walking around the farm. I could hear the pigs oinking in the background while Tillie barked at a deer outside my office window.

"Time is not linear. Time is holographic. All lives, past, present, and future, are going on right now. People who experience past lives are just watching a different video screen."

I had, of course, called Lory to give him a report on my apparent past life experience with Harrison. It was a subject we'd never discussed before, and I had no idea what the Holy Pig Farmer really thought about the very Eastern concept of recycled souls. Lory chuckled.

"When people ask me if I believe in reincarnation, I always say no ... but maybe I will in my next life."

"Lory! This is serious. I mean, it wasn't a dream. I *was* there. With Harrison. In Virginia, we think. Two hundred years ago!"

I was sure that this experience held the key to my otherwise unlikely relationship with someone like Harrison.

"Okay, say you've had nine or ten past lives with the same person," he replied as if he were talking about how many eggs a hen had just laid. "And say you were never able to forgive him and bless him and let him go. Then you meet the same person—Harrison in this life—and you're able to forgive him and bless him and let him go."

"Let him go?"

"All work is to be done in this lifetime," Lory replied, "and the things we need to learn are presented to us in this lifetime. So, in a way, past lives don't matter. And they're very seductive, because when we get caught up in the drama of past lifetimes ... " *Especially if they took place during the American Revolution!* I thought, "they take our attention away from blessing and forgiving and letting go right now."

"Another ego trip?"

"Yeah."

The words "let him go" continued to dart around my mind.

"So," I began carefully. "That life in the South with Harrison was ..."

"... was about what you need to do in this life," Lory finished.

The strange and powerful grief embedded in my relationship with Harrison stopped after our mutual antebellum flashback, never to return. As if the Holy Pig Farmer had predicted it, quite suddenly, I had no tolerance for Harrison's self-absorption, and just as suddenly I decided it was time for me to get my own place—and my own life—and move into town.

Part III

My Lunch with Deepak

*I came to realize that without a vessel for my beliefs,
without an unequivocal commitment to a particular community of faith,
I would be consigned to always remain apart, free in the way
that my mother was free, but also alone in the same ways
she was ultimately alone.*

PRESIDENT BARACK OBAMA, *THE AUDACITY OF HOPE*

*A church is like a finger pointing to God. After a while, people begin
worshipping the finger. And then they poke their eyes out with it.*

THE HOLY PIG FARMER ON THOMAS MERTON

16

THE CHURCH OF GREG

February 1998

Would you come pick me up and take me to church with you?"

"Really?"

My pal Greg Tatman was caught off-guard.

"Yes . . . really!" I replied, and the force of my own conviction surprised me even more than it did Greg.

It was early 1998, four years since my Christ-on-the-Highway experience, and it had never occurred to me to do anything formal about it until now. For reasons I couldn't explain then and still can't, on that wintry Sunday morning I simply got the call, as preachers say, to go to church.

Some might chalk it up to the fact that I'd just moved into my pretty seventh-floor downtown apartment and everything was new and I was trying to make friends and establish new routines (something that sounds a lot more fun than it really is). But the call to call Greg really was a call, much like the mysterious magnetism that draws men and women into the ministry. Rabbis, imams, monks, nuns, priests, pastors—ask any of them why they chose the road they did and they'll tell you they "got the call." Meaning that they literally felt God calling them to serve spiritually. Most interesting are those who are drawn to the idea of going into the ministry but in the end decide not to go because they didn't have the call. And so it was that on that vaporous morning, while the Pacific mist went about its usual February business of turning everything outside my windows into fluff, for the first time in my life I woke up to a powerfully distinct call to public worship.

I had no idea where Greg would take me. I didn't even know to which denomination he belonged. And I knew nothing at all about church. My sum total experience in houses of worship was the few times my father had tried to take my sister Valerie and me to some nice church when we were little kids, where the pastor looked so much like Colonel Sanders we inevitably got the giggles and had to be taken out. So, this call to worship was both out of the blue and out of character, but there it was.

As soon as we walked into Central Presbyterian Church that morning, I felt it. That quiet, rooted sense of peace that Greg and the Holy Pig Farmer each radiate. Peace. It always gets back to peace.

Central wasn't a fancy church. In fact, it struck me as rather plain, as traditional Protestant churches are wont to be. But the spiritual vitality I immediately felt there had an almost rococo liveliness. I seemed to have come to the right place.

Of course, I had no idea what to expect. Or what to do. I followed Greg to a pew on the left side, self-consciously taking a seat beside him. People young and old—mostly old—were already settled in. There was a hushed sense of anticipation, but no discernible cowl of fear or guilt as I had long imagined to be the creepy under-coda of all church services. There was reverence, but no holy-holy-holier-than-thou superciliousness—thank goodness, or we would have run the risk of my falling into yet another sacrilegious giggle fit. Things were certainly social, as latecomers were greeted with smiling affection and "sit here with me" gestures, but the obvious timbre of the time was reflective. And the music! Some very accomplished—and passionate—musician up there was totally acing Handel's Organ Concerto in B Flat Major. But the best part was that all these people had gathered together in a clearly sacred act that seemed as natural as morning to them. As for me, once the service started I might as well have landed on Pluto.

Central Presbyterian's Sunday morning protocol was so complex they actually handed out little guides intriguingly labeled "Epiphany." They opened with a quote by Jesus: "I will never turn away anyone who comes to me." Sure reminded me of Lory's "Just a little bit of willingness is all He needs."

But even with my handy bulletin, I had a terrible time keeping up. Things zipped along at a most confusing clip. First there was a "Prayer of Preparation" to be done in silence. I was still doing that when without warning the pastor launched into "Welcome and Announcements," opening with an invitation to enjoy coffee and somebody's homemade Epiphany sticky buns after the worship service in the Fellowship Hall where—lo!—a free diabetes clinic would also be going on.

Then the pastor detailed someone's unfortunate emergency surgery and closed with the hope that "the Lord be with you," which drew such a fast and loud "and also with you" from the whole congregation that I about jumped out of the pew.

Next a man who looked just like my high school geometry teacher strode up front and read: "With profound happiness we welcome one another. How good it is to approach the courts of our God!"

And everyone else responded with "Happy are those who live in God's house! Singing our praise to God fills us with joy!"

Mr. Math continued with "Here we welcome both friend and stranger. All peoples of the earth are God's children. Open your hearts to receive new strength. Open your lives to renewed understandings."

"That's from Psalm eighty-four," Greg whispered.

Not bad.

A tiny turquoise-eyed woman with a helmet of white hair and a piece of paper clutched in her hand bobbled up, took her place behind a lectern that was almost as tall as she was, and began reading:

"Life in the spirit begins a deepening process of internal transformation whose central quality is compassion."

A few heads nodded in agreement, and a grinning middle-aged hippie with his long hair swirled into a topknot at the crown of his head shouted out: "Amen!"

Undaunted, the little woman read on: "Indeed, growth in compassion is the sign of growth in the life of the Spirit."

"Marcus Borg," Greg noted.

"The cheese?" I asked, straining to hear him.

"What a friend we have in cheeses!" he sang back.

The woman at the lectern suddenly stopped reading and looked up, and I thought we were in trouble. "The church," she began more slowly now, "is to be ... to be a vessel of God's passion for healing the world. It is to be a family of transformation. And I think," she concluded, "I think that God can get along just fine without the church. But we cannot."

The man with the topknot applauded. No one else joined him, but now I saw waves of undulating heads nodding their approval. We sure were off to a rousing start.

We were also standing. Without warning, everyone in the sanctuary had just stood up, apparently to sing something. Startled again, I stood too, my bulletin fluttering to the floor like a wounded bird as I stepped on my purse, lost my balance, and crashed into Greg.

"This really moves along, doesn't it."

"Time flies like the wind," he replied sagely. "Fruit flies like bananas."

"Brightest and best of the stars of the morning," sang the congregation. "Dawn on our darkness and lend us your aid."

I scrambled to find the hymn in the hymnal, after I found the hymnal, which looked just like the Bible that was also in the pew rack in front of me, and I was surprised to see that the hymn du jour was written way back in 1811 by someone named Reginald Heber.

"English," Greg said. "Got made Bishop of Calcutta and dropped dead one day after he'd baptized forty-two people."

"Did he drown?" I asked, but Greg didn't answer because suddenly we were sitting down again and everyone had begun to read something called the "Call to Confession" out loud:

"God has called us not to a set of beliefs but to a relationship of trust. We are drawn to the Spirit whose will for us is life at its fullest, attuned to all that is good and true."

These guys weren't messing around.

There was another silent prayer, again way too short for my taste. Then still another hymn—this one in Spanish!—all about *el Niño de Dios* and some kind of perfume. No sooner had we macheted our way through that than the pastor assured us that "God is ever willing to grant us forgiveness, but we cannot receive it if we are unwilling to be changed by it. As long as we focus on preserving our lives," boomed his rich, strong voice, "and protecting our own advantages, we will be lost …"

We can't receive God's forgiveness if we are unwilling to be changed by it? That was huge! That was … gigantic! He meant, I was sure, that God would forgive us for anything … but it was up to US to be willing to take it—and its enormous implications for changing our lives!—in.

I really needed to think about this. Alas, we were standing yet again. And shaking hands this time! A massive tan guy lumbered over and my hand vanished in his, which was more like a heated baseball mitt, while he cranked it and said he wished the "peace of Christ" to be with me.

"Ow! … thanks."

"That's Lance Deal," Greg said as the guy bear-walked away. "He's a big Deal."

"I can see that."

"Won a silver medal in the Olympics."

"For handshaking?" I asked, massaging my thumb.

"Hammer throwing," Greg replied. "You're supposed to wish him peace back."

"Oh … peace!" I called out to Lance's barn door of a back. He turned around, grinned, and flashed me the peace sign, so I flashed it back.

"Hey, this isn't a Dead concert," Greg said, but he was smiling.

Four more sweet-looking elderly people came over to wish me the Peace of Christ, apparently because I didn't look like I already had it. Then each one hugged Greg. He sighed.

"That's why I love it here. It's like having three hundred grandparents."

When everyone settled down again, someone in a black pastor's robe—but not the head guy—appeared with a guitar and called all the children to join him up front for a fun sing-along called "Time for Discovery." But only a few little feet flew down the aisles, which didn't seem to bode well for the future of the church.

Next it was time for the choir's big number, which in church, I learned, is called an "anthem." Dressed in white robes and long white satin ribbon-like scarves, the mixed-age group rose in unison, and with a signal from the young conductor—who turned out to be the same guy who had played the organ so divinely earlier—they opened up with a lilting, waltzing thing called "River in Judea." The harmonies soared, the choir robes swayed, and the words, O the words, how they took us all away with them:

> *There is a river in Judea*
> *That I heard of long ago*
> *And it's a singing, ringing river*
> *That my soul cries outttt . . . to know.*

I was ready to burst into applause at the end, but no one else did—not even Mr. Topknot—and then the main pastor was before us again, his powerful baritone calling out:

> *Hear a just cause, O Lord, attend to my cry;*
> *Give ear to my prayer which is not from deceitful lips . . .*
> *Uphold my steps in Your paths, that my footsteps may not slip.*
> *I have called upon You, for You will hear me, O God;*
> *Incline Your ear to me, and hear my speech.*
> *Show your marvelous loving kindness . . .*
> *Keep me as the apple of Your eye;*
> *Hide me under the shadow of Your wings . . .*
> *I will see Your face in righteousness;*
> *I shall be satisfied when I awake in Your likeness.*

"Psalm seventeen," Greg said under his breath.

"This is the witness of scripture," the pastor concluded. Everyone in the church chanted: "Thanks be to God!" To my surprise I was near tears. It was "I will see Your face in righteousness" that did it. Never had I heard anything so "officially religious" catch the moment of seeing my father's face in the sky. Could there be anything more righteous?

The sermon came next, and I am here to report that the first sermon of my church life, preached by the Reverend Bo Harris, was as stirring as reading any feature story in the *New Yorker*. Lucid, potent, witty, informed, timely, challenging, and crafted like a piece of world-class literature, it was nothing less than a work of art. In twenty minutes flat, that sermon deleted forever my life-long assumption that churches, even good-hearted ones, were by definition intellectual wastelands. This fact has continued to reconfirm itself ever since. Eleven years after my introduction to the erudite sermons of Bo Harris, an interim pastor, Scott Dalgarno, dazzled me witless with his poem "Exquisite Corpse," published in the monthly church bulletin during Holy Week:

> *Jesus came to Bethany, where Laz'arus was, whom Jesus had raised from the dead. There they made him a supper.*
> **JOHN 12:1-2**

Four days dead and sipping soup, Lazarus
sits up, grunts, asks, "What's today?" He reeks
of tomb, but no one blanches at this banquet.

Sister Martha feeds him, wipes his chin, reminding him
of time and mass and the unforgiving weight of resuscitation.
There's that late-charge he thought he was clear of,

and the pruning, and that long look a bar-maid
once gave him, but that's all in Lazarus' moldy brain.
The guests merely gape; the vacuum of the tomb

has sucked every verb from the house, but Mary
has an idea. She produces a jar of nard, pure, priceless,
and gloppy as death. She smashes it like some Jeremiah,

peeling the fractured alabaster, lavishing the ooze
on Jesus' chapped knees and feet. All stand transfixed,
but Lazarus' eyes are still on Martha's spoon,

Hovering a bit out of reach. Slowly he searches the room
for an explanation. There's Mary, as busy as a Martha,
and Martha, nonplussed, her heart churning envy and disgust.

What kind of household is this, Lazarus wonders,
where the dead are fed and the living embalmed?
Nothing sealed is safe; nothing at rest left undisturbed
by the merciless provocations of the living.

As usual, there was no time to ponder the wild implications of my first foray into sophisticated scriptural thought because the members of the congregation had jumped to their feet once more, this time for yet another hymn. I could see why Central Presbyterian Church attracted Olympic athletes: this service was a serious quad and abs workout.

Greg watched me dig through my hymnal like a frantic squirrel trying to find our next hymn.

"You're lost ..." he offered, "but now you're found?"

Maybe so. Miraculously, I managed to locate the hymn before we finished it. It was called "The Kingdom of God on Earth," written in 1873. Yet the words still glowed on the page.

Onward through the darkness of the lonely night
Shining still before them with Thy kindly light
Guide them all, Thy children, homeward from afar
Young and old together, by Thy guiding star.
Light of life that shineth ere the worlds began
Draw Thou near, and lighten every heart of man.

In the words Dick Cavett used more than a decade later to describe his own emotional stealth-attack while witnessing Barack Obama's inauguration: "I had neither planned nor expected to cry." But, as Cavett says, music does bypass the brain and go straight to the heart. Indeed, "as suddenly as a hiccup," I, too, erupted with "an audible, gurgling sob."

When the offertory plate came around, accompanied by a brilliant piano solo of Beethoven's "Ode to Joy," I dropped a twenty-dollar bill into the polished brass bowl, and a few tears too. And when we rose to sing our final hymn—an old-timey Southern song even I had heard before—I stopped lip-syncing and let my own thin-and-watery eternal disappointment of a voice cut loose, because with the power-punch of a choir leading the charge, I was ready to fly away, hallelujah by and by, I'll fly away!

So this was church.

Who would have thought that it was sacred ceremony, and family. Performance, and truth. Illuminating, transformative, authentically sacred, and down home, not to mention a virtual lesson in music history. That so much shared goodness could be packed so gracefully into one short hour absolutely floored me. There was no doubt about it: my first-ever church service had rocked my soul, if not in the bosom of Abraham then at least in the rain shadow of the Holy Pig Farmer. And it was a darn good time too. If Bo Harris had walked out disguised as Colonel Sanders, everyone in the place would have guffawed right along with me. Not that anything that goofy was likely to happen in a Presbyterian church, but ... you never know. One thing was sure: this was no bastion of guilt-inducing hellfire-and-brimstone so busy judging everyone while protecting its own advantages that it didn't have time to be a vessel of God's passion for healing the world.

Like a wonderful book you don't want to end, I couldn't wait for the next church chapter, even though it was a whole week away.

"That was fun!" I told Greg.

"Epiphany is supposed to be fun," Greg replied. "It's a time of great celebration, you know, given that the birth of Christ was bringing fresh light into the world before the darkness of Lent descends. So Christians are supposed to practice new openness and inclusivity and charity and goodness ... and Bob's your uncle!"

I'd heard of Lent, but I truly didn't know what it—or Epiphany—was, any more than I knew what the Holy Spirit was before the Holy Pig Farmer explained it to me. All I knew was that I liked this church very much.

"It's a sweet place, isn't it," I said.

Greg nodded. "Oh, yes. I had to look long and hard to find this church. Trust me, very few churches are like this one."

I just couldn't understand why the place wasn't packed to its holy rafters. Especially with people like me who naturally held "Christian" values long before I even knew what they were.

17

CASTING OUT DEMONS

March 1998

Not long after my first Sunday-go-to-meetin' I woke up in the middle of the night with a roaring sore throat. There, hovering above my bed was another apparition—but it wasn't a Red Light Being, and it wasn't very nice. This time my night visitor was a fearsome thing, a big dark-gray dull blotchy circle with a serrated edge suspended in midair above my feet.

Pulling my mind out of the sweet nest of sleep, I forced myself to focus my attention on this icky entity. Then a string of words I'd never uttered in my life came flying out of my mouth: "In the holy name of Jesus, I cast you OUT!" My body jerked violently, and I saw that the horrid Gray One had faded to about half of what it had been. I summoned all my will and assailed the vile thing once more, and, as foreign as it was to me at that point, I called on Jesus's help one more time. This time my body convulsed so hard I was lifted off my bed. The lightless blotch made a silent visual pop and vanished.

And my sore throat was gone.

"Oh, my God," I breathed. "I just cured myself of a sore throat!"

Like everyone else, I'd heard that Jesus supposedly "cast out demons," but the concept wasn't remotely in my personal conceptual lexicon. In fact, I'd never really thought about it, much less taken it seriously. Now I felt as though I had just been made privy to one of the great secrets of the universe.

"Wow," Rande said when I called to tell her the next day. Then she laughed and said: "Well, you always wanted to be a doctor!"

In August of 1999, the strange hierarchy of Gray Ones was revealed to me in the most dramatic of ways. Ever a fan of Chinese medicine, I went to see a respected local acupuncturist for a routine summer "tonification" treatment, sort of a seasonal tune-up to keep things in balance. The idea is that your bioelectrical system is the subtlest system in the body, and the most fundamental. As the saying in Chinese medicine goes, "Matter (i.e., blood and lymph) follows Chi'i—or energy. A number of things can interrupt the flow of Chi'i, which in turn causes discomfort and dysfuntion: a physical blockage, an emotional reaction, exhaustion, depression, an infection, a pet that will not stop scratching your favorite sofa (which goes back to emotional reactions). Acupuncture needles inserted at specific energy points act like little antennae that jump-start its corresponding energy circuit and, done right, get things moving again. Keep your bioelectricity moving, and everything else moves with it, which, by the way, is the real explanation for why Chinese obstetricians are able to do C-sections with only acupuncture: keep the Chi'i moving and there is no pain. Not a bad life philosophy when you think about it.

When last I'd seen this particular acupuncturist, her own circuitry appeared to be zinging right along and she seemed perfectly healthy. Now she looked terrible, emaciated and fragile, with a sickly yellow cast to her skin.

"What happened to you!?" I blurted out.

"Oh, I caught a nasty virus," she said, "and right afterward I was diagnosed with this weird viral lymphoma."

A cancer caused by a virus?? What she told me next was even more chilling. Another healer in town, she said, had come down with the same virus, and then the same cancer, and the woman had quickly died of it. This doctor looked so awful I felt guilty having her work on me; she's the one who should have been on the table!

That night around 2:00 AM, a Gray One of apocalyptical proportions woke me up. It was bigger, denser, and more maniacally active than anything I'd seen before or have seen since. Nasty didn't begin to describe it. It was horrific. It had huge limbs the girth of big tree branches with which it violently thrashed the air in my bedroom like some kind of demented octopus. And the thing emanated absolute malevolence. If ever there were an image of aggressive evil, this was it. I was quite sure that I was looking at the shadow-twin of the very dangerous virus that had assaulted the acupuncturist and killed her colleague.

This was no time for hysterics. With all my might I summoned all the healing power I could think to call upon—Christ's first, and not wanting to take any chances, I threw in the Buddha and Moses and the Virgin Mary and Muhammad and the Holy Pig Farmer, too, though I was loath to expose my dear spiritual teacher in any way to this truly horrific entity. I focused as hard as I could and mentally let fire. "Get out! GET OUTTT!"

It's no surprise that the Gray One was almost unmovable. Almost. After mentally blasting it a few times—again, with all the help from above and beyond I could muster—I sensed the slightest lessening of its power. So I kept at it. After more than an hour of spiritual combat and who knows how many blasts, even this monster began to fade. Finally, with the soundless popping sensation Gray Ones always make when they're bested, it was gone, leaving a sick dull vacuum in its wake. And I was utterly exhausted. Safe, but spent.

This Gray One made the basic gray blotch associated with sore throats look like kindergarten. No, day care. I had, I knew, now entered the realm of life and death. Are there negative energy forces—"demons"—that attach themselves to our energy fields and cause serious, even lethal illnesses? Are they especially able to attach themselves to our energy fields when we're emotionally upset or worn down or undernourished? Is this what we're really saying when we declare, "I got sick because my resistance was down"?

More important, by my being able to literally see them, albeit only when awakened from the altered state of sleep, was I being made privy to one of the most fundamental inner workings of health and sickness and healing, at least spontaneous healing, both the kind Jesus was famous for and the sort all medical doctors have witnessed but can't explain? Is all of this somehow related to why as a child I always wanted to go to medical school, why I had finally enrolled in acupuncture college, why I had followed the progress of bioenergetic (energy-based) medicine for twenty-five years? Like many other intelligent modern people, I'd always considered the idea of Christ "casting out demons" as a manipulative lie at worst, a symbolic gesture at best. What if it's neither?

What if, in fact, it is the truth?

Then I remembered something I'd read in *Omni* magazine back in the early 1990s when I was writing for the publication myself. A Russian study had decided to explore the way pathogens spread. The scientists had set an open bacteria-infected petri dish beside an open clean one. Naturally, the uninfected one became infected. Then the researchers put an infected dish inside a glass case, and set an uninfected dish next to the case.

To their astonishment, the uninfected dish still became infected! It wasn't until they built the case out of glass treated to screen out ultraviolet light waves that the clean petri dish stayed clean. So there are physical pathogens, but there are also some sort of shadow entities associated with physical pathogens that, apparently, travel on light. Could these be the "demons" Christ and other healers "cast out"? Is that what Gray Ones are? Whatever they are ... they *are.* That is the main thing. They exist, if hidden away on a far edge of the light spectrum. And our great good comfort lies in knowing that Gray Ones large and small are no match for the iron will of love. Or, as Master Bassui put it: the supernatural power of your own nature destroys evil demons.

18

My Lunch with Deepak

May 1998

Spring at last was poking its green nose up through the endless neutral field of Northwest gray. One of the unexpected new beginnings that always seem to emerge from the annual amping up of springtime was an unexpected call from an Oregon Public Broadcasting producer. She wanted to make a pilot video for a possible TV series based on my fly-fishing book. A meeting was set at OPB's Portland studios for May 1, and, despite obvious "May Day! May Day!" implications, I arranged to have lunch with a Portland-based girlfriend afterward.

The meeting was fun, but the studio reading session I had been asked to do took forever. Once it was over I was starved. But when I called my friend, I found her in the midst of a sudden "office crisis." "Give me two hours," she said and suggested I have lunch on my own and then meet her at her downtown office.

Disappointed, I decided to treat myself to lunch at the riverside restaurant in Portland's RiverPlace Hotel. Visions of the Willamette's peaceful green danced in my head. Yet when I arrived, an apologetic hostess greeted me with further disappointment: "Oh, I'm sorry, we just stopped serving lunch. But I can seat you in the bar." Could this day go any more sideways? Too hungry to go anywhere else, I ignored my dislike of bars and submitted to dining sans river view. At least this bar was smoke-free.

But much to my mortification, the hostess sat me at a table just inches from the only other person in the bar, a tall dark man wearing an expensive tracksuit and new Nikes. If I stayed I would continue to completely invade his private space, but if I asked to be moved he might think I was some kind of racist! Oh bother! As I silently fretted, I turned to check his face for any signs of distress and found none. Then it struck me: he sure looked an awful lot like ... Deepak Chopra.

My heart did a little cartwheel. Is this another one of those wild mystical moments I keep bumbling into? A white-gloved hotel bellman approached the gentleman beside me and presented him with a message.

"For you, doctor," he said.

Well, Deepak is a doctor. But how could I be sure he's, you know, Dr. Chopra?

Our server came over to take our lunch orders. I hadn't even glanced at the menu.

Mr. Maybe-Deepak nodded politely in my direction.

"Uh ... I'll have the ... uh ... Caesar salad with ... salmon!"

"Just as I already ordered," Mr. Maybe noted calmly, "but with chicken."

Okay, chicken, I thought. *He's not a vegetarian. But then, he hasn't lived in India for a long time ... assuming he is Deepak Chopra.* At that, my mind seized upon the perfect way to find out, a solution absolutely brilliant in both its simplicity and verve.

"Excuse me?" I said.

"Yeeeees," the nice man replied with a wry smile.

"Uh, are you from ... India?"

"Yeeeeees," the man answered.

"Oh! Then you must be Deepak Chopra!!"

"Yeeeeesss ..." he confirmed with a broader smile.

Now what. My planning hadn't gotten past the subcontinent. I turned to fully regard my new lunch buddy. And let me tell you, up close Deepak Chopra is one very good-looking man. I think he's one of those guys who never quite photographs as well as he looks in person, largely because his features are full and round, unlike the severely alpine elbows-and-knees faces of supermodels.

No, Deepak's face is sensuality personified, though in a very privately held sort of way—there was nothing "hey, baby" about him. His is an extremely masculine energy, but it runs at frequencies as gentle as jasmine blossoms. The result, of course, is that Deepak Chopra radiates a very grounded peace, just like—you guessed it—the Holy Pig Farmer. But the Holy Pig Farmer is a lanky, tall drink of Americana, and Deepak carries within his handsome fleshiness the powerful exotica of India. His strong jaw rolls into a rajah's chin with a cleft broad enough to hold the Ganges and deep enough to make Cary Grant's look like a little storm ditch. His full manly nose points to even fuller lips with undulating curves. His high, rounded cheekbones could be the Western Ghats. He has, of course, a full head of glossy East Indian black hair and eyebrows to match, these arching inquisitively over eyes filled with so much bemused Spirit you could imagine him writing a book someday called *Why Is God Laughing?*, which, of course, he has.

"So," I began, hoping to sound profound, or at least not lightweight, "what would you ask the Dalai Lama if you met him?"

"I would ask him if he likes his steaks medium-rare or well done," Deepak replied without a pause. Then he did pause. "He has a good sense of humor," he added. *Uh-oh. He's already met him.*

"So," I ventured again with neither a plan nor a net, "with a schedule like yours, how do you stay so centered?"

"Silence."

"Silence?"

"I go into the wilderness."

"You travel alone, then?"

"Yes, mostly."

"You don't mind being alone?"

"No, I'm happy alone."

"You're self-sufficient?"

"Yes."

"How do you stay that way?"

"Silence."

"Am I ruining your lunch?!!"

"No ... no," he with a patient smile.

I had asked Deepak these things because this was what I was struggling with at the time. Living solo had brought me face to face with an uncomfortable fact: I didn't like being alone. Worse, earlier declarations of "wanting action and playmates"—my reasons for calling Harrison in the first place—proved to be a gloss-over for a deeper truth: I was afraid of being alone. It wasn't a big step from that to compulsive wanderlust.

"You strive against loneliness," writes adventurer Beryl Markham in *West with the Night.* "If you read a book, or shuffle a deck of cards, or care for a dog, you are avoiding yourself.... Being alone in an aeroplane for even so short a time as a night and a day, irrevocably alone ... can be as startling as the first awareness of a stranger walking by your side at night."

My apartment was the cockpit of the plane I alone inhabited, closed off and claustrophobic. The road was my liberation. There was, I knew, authenticity in my love of the world, and my fearlessness about going out to look at it by myself was, perhaps, admirable, especially to women, since the idea seemed to frighten most of my girlfriends. Of course there is great natural goodness in loving the company of others, and in being part of a larger community. "The abhorrence of loneliness is as natural as wanting to live at all," Markham adds. "If it were otherwise, men would never have bothered to make an alphabet."

Two years later, when my Bhutanese friend, Yangzom Rinzin, came to live with me for a month, the amount of time Americans spend alone shocked her. "In Bhutan, we never go anywhere alone," she told me. "Even if you go to the store, your sisters, your aunties, everyone goes with you." She found American individualism fully unnatural.

Nonetheless, most of us Westerners find ourselves living alone at various junctures in our lives for various reasons and lengths of time. As uncomfortable and unnatural as these periods might feel, I knew one should be able to face them with courage, if not the quiet enjoyment of, well, quiet, just as Deepak was saying. But all I could seem to muster was a sort of tortured hyperactivity reminiscent of, say, a hummingbird trapped in a sunroom.

Meanwhile, the deadline of a second adventure book (golf, this time) was upon me, and so, therefore, were many long hours of stationary, solitary work, writers not even having the benefit of seeing officemates five days a week like normal worker bees. Truth be told, it was my terror of solitude that was bullet-training me directly into the arms—or, at least, the general zip code—of God. Basically, I was getting very tired of bashing my head against the windows.

"So ... " I said. "Why did you want to know God?"

Deepak regarded me with a raised eyebrow, and new interest.

"I didn't want to know God ... at first," he replied plainly. "I wanted to have an adventure."

Have an adventure? And I wanted to slap my knee like Calamity Jane and holler: "Well, goll-durnit, Packy, you sure as shootin' is havin' yerself one now, ain't-cha!"

I resisted this impulse. And just smiled and said: "So did I, Dr. Chopra. So did I." And then in a moment of stark honesty I added: "I just don't like living alone."

"The space between thoughts is the window to the soul," he offered kindly, but his eyes were now practically shooting sparks. "Thought comes from silence, from infinite possibility, the Akashic Records."

"Did you say ... the Ass Kick Records?" I asked, wondering if my ladylikeness had just been insulted.

Deepak laughed.

"The Akashic Records," he repeated, then he spelled it out for me.

These are, he explained, a concept from Hindu mysticism that refers to the existence of a sort of cosmic computer program that records, well, virtually everything—every thought, deed, really bad waffle recipe, all of it—much like Carl Jung's collective unconscious or what some people call the Universal Mind. According to Deepak, many believe that clairvoyants are clairvoyant because they can access the Akashic Records. We all access them occasionally, when, for example, we know someone is going to call us seconds before the phone rings and it is that person. Or when we have prophetic dreams about events that really do happen. Or when we just know the Ducks are going to peck right through the shields of those darn USC Trojans!

"There are states of consciousness that allow us access to the Akashic Records," Deepak explained. "In deep meditation, in sleep."

"And in silence?" I offered.

He nodded.

"As in," I said, quoting Holy Pig Farmer scripture, "leaving behind the Little Self in favor of the Big Self, the classic spiritual quest?"

He nodded again.

So, I wanted to know, what did he think of the general spiritual condition of America?

"I think Americans are becoming more and more spiritual, and less and less religious. So many in the West already have all the material things."

"Boy, you're not kidding!" I agreed. "And so many people who have everything end up always finding something wrong with their lives."

"Melodrama," Deepak declared.

"But why do they do that?" I said, thinking of Harrison.

"Attention. It turns attention back to the self."

"The Little Self?"

"The very Little Self."

"So, do you think it's more difficult for women to keep our minds on the Big Self?"

"Easier. But then, you always want children."

"And I suppose that messes everything up!?" I asked laughing.

He shrugged. "It's biological."

"Do you . . . ever get bored?"

"No. I am always thinking, writing."

"Well, I think God was bored—I think that's why He or She or Whatever . . . that's why God created the world!"

Deepak actually grinned.

"I agree," he said with a nod of approval.

Encouraged, I told him I was convinced boredom was the mother of golf, and I explained that I was in the middle of writing a golf book and found the game so difficult I was boring myself silly with it.

"Do you play golf?" I asked with a bit too much hope in my voice, imagining a fun new chapter that, at least, wouldn't bore me to death, perhaps: "Chipping with Chopra."

"No. Golf is too slow."

"Tennis, then?"

"No, skydiving. Skiing. Scuba diving."

"Adventure sports!"

"Yes."

"That's why I love fly-fishing! That's actually why I'm in Portland."

Then something dawned on me.

"Why are you in Portland, anyway? Are you giving a talk or something?"

"Yes," he said. "Tonight. Aren't you coming?"

"Oh ... gosh, well, I live down in Eugene—that's two hours south— and I didn't know you were talking in Portland, so no, I hadn't planned on going."

"That's too bad. If you want to come I will get you a ticket."

I explained that my mother's sister was coming in from Texas for a visit and one of my sisters was flying into Eugene that night from California and I'd been nominated to pick her up. And, you know, I didn't have any nice clothes with me. And now I was going to have dinner with the girlfriend I was supposed to be having lunch with but she couldn't make it ... but, gosh this was even better because I could have lunch with her any time ...

Deepak Chopra fixed me with that princely gaze of his and said: "You must come. It will change your life."

I guess I took that as a sign to tell him about another life-changing event—seeing my father's face in the sky—because out came the story. He listened with intense interest.

"Your father's face?" he said.

"Yes."

"In the sky above you?"

"Yes!"

"Three days after he died? Just like the resurrection."

"Yes!! Yes! I know it's crazy, but it really happened. My sister saw it too. And she lives in L.A. .... she's the one I have to pick up at the airport ..."

Deepak swiped the air in front of him.

"That is a very good story. I'll use it!"

"Oh, but not tonight, I hope. I'd be ... embarrassed."

"You're coming, then?"

How could I not?

"Good. Meet me back here at six-thirty and I will have your ticket."

Our server arrived and asked if we wanted dessert.

"I'll have some hot tea, please," I replied.

"A cappuccino," added Deepak.

"How funny!" I said. "You're from India and you order coffee, and I'm from, like, Starbucksville and I order tea—but then, America doesn't understand tea at all. You have to go to England for that."

"Not necessarily," Deepak replied. "My father is a great tea aficionado, and he was once in London at a very good restaurant and ordered tea. When it arrived he took one sip and said to the waiter: 'If this is tea, I would like coffee. If this is coffee, I would like tea.'"

And with that, he paid for my lunch.

"I don't believe you, Jessica," my friend half-yelled. "I leave you alone for two hours and you end up with Deepak Chopra??"

I had showed her his handwritten name and office number to prove it.

"Jeeez," she hissed, shaking her head.

A few hours later she and her husband—who also wanted to witness this miracle—escorted me back to the RiverPlace Hotel where we had drinks in the bar and waited. A little before 6:30 I decided I'd better go to the front desk so I didn't miss Deepak, and as I passed the elevators one opened and out he stepped, now in a beautifully cut suit.

"You're here," he said. "Good. Let's go."

"With you?" I asked, shocked.

"Yes, yes. Come on. My driver is waiting."

We dashed to the front door with my incredulous friends watching as I waved and mouthed the words: "See ya!"

Deepak's driver delivered us to a secret entrance around the side of the auditorium. Of course everyone thought I was *somebody*, walking in with Deepak like that.

"Would you please find Miss Maxwell a good seat," he instructed a woman who seemed to be in charge of things backstage, and she spirited me away to the last of what seemed to be reserved VIP seating in the very front row.

The house was completely packed—I still don't know how that woman even found one vacant seat—and jittery with excitement. What would these people do if they knew I'd just had a two-and-a-half-hour private lunch with their spiritual hero!

The stage was broad and at its middle was a pedestal topped by a glorious bouquet of tropical flowers. When Deepak took center stage I fought an impulse to wave. For the next three hours the genius of Deepak Chopra flooded out into the opening minds of his audience. And he did it without a note, just like the Holy Pig Farmer does. If you haven't heard Deepak Chopra speak, do yourself a favor and the next time he's coming soon to a theater near you, go. And take a friend with you, because you will want—and need—to discuss what you learn with someone smart afterward.

"We created the software of our souls," he told us that night. "We are the stuff that dreams are made of." Our deepest desire, he said, at the deepest level of memory, is to reunite with the Source. "That is where healing comes from."

Spirit is everything, he said. It is always fresh. It is the memory of creation. The whole, he went on, is contained in every part. The holographic universe is a three-dimensional projection of energy and information. "It is nothing less than the mind of God projecting itself holographically as the universe."

That described the vision of my father's face perfectly: it was a holographic projection of energy and information recognizable to me and to my sister. The Holy Pig Farmer was right: Daddy was with God. And of God. Bringing my sister and me back to God, as the last and most lasting parting gift a father could give. No wonder Deepak was so interested in my Daddy sighting.

Then he said something about vibrations uncovering the "secrets of karmic connection," which then transfer themselves to a prism of the past. "Detach from the past," he beseeched us. "It's not here."

Wasn't that like the Holy Pig Farmer cautioning us not to get caught up in the old dramas of past lives because "all work is to be done in this life"?

What Deepak said next was startling: "Sinner and saint are exchanging notes" because creation is made of opposing energies. "If we are intimate with our shadows, we will never judge anyone."

Take that, you old fire-and-brimstone us-against-them glass churches!

As if that weren't hot enough, he went right into claiming that "Spiritual and sexual energy is the same thing" and describing the spiritual nature of the orgasm, which, he said, represented timelessness, loss of ego, naturalness, the surrender to mystery, communion, and defenselessness. "The lover and the beloved become one," Deepak surmised, which I was sure he meant in more than the usual way because I suspected he was quoting the Persian poet Rumi, who so often refers to God as "the beloved."

Onward he marched our minds, describing the "intelligence of Spirit" as able to "eavesdrop on the universe." He discussed the inherently poetic rhythms of the seasons and of natural cycles. Then he came to what he called the Seven Levels of Consciousness. I can remember only four of them. One was a glimpse of the soul as witnessed through "the gap that connects everything to everything else," or, as he had put it at lunch: "the space between thoughts is the window to the soul." Another was "Cosmic Consciousness," which had him paraphrasing St. John's "I am in this world, but not of it." Level Six was "God Consciousness," which is where, he said, healings and miracles occur. And Level Seven? This was "Unity Consciousness," in which "the witness and the object become one."

With that, Deepak Chopra turned to the bouquet of flowers behind him and said: "It would be as if you were looking at this hibiscus and you couldn't tell if you were it or it was you."

I slid down in my chair and wept.

Rather than try to wade through the thick crowds around Deepak to say good-bye at the evening's end, I slipped outside and ran through the sweet holy night all the way back to the hotel. I had no fear. And just as after my first evening in the presence of the Holy Pig Farmer, every cell of my body was on fire. In the words of bluesman Taj Mahal, ask me was I running? I was flying! I left the copy of my fishing book I'd used at the

OPB studios with the front desk as a thank-you for Deepak, then drove home in a blaze of happiness.

He was right. What he taught us that night was life-changing. His talk was nothing less than a shout-out to the deepest thing we know, the thing the Holy Pig Farmer says we're here to remember, the thing that gives so many intellectuals fits because its mystery cannot be understood by the human brain—which, like the banker lobbying for his own bailout, knows with exquisite clarity how much anointing itself the King of Reason is in its own best interest. In a display of dazzling mental judo, Deepak used his own feast of an intellect to flip Western science into the waiting lap of Eastern wisdom and tell every rational mind with eyes to see and ears to hear that what is beyond the mind is, in fact, far grander than even it ever imagined it was, and thanks to its divine origins, far more important. Then he graciously implored us to revel in this miraculous—and liberating— irrefutable fact.

As for the hibiscus, it was clear that Deepak had managed to both access the Akashic Records and play one of my own on his jukebox. How else could he have managed such a surgically precise reference to my first reported spiritual experience (not to mention the curious reading of big league pitcher auras, albeit with a little help from some secret pitcher's mound dirt)? And to pronounce it an example of Level Seven? Highest of the high? Holiest of the holies? Holy Moly! How much are these peabrains of ours actually capable of, anyway?

Two years later, while reading his then-new book, *How to Know God*, I came to the last paragraph of page 243 and was amused to find a kindly if slightly misremembered description of my having seen my father's face in the sky. The name of the chapter is "Strange Powers," and its lead quote is scriptural, from Mark: "... for all things are possible with God."

19

THE BLUE LIGHT

May 1998

"And this book that he appears to be writing," the priest interrupted,
"... did the pages, by chance, have blue light surrounding them?"

KATHLEEN McGOWAN
THE BOOK OF LOVE

Four days after my lunch with Deepak, Aunt Katy arrived. She was tired from the several flights it always takes to get to Eugene from practically anywhere, and from the long drive upriver from the airport. So we all sat with her, scattered about my parents' living room in that sweet deep comfort of just being in the presence of much-loved family members you don't see very often. Aunt Katy closed her eyes.

"You know," she said, "for as long as I can remember, every time I close my eyes I see a room. It's always the same room, but I don't know where it is."

"It's not a room in your house?" Mother asked.

"No. It's nowhere I know. I wish I knew where it is."

"We can find out," Valerie offered. "I can hypnotize you and see if you can tell us where the room is."

"Oh, nobody's ever been able to hypnotize me," Aunt Katy scoffed. But she was game. So we led her to the guesthouse next door where I'd lived only six months earlier—it was a little spooky to be back there. Once she was settled into a comfortable armchair, I readied a notepad and pen and Valerie got to work. Within minutes Aunt Katy's chin was on her chest. She was out.

"So, Katy," Valerie began. "Where are you?"

To our complete astonishment Aunt Katy replied: "Church. I'm in a church."

Valerie and I looked at each other.

"There's a beautiful glass door," Katy went on. "Stained glass. I'm sad ... I'm with God. Oh, I'm not afraid. He's here."

Suddenly her left arm shot up above her head and she reached toward something she alone was seeing.

"Such a beautiful ... beautiful shining blue light. It's peaceful ... but I wanna cry. I don't know why. There's so much love."

My sister's eyes were big as cupcakes. "I've never seen anything like this," she whispered to me. "I think she's in a different lifetime," I whispered back. "She's not a church person." Valerie nodded in agreement, then went back to her work.

"Surround yourself with this feeling," she told Aunt Katy, but Katy didn't seem to hear her and kept on talking.

"I don't see God. But He's here."

Katy clutched her hands to her chest.

"Oh ... oh!"

"What do you understand?" Valerie asked.

"People should believe. People don't find peace. They should go where it is. Some people are so cruel ... but I am so happy! Oh ... !"

"What?" Valerie asked, but Katy had moved on.

"Wood floors. It's old. My mother's ... she's with me. She's there—you see? She needs a new dress. I love her so much!" Grandma had died a dozen years earlier.

Katy shook her head. Like the needle of an old phonograph skipping from the middle of one song into another, she jumped to a new reality. And she had a new voice. It was the unmistakable backcountry drawl of east Texas circa 1920s, a throaty southern pitch we had never once heard come out of our aunt's mouth before. Her head began to thrash back and forth as if she were in great pain.

"I cain't do that. It's so hard. I cain't understand," she wailed. "They don't know that I'm trying. I'm not very smart, not like May-ree. It bothers me so much."

With that Katy broke down, and so did we. We knew our aunt was reliving the shame the nuns at her childhood Catholic school had shackled her with as a child. We'd heard the story many times. Katy had been born a "blue baby" with the umbilical cord wrapped around her neck. The resulting oxygen deprivation left her with some minor learning disabilities, though she was great at math and became a professional bookkeeper. Nonetheless, the sisters at the Catholic school she and our mother attended would whip little Katy mercilessly because she couldn't remember her catechism. Finally, our mother refused to take her baby sister back to that school, and refused to return to it herself. The whole experience soured both of them on religion, especially Mother, despite the fact that she had been named after the Virgin Mary. I had too, for that matter—my birth certificate reads "Mary Jessica."

"Breathe it out," Valerie told Katy gently. "Let it go. You've carried this long enough."

Aunt Katy cried and cried and cried. And so did we. It was one of the most pitiful things I've ever witnessed, a seventy-year-old woman finally sobbing out the hurt inflicted on her as a seven-year-old child by a bunch of ignorant so-called brides of Christ who didn't even know the Golden Rule. No wonder people distrust religion.

Katy's needle jumped again and she was singing yet another song.

"We're goin' undah the house an' we're goin' to play cars!" Katy announced. "I'll build a road for Junior. Yeah. No! Don' put your hand in your mouth!"

"They're little kids!" I breathed. "She's with Uncle Junior!" He was Katy's and our mother's little brother. Katy was reliving a conversation from their childhood, word for word.

"Mama's callin'!" she continued. "Okay. No! If it rains it'll get dirty. You gonna get in trouble."

The next moment Katy was placing her hands on her head as if she were adjusting her hair, or a hat.

"Goin' to church," she said in a more grown-up voice now. "Ah don't like that much. Cain't tell Mama—she's Catholic. Ah have to ... but I'm tired. I'm so tired."

Now she straightened up in her chair. With resolute command she now appeared fully in charge. In a voice much like the one we knew, she loudly proclaimed: "Ah'm buyin' shoes. High heels. Green suede. To go with mah green purse. I Cain Buy Whatever I Want."

Valerie smiled. "It's beautiful here, isn't it, Katy?"

Katy smiled too, and leaned back. With her eyes still closed and her hands folded peacefully in her lap, she replied:

"Oh yeah."

My sister had managed to complete years—if not lifetimes—of successful therapy in fifty minutes flat.

When she came to, Aunt Katy was exhausted. Valerie helped her onto the guest bed while I ran to get Mother so she could hear what had just happened. Tillie the Wonder Corgi followed Mother and me back to the guesthouse. Mother and I sat across from Valerie and Katy as Valerie recounted the session. Then I noticed that Tillie was doing something odd: she was quietly padding around the armchair Katy had been sitting in and looking up at the wall behind it with a goofy doggie smile on her face. I searched the wall, and even the ceiling above it. But I saw nothing. Not even a bug. Nonetheless, Tillie kept walking slowly around and around the chair while smiling at the wall. Then I realized she was looking exactly where Katy said the blue window was, where she herself had just been reaching. Was Tillie seeing something we weren't? A light being? Perhaps a blue light being?

Mother and Valerie, with Tillie on their heels, walked back to the house to finish making dinner, and I stayed with Katy. When she was ready, we got up together and headed back as well. Partway there, Aunt Katy stopped and turned to me with a strained look on her face.

"I've never told this to anyone before," she said. "But I've always known I was there. With Jesus. When He was alive. I wasn't anybody, just a nobody in the crowd. But I know I was there. When He was on the earth. I saw Him. I was there."

When I had a moment alone with my mother, I shared what Katy had told me. My mother bit her lip. "Did I ever tell you that once when Heather was just a baby, Bob and I were watching her play on the floor, and I looked up and saw that a blue spirit was watching her too? I tried to get Bob's attention so he could see it—if he could," she said laughing, "but it vanished before he saw me. And," she continued, "you remember our neighbor who lived in the old house just north of ours?" I did. "Well, every time I stopped in to visit her she had me open the Bible and read a passage, and every time I opened to the same passage." My mother was now talking through tears. "It's the one that says the angels will lift you up lest you dash your feet upon the stone."

"That's from Psalm ninety-one," Lory said. I had called him to tell him about Aunt Katy's unexpected Messianic regression, and then my own anti-religious intellectual mother's personal connection with both light beings and the Bible!

"This would explain things," Lory said calmly. "I believe spiritual gifts come down via genetic lineages. Your Aunt Katy's and your mother's spiritual energies have been passed down to you. And yes, I think it's true that your aunt was touched by Christ when He was alive. I've experienced these people before. They usually don't want to talk about it, just like your aunt.

"There's a problem today," he went on. "It's the amount of shame people have for what they know spiritually, and what they've experienced. I'm actually working on a new program designed to release people from their spiritual shame and guilt, and allow them to be the mystics they are. We should talk about it sometime."

He was ready to get off the phone.

"Wait," I said. "There's one more thing. When I was still living in my parents' guesthouse where Katy had her regression, her husband, Uncle Bernie, came to me one night in a sort of waking dream. He had died in a car wreck when I was ten. He was sitting peacefully in the chair beside my bed, and he said he was there to answer any questions I had about ... anything. So I asked him if we should be afraid of death, since he was, you know, dead."

"What did he say?" Lory asked.

"First he laughed, and then he shook his head and said: 'No.'"

"You uncle is right," Lory replied. "Now I need to go feed the pigs."

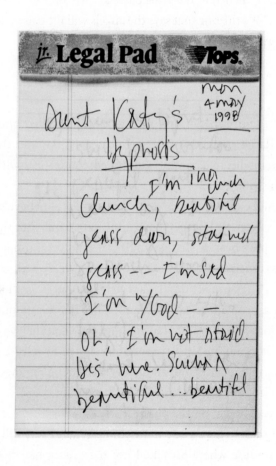

20

THE COLOR RED

May 1998

You had lunch with Deepak Chopra … and your aunt had a past life with Jesus?!"

Even my superspiritual best friend was twitterpated by this latest news. When Rande finally stopped laughing she took a deep breath and said: "Jeez, Jess, you're like Lucille Ball tripping over God!"

"I know! And the weird thing is, I don't know how any of these things happen. I mean, all Valerie was trying to do was find out why Aunt Katy sees some weird room when she closes her eyes, and I ended up sitting next to Deepak because all my own plans mysteriously went completely whopper-jawed. He's really cute too," I added. "And he scientifically explained almost all of the stuff I keep experiencing. Except for casting out demons. I forgot to ask him about that, darn it. And I still have no idea where asking Jesus for help came from. I just don't think that way."

There was an interesting pause.

"I do," Rande replied slowly. "If I walk into my classroom without asking Christ to be in my heart first, things don't go very well."

Rande talks to Christ?

She had been my best friend for twenty-five years and never once had she mentioned any sort of personal connection to Jesus. In fact, she'd always seemed as allergic to religion as I was. But there she was confiding that she, too, was tapped into the living, or, at least, still-available essence of the spiritual master we call Christ, whose mysterious, protective energy somehow aligned with hers in a sort of heart-level partnership that allowed her to manage some very difficult high school kids.

"You don't have to go to church to be with Christ," she said softly, sounding an awful lot like the Holy Pig Farmer.

"Oh I know," I said. "But that's another weird thing—I really like church. At least Greg's church."

I told Rande how the Church of Greg was this remarkable place filled with hundreds of grandparents who work nonstop to help people who really need it.

"And the music is wonderful!" I added.

It was true. I had fallen in love with sacred music. Being only blocks from the University of Oregon, Central Presbyterian Church had a tradition of hiring a graduate student from the school of music as its choir director. Inevitably, this young person was in the passionate stages of an early love affair with music, hence Central's choir was well known for its complex anthems and ambitious classical performances, often in Latin, which I adored. But I loved the simple old hymns and spirituals best. Sometimes you could hear the roots of the blues in the haunting repetition of early Christian chants. Like the water-song of rivers and the metronome of casting a fly rod, when sung by a great choir these good, deep songs had the power to push minds into the higher registers for days on end.

There is a balm in Oregon.

I just wished I had a singing voice worthy of being part of a choir as good as Central's. "My voice is so wimpy," I whined to Rande. "You've always had such a great singing voice. Why can't we both have great singing voices? We share everything else!"

It was my blossoming interest in sacred music that a month later glued my attention to an obscure National Public Radio report on the twelfth-century Christian mystic and composer Abbess Hildegard von Bingen. Given to visions from the time she was a young girl, when she was forty-two years old she reported hearing the voice of God, telling her to "write down everything you see and hear." From that point on she was a firestorm of sacred creativity, constantly composing passion plays and monastic chants. We still have records of about eighty of her musical compositions, and some of the most haunting, the radio presentation instructed, were available on a new CD. I ran right out and purchased it, only to be floored more by something I read in the jacket notes than by the music itself. Apparently von Bingen had a special fondness for the color red: she believed that as people grew closer to God, they quite literally "reddened."

Was red also Hildegard's holy color? Did she see Red Ones too?

It was now early June. Summer had arrived on a cloud of grass pollen, my allergenic nemesis. My eyes were now as red as my hair. When I went to church the following Sunday, I was shocked to see the sanctuary all decked out in ... red!

"What the heck's going on?" I asked Greg.

"Pentecost Sunday," he replied.

"Uh ... what is Pentecost?"

Greg regarded me with an I-realize-I-could-tell-you-this-is-the-day-we-all-eat-noodles-and-wear-Groucho-noses-and-you'd-believe-it-but-this-is-too-important-to-mess-around-with look and finally said: "Pentecost is the fiftieth day after Jesus ascended into heaven, and as His family and the Apostles and other disciples were inside praying together, the house suddenly filled with the sound of wind rushing through it and then the Holy Spirit sent down tongues of flame—hence the red—that touched the heads of everyone there."

"You're kidding."

Greg smiled.

"Nope. And the holy flames made them all want to go out and preach the gospel of the risen Christ ... and they did and got three thousand converts right then and there. It's also," he added, "why we're both redheads. Let us pray."

Not long afterward I learned that on Pentecost one year, the huge wooden cross high on the wall above Central's choir loft suddenly burst into flames. It proved to be just a faulty lighting wire ... but still.

21

THREE KINGS AND THE
PENDULUM SWINGS

June 1998

By late June school was out and Rande could finally escape for our annual Girlfriends' Summer Getaway. This also got me out of the south end of the Willamette Valley where the pollen from scores of ryegrass farms always piles up in the breezy sneezy wheezy month of June. I might be able to cure myself of sore throats, but grass pollen allergies were a hoarse of a different color. "That's because they're genetic," Rande offered, "and not caused by demons."

This time we had rented a cabin in an old mountain retreat in rural Montana. A nice couple had the cabin across the dirt road from ours, and it happened that the man of the couple was a professional psychic ... when he wasn't working as a Missouri fireman. (Does everyone have a secret spiritual life?)

Chris Goldsmith took one look at me and insisted on giving me a reading using tarot cards as his guides. He asked me to choose nine cards, then laid them out one by one on our beat-up kitchen table in what he called the Celtic cross formation. As he turned each one over he talked about the usual things—success, obstacles, luck, and love ... mostly love. Suddenly, he became very agitated. He actually started bouncing in his seat. "Three Kings!" he said as if he were making an important announcement. "Three kings are coming to you. I don't know when—there is no time in Spirit. But they're coming."

"One king will be more than enough, thank you."

"No, there are three. Three kings. Three."

Then a wisp of doubt swept his eyes. His eyelids fluttered, then dropped, and his head moved from side to side as if he were watching a mental tennis game. Knots of spittle formed at the corners of his mouth.

"There's a man," he began. "You're still attached to him—energetically. No, he's attached to you. This is very bad. No, no. You must cut this cord. This man cannot give. And this man, if you don't cut this cord he will block the way and the Three Kings won't find you."

Then the psychic fireman began to weep.

"Oh my," he said. "And when I cry like this? You can take the reading to the bank."

"Harrison!" Rande breathed when I gave her a report on the reading.

"But ... we split up months ago!" I protested. "I haven't seen him since!"

Rande's normally kind expression hardened, and a strange little smile crept into her eyes.

"Well, my lovely, looks like the devil is still with us, isn't heeehehehe ..." she said, letting loose a Wicked Witch of the West cackle.

"Stop it!"

"I think. We need. To perform. A little cleansing ritual ... gnaw, gnaw, gnaw!" she added, now sounding a little too much like Curly Joe. The next thing I knew, I was flat on my back on the sofa and Rande was running her palms through the air half a foot above my body. Years ago she had studied a traditional Hawaiian hands-on healing technique called Huna. She was good at it, and she was determined to use it to try to free her best buddy of some kind of invisible fallout from getting a little too close to the Creature from the Blocked Lagoon.

"Here," she announced, stopping above my solar plexus. "My God ..."

"What?"

"The energy. It's really strong. YUCK!"

"What do you mean!?"

"Well, it's really big too," she went on, "like a giant yucky ropey cable! And, Jess," she added, "it's made of ... GRIEF."

"But I feel so ... happy!"

This was true. It was also true that I still secretly pined for Harrison— or, rather, for the romance he represented. Stupid, I know, because he had proved himself to be a narcissistic creep of the first degree.

A few months earlier, on Valentine's Day no less, I had finally blown up at him for the two years of misery he'd caused me ... and yes, I had tolerated. Two years of keeping me in the wings, two years of listening ad nauseam to his endless problems with his divorce, and his relatives, who, according to him, ran the family business with eternal disregard for his own talents and contributions. Somehow, Harrison was always everyone's innocent victim and I was always his personal cheerleader. While this had, at first, passed as intimacy, it had finally dawned on me that this particular version of intimacy was all about him but never about us, which is the true definition of intimacy, isn't it?

So when I called him on his lopsided idea of a love relationship on a day usually devoted to hearts and flowers, his chilled response was simply: "I can't take you anywhere," followed by: "We have no relationship." A period of frantic damage control on my part had ensued, but my phone calls were rebuffed, as he was still "too raw" from my "anger"—precisely the kind of pitiful-poor-unaccountable-me Rande, Greg Tatman, and even my new friend Val Brooks had warned me about.

I'd met Val at a book-signing fundraiser I was invited to after the publication of my fishing book. She was with her close friend, Jan Eliot, the famous Eugene-based cartoonist who draws *Stone Soup*. Val, in fact, is the model for "Val," the cartoon strip's lead character. True to Jan's story lines, the real Val is a brilliant redhead, but in person she also has Marilyn Monroe eyes and lips, with a broad laugh and a hooting sense of humor. And she's a very devoted novelist. Much to my delight, we started having literary lunches every Tuesday at a downtown café called Zenon.

"Of course he's not accountable," she had concluded with a near-hysterical laugh. "He's an *alcoholic*." Val had, it turned out, married one herself when she was still a teenager and learned all about the alcoholic personality the hard way. "Control, abuse, denial, victimization," she intoned, as you could imagine her *Stone Soup* character would, but Val wasn't smiling. "They keep you isolated to control you, then they abuse you, and when you call them on it they deny it and magically become your victim for being mean to them or raising your voice or some baloney, even if they've already beaten the hell out of you. It's all ego-ego-ego unless they actually recover spiritually, and don't count on that. My advice is: run."

For an embarrassing amount of time—months, to be honest—I had remained beside myself with angst at Harrison's odd response to my justifiable blowup. Finally, I'd worked up the courage to go to his apartment, only to have him open the door wearing the expression of a madman. Something clicked. I stepped out of this pathetic drama and said: "I don't know what's wrong with you, but I don't want anything more to do with it." And then I took myself out to a nice long gourmet lunch at Café Zenon, feeling for the first time since I'd gotten involved with Harrison that I was free of him at last! But. When I arrived back at my apartment and listened to my phone messages, all seven of them were from Harrison. Apologizing profusely. Blaming his state of mind on the stress of his divorce, which was still taking forever and remained the central drama in his life. Telling me all the blah-blah-blah love things he should have told me on Valentine's Day.

When I didn't respond, he called again that night. When I held my ground about his self-centeredness, he defended himself with the kind of exquisite self-understanding and self-forgiveness that real love is supposed to offer its lover. When I told him as much, a cold stone fell into his voice, and the things he said, the names he called me are nothing I care to repeat. And that, for me, was the end of the end that had begun on our national day of love. Which should have been a clue.

Sometimes I wondered what had happened to the sweet soul I had apparently married in the Deep South as an innocent hoop-skirted girl centuries ago. Harrison Brandt was certainly no longer the man he was then, a fact that obscured an already confounded "reality." But when my thoughts circled back to that exalted antebellum vision, they inevitably cycled back to Harrison, something I found too humiliating to tell even my best friend.

I didn't have to.

"He's still got his hooks in you," Rande declared. "And you're still grieving."

"But ... why?!" I sputtered. "That past-life grief thing is supposed to be history."

"I think most of it is, but you smushed some of it into this cable thing and it's definitely still there ... like an Umbilical Cord to Hell!"

That did it.

"Oh, ICK!!!!!!" I wailed. "Get RID of it!!"

Rande squared her shoulders and shook her hands.

"Okay, fasten your seatbelt."

She closed her eyes. Her head began to roll a little from side to side and she started making a low um-um-um sort of sound.

"Are you humming?"

She shook her head. "Chanting."

"Sounds like 'La Bamba.'"

"Quiet! This is serious!!"

I was about to make another wisecrack when Rande's voice fell into a new register.

"OhhhhmmmLordJesusChristSonofGodhavemercyOhhhhhhmmm mmmmm.

"LordJesusChristSonofGodhavemercyOhhhhhmmmmmmmm."

"Rande?"

"OhhhhhhmmmmmmmLordJesusChristSonofGodhavemercyOhh mmmmm."

The space on my abdomen beneath her hands began to feel warm.

"What's happening?" I asked, a little panicked.

Before she could answer I was seized by a spasm of pain.

"Owww!" I yelped.

"OhhhhmmmLordJesusChristSonofGodhavemercyOhhhhhhmmm-mmm," Rande chanted, and then began scissoring her hands over my stomach like an unusual version of the Macarena. The area beneath her hands now felt red-hot, and the pain intensified until it felt as though something was being torn away from my body.

"Is this like ... psychic surgery?" I groaned.

"Sort of ... OhhhhmLordJesusChristSonofGodhavemercyOhhhh mmm ..."

Finally, the invisible cable or whatever it was broke, and a tidal wave of grief broke with it. I howled, and to my surprise Rande howled with me. Together, we wept and sobbed and cried out until, in an instant, this strange sorrow vanished as quickly as it had arrived and we opened our eyes. I felt spent ... and refreshed ... and ravaged ... and euphoric. I also felt as though I'd just lost a thousand pounds. Rande said she felt "light" too.

"Hey, this is like contact weight loss! You and your friend can take turns dieting and you BOTH still lose weight nonstop!"

We were giddy with joy.

The only discernible negative from the entire Huna Healing experience was that we'd ruined our mascara. Tears sure seemed to be a regular visitor on the spiritual scene.

"Have you noticed that spiritual people weep a lot?" I asked Rande.

"Yes," she replied. "It's because your heart's opened up, and things touch you."

I guess that settled that. There was, in fact, another downside to my friend's healing session: for the rest of our vacation I walked around feeling as though I had a hole the size of a cannonball through the center of my body. It was, shall we say, a little breezy. I felt a bit weak. But soon the circular space seemed to mend, or, more accurately, to fill up again ... which felt both comforting and strange. "Rande, do you think we're pixilated?"

My best friend looked at me over her Mardi Gras–colored bifocals like a wise little tropical bird and replied: "Of course."

When we saw Chris Goldsmith in front of his cabin as we left the retreat on our last day, he flashed us the peace sign and called out: "Three Kings, baby. Three Kings!"

I arrived at church the following Sunday feeling more settled than I had in several years. Alas, for the first time, Greg wasn't there, and my church-shyness returned, sending my newfound spiritual peace reeling.

There wasn't even anyone to lead our singing, the choir having adjourned for the summer. What was I going to do!

You big chicken, I thought. *You're in church, for Christ's sake . . . literally. Anyone here would be happy to help you, so sit down and shut up . . . until it's time to sing!*

I took a seat by myself in the back. But when we stood for a hymn I felt completely insecure. The hymns were all still new to me, and lord knows I couldn't read music. I was so flustered I couldn't even focus enough to read the lyrics and just flubbed along not having a clue about where we were . . . until an impossibly loud voice boomed forth directly behind me, pronouncing every word with clipped precision. The singer was also singing the bass part all by himself. How odd. Stifling a laugh, I turned around to see who on earth would dare to sing so boldly and came face-to-face with a tall, relentlessly handsome, blue-eyed man in a suit and a bow tie. Faster than I could possibly make any sort of conscious assessment of my own, these words shot through my mind:

"Now, that's the sort of man I should marry."

Part IV

Dharma Object Lessons

Jessica's prayer wheel from Bumthang, Bhutan

Everyone is our neighbour, no matter what race, creed or colour.
Her Majesty Queen Elizabeth II

All the religions of the world command us to take care of one another.
Karen Armstrong
Author, historian

What we do to everything, we do to ourselves.

BLACK ELK
OGLALA SIOUX HOLY MAN

*This is the sum of duty: do not do to others
what would cause pain if done to you.*

MAHABHARATA 5:1517
HINDUISM

Hurt not others in ways that you yourself would find hurtful.

UDANA-VARGA 5:18
BUDDHISM

Be charitable to all beings, love is the representative of God.

KO-JI-KI HACHIMAN KASUGA
SHINTOISM

Blessed is he who preferreth his brother before himself.

BAHA'U'LLAH
BAHÁ'I FAITH

*None of you [truly] believes until he wishes for his brother
what he wishes for himself.*

43 SAYINGS OF PROPHET MUHAMMAD
ISLAM

Do unto others as you would have them do unto you.

LUKE 6:31
CHRISTIANITY

*That which is hateful to you, do not do to your neighbor.
That is the Torah. The rest is commentary.*

RABBI HILLEL THE ELDER
TALMUD, SHABBAT 31A
JUDAISM

22

THE CENTRAL ANGEL

September 1998

W ith summer over and the first rains of the year threatening to begin anew, all Northwesterners were in their places with perhaps not the most sunshiny faces. It was a particularly bittersweet time for me because, besides living alone and not liking it, back-to-school time both sent Rande into the vortex until Christmas vacation and reminded me of my deepest nadir: I wasn't able to have children. Infertility was not the problem: I could conceive with the best of 'em. I just couldn't carry a baby to term. In my first marriage, after losing five pregnancies with no medical explanation, I began researching adopting a baby girl from China, an expensive proposition at best. When my ex-husband's parents surprised us with a generous monetary gift, I called an adoption agency right away. And when my ex-husband used the money to build a new deck instead, I gave up. To this day I keep the beautiful baby clothes I bought for my future daughter in a special box, and her gaily painted high chair is still in my basement. So September always hurt a little. And it put a bit of a damper on my love of the golden approach of fall, which, as it is for so many of us, is my favorite season of the year.

This, then, was the murky ferment from which emerged, like a catfish crawling blind out of the mud, a disciplined spiritual routine that has served me to this day. I soon knighted it: "Mornings Are Mine." Still abed,

I would force myself to spend at least an hour in meditation and prayer. First I tried my best to clear myself of any negativity—physical and emotional. Then I turned to praying wholeheartedly for others, a practice I found supremely rewarding, mostly because, as religious scholar Karen Armstrong puts it, the process instantly "dethrones yourself" and offers up the great relief of thinking about others instead. Finally I asked to be shown the way to accomplish whatever needed to be accomplished that day. Somehow, the Holy Pig Farmer's words "show me the way!" had a ringing effect on ... well, Whoever was listening out there, because every time I asked, the way was surely shown, often with all the lovely playfulness of Divine creativity. You never knew which sign or wonder would show up next!

Besides Mornings Are Mine, the structure of my weeks orbited around the twin highlights of Tuesday "Literary Lunches" with Val Brooks and Sunday mornings at Central Presbyterian Church, events I looked forward to like twin treasure hunts. Val and I punned and roared our way through each lunch date—at least we thought we were funny—and she always enjoyed the latest installment of my little ongoing spiritual adventure.

Along the way I managed to collect a curious cadre of would-be authors: a poet-biologist who had agreed to guide my little nature-loving nephew Jesse and me on a salamander hunt, the detective mystery writer uncle of a former journalism student, a couple of literary church buddies, even the brilliant former financial columnist wife of the nice guy the local electric company sent over to help me improve my energy efficiency. Enough, I thought, to form a little authors' support group. So I invited everyone over to my apartment for a first meeting. When the biologist arrived he informed us that a lunar eclipse was in progress, so we all dashed up to the roof deck to find a scarlet moon hanging in the night sky like a tomato from another planet. Charmed, we knighted ourselves the Red Moons, a magical name that's stuck for a dozen years and counting. Thus did monthly Red Moons meetings sluice more juice into the strengthening trickle of my new social life, proving yet again, if you don't have one, start one!

Meanwhile, my love of church grew weekly. What a comfort to know that the same collection of good people would be there at the same place and same time every Sunday morning, all come to worship something a bazillion times bigger than themselves. It reminded me of something the jazz sax–playing copyeditor at the *Los Angeles Times* told me when I worked there after college: "Rock stars think they're the music. Jazz stars know the music is much bigger than they are."

Always, church as Central Presbyterian does it pushed you far beyond the boundaries of selfhood toward a practical and applied confirmation that we truly are all in this thing together. The experience really made you want to behave. And be thoughtful, kind, and giving. No wonder the Dalai Lama always says the point of all religion, really, is to produce better human beings.

And how I looked forward to our superprogressive pastor's weekly sermons. Inevitably, they reminded us of our responsibility to the world and to each other, usually just after the choir delivered yet another slam-dunk ring-the-rafters anthem. You never knew what those guys were going to do—could be Mozart, could be Mozambique! I even liked "Minute for Mission," the church's version of the dreaded public television fund-raiser. They were just little commercials, really, given by church regulars imploring us to join in the dazzling array of quiet work projects for people in need all over the world. What a bunch of Good Guys ran this place. What a bunch of unsung heroes!

To my unchurched self, the rich offerings of church life continued to seem like a miraculous waterwheel that kept on turning of its own accord, always moving, always contributing, always there offering whatever level of participation of which any member of the congregation cared to partake. I knew the Holy Pig Farmer would approve of Central Presbyterian Church. And I still couldn't understand why progressive sanctuaries like this one were dying out. Could the ringing rings of cruelty from church experiences like my Aunt Katy's really have so tainted religion for sensitive, thinking people?

The slow but reliable machinations of Mornings Are Mine sessions and church services were the engines that drove my own spiritual growth. It was not a flashy road. It was more a long, measured slog across a Serengeti of the sacred: a lot of beige landscape and steady weather, percussed by the unexpected appearance of a wildebeest or lion—

another message from a Red One, more uncanny "coincidences"—whose accompanying glee would see me through another thousand miles on The Plateau.

And make no mistake; it is precisely the long distances on The Plateau that bring forth the occasional wildlife sighting, spiritually speaking. Spiritually speaking, it didn't take too long to learn that the metronome of church—and of all spiritual practice—is to the spiritual student what devotion is to the happily married: the isolated electricity of a tryst with a stranger is nothing compared to the abiding comfort—and thrill!—of the beloved marriage bed. (Not to mention the smart idea of putting real love in making love.) Slowly, I knew I was being readied for the first healthy relationship of my life, though I had no idea who my future husband might be or where on earth I'd meet him.

"Argentina, probably," Rande offered more than once.

But the lovely new routines of my budding spirituality gave me a kind of patience I'd never had. Patience with The Plateau, patience with the quietude there between bouts of spiritual fireworks, and general patience with what often seemed to be the Paleolithic pace of my own life. How acutely do we want what we want! How desperately important our desires seem and how they haunt us. How easy it is to eternally count our longings and miss our countless blessings altogether. And how miserable it makes us!

The Holy Pig Farmer has a sure-fire cure for the Self-Pity Blues. He calls it his Thank-You Exercise. For one full day you have to silently thank everything you already have, everything that's already in your life. Everything. You thank the chair you're sitting on for being there. You thank the table on which you set your tea and you thank your tea. You thank the air you're breathing, the light that lets you see, the floor that supports you, the roof over your head. You thank the water in your faucets, its heat or coolness, and the fact that you are allowed both. You thank the smooth chill of your porcelain bathtub, the fizzy delight of a simple hot shower, the sturdy reliability of your bar of soap, the bubbles in your shampoo. You carry on like this nonstop, and Lory guarantees that by the end of the day you are so darn grateful for all the things you do have that you've forgotten all about the things you don't.

"This exercise puts the focus of your mind outside itself," he explains, "and anchors it in gratitude. And if there's anything the Serious Dude in the Sky likes, it's gratitude."

But wrestling one's eternally self-centered mind into spiritual submission is very hard work. It takes time. And so you have your regular, everyday spiritual practice and what I call your Special Circumstances Practices (more intense prayer and meditation for crises, lost objects, getting rid of especially annoying telemarketers, and so on) and you have your once-in-a-blue-moon revelations, and in the interstitial space between them all dwells the cliché we call "inner peace," the most powerful and elusive personal accomplishment known to humankind. This is the real prize won by keeping your restless feet firmly on The Plateau and your mind on "much obliged." So, you know, like, whistle while you work!

As for personal revelation, as sexy as it is I was absolutely clear that signs and wonders are the carrots, not the goal. The goal, of course, is peace.

Revelation can, of course, arrive anywhere at any moment, and one could make a good argument that it's more apt to show up at your regular place of prayer because it knows where you are, a little spin on author Tom Robbins's mandate to write every day at the same time and place "otherwise your muse won't know where to find you." And so it was that the constant and subtle ways of the good people at Central Presbyterian Church showed me the immeasurable value of decidedly unglamorous regular spiritual effort. And it was my acceptance of and pleasure in business as usual that almost made me miss the most spectacular thing I've ever witnessed at my own house of worship.

The moment I walked in that holiest of Sundays, I felt giddy. Just going to church made me happy, but this was off the charts. Oddly enough, everyone else seemed giddy too. People were laughing and hugging each other and behaving in a decidedly non-Presbyterian fashion, which is defined by the domination's motto that all is to be done "decently and in order." Soon I was so gleeful it actually occurred to me that I'd better be careful or I would float right up to the ceiling! And that's where I saw it. Hovering over the entire congregation high above us all was the most beautiful Red One I'd seen since that first holy visitation upriver.

But this one was not a slowly orbiting ovoid. And it didn't look like an indoor galaxy. It was more classically angelic. But it was not in the image of a silly Hallmark angel with golden locks and a halo floating peacefully up there like the Good Fairy. It was, in fact, a very active Red One, in a slow-motion sort of way, and if I were pressed I'd say it sort of resembled a modern dancer like an abstract Martha Graham waving yards and yards of red silk that billowed around her in great slow arcs.

Remember that these angelic visitors are made of light. Looking at them, your eyes are constantly trying to make out their form, which tends to have fuzzy edges and shift around as light waves do. But none of that is as important as the real evidence of a heavenly visitation: How You Feel. Which is always and unequivocally euphoric. But it's one thing to report that you, yourself, felt that way in the presence of a friendly visiting entity; it is quite another to report that an entire congregation felt that way, whether they knew why or not (they didn't). And there we were, an unsuspecting group of some three hundred souls, sharing a few moments of absolute rhapsody on just another Sunday morning in spring.

I was, I confess, dumbfounded. This was the first time I'd ever experienced the presence of a Red One, or a Gray One for that matter, with other people around. I wanted to ask if anyone else could see the Red One, but then thought better of it. The pastor still had a sermon to preach, after all.

And the experience both answered and begged new questions. My ongoing wish that those to whom I'm closest could see what I saw had almost been granted—it was clear that they had at least experienced it. *If only*, I thought, *secular America could feel this! Then maybe good churches like Central Presbyterian would satisfy the deepening hunger for authentic personal spiritual experience.*

Regardless, I was obliged to consider the possibility that perhaps the glorious Red One I had been so honored to see in fact served as the church's resident guardian, always there but rarely noted. Are Red Ones, I wondered, actually assigned to places where people gather to do genuine good—perhaps those more devoted to helping the world as they are to helping themselves? Are these exalted beings always present at churches and temples and other gathering places that deserve them whether members realize it or not? Or do these benevolent visitors just make random house-of-worship calls? Finally, I couldn't help but wonder if the Central Angel was the source of the sense of sparkly goodness I had experienced the very first time I walked into this sanctuary with Greg Tatman, and if it was, in fact, what had made me stay.

Or was it what had called me to this church in the first place, and yet another bit of evidence that there's much more to reality-as-usual than usually meets the eye?

At home later that afternoon my phone rang.

"Don't you just love bein' right? Don't you just LOVE bein' right!"

It was my Seattle musician friend Chic Streetman, calling to share the miraculous news that his wife was pregnant, despite his doctors' emphatic pronouncement of his permanent chemo-induced sterility three years earlier.

"And," he added with a laugh, "it's a boy. Just like you said it would be. Just like what you saw."

On February 21, 1998, Julien Streetman arrived in the world, and in three years he had grown into the material version of the handsome, lanky, energetic spirit-boy who had almost knocked me down in his parents' kitchen on Thanksgiving 1995.

Julien Streetman

23

DHARMA OBJECT LESSONS

November 1999

It was on the flaming heels of this flourish of Christian mysticism that I was flung into the rarified world of Himalayan Buddhism.

My fly-fishing coach, Guido Rahr, was finishing up a master's degree at Yale University's super-progressive Forestry and Environmental Studies Department, and was raving about his fellow students from the Buddhist kingdom of Bhutan. "They knew the answer to every question our profs asked," he told me. "They're enviro-brainiacs!"

By November of 1999, I was on a plane to the Inner Himalayas for *Audubon* magazine to see if Bhutan's environmental policies were as good as they sounded.

The mountains looked like inset diamonds on a bracelet of blue. I talked my way into the cockpit of our small jet to get a better look.

"That is Everest," our Bhutanese pilot recited. Like almost everyone in the Land of the Thunder Dragon, as Bhutan calls itself, he spoke the Queen's English. "That is Kanchenjunga, the third-highest peak in the world," he continued. "And that is our own Jhomolhari, only five thousand feet less than Everest." He smiled. "Right now we are over Bangladesh. But once we reach those mountains? We're in Bhutan."

Waiting among those glowy, snowy mountains was a score of knife-blade river valleys still blessed with wildlife species that have been extinct elsewhere in the Himalayas for decades. Winging across a blue-silk sky toward this secret garden at the top of the world was enough to give any Westerner emotional vertigo. I could hardly wait to get my feet on the ground.

On a map, Bhutan floats jewel-like and remote on the southern slopes of the Eastern Himalayas. Tibet lies to the north. To the east and south is the Indian state of Assam. To the west is the former Buddhist kingdom of Sikkim, its king having been voted out by a majority of Indian nationals who had taken up residence there; the king died seven years later, it's said of a broken heart.

The mountains have always played an impressive role in preserving Bhutan's rich native culture and its extravagant natural beauty. They made invasion nearly impossible, thus helping Bhutan maintain the distinction of being the last independent Himalayan Buddhist kingdom, the only one not to have been absorbed by China or India, or colonized by Europeans. To this day, the Bhutanese believe that proper daily worship of the mountain deities protects them from evil.

As our kamikaze landing would soon prove, the mountains still do deter invaders. Suddenly we were dropping through the clouds and swooping in a hawk-drop toward a valley that barely seemed wide enough to farm ... much less land in. But this one—the Paro Valley—is the only one in the country long enough to accommodate jets. From north to south, the winter stubble of red rice fields rustled around square old white farmhouses. The mountains marched east and west. Down the middle ran the onion-colored rush of the Paro Chhu River. The shriek of our turbines seemed an unpardonable insult to this ancient Buddhist settlement. I'd been in Bhutan just two minutes and already I felt she-bear protective of its otherworldly peace.

And well it should be protected. In a distance of some 100 miles, Bhutan's altitude drops from 24,784 feet to 700. Nearly three-quarters of this Switzerland-sized country is forested, and 60 percent will remain so by royal mandate—that's how serious the king of Bhutan is about preserving his kingdom. Red pandas, blue sheep, and snow leopards still dwell in the cold boreal forests. The southern jungles are home to Bengal tigers, leopards, Asian elephants, golden langur monkeys, pureblooded Asiatic buffalo, and four species of dramatic and colorful hornbills.

But I was there to see the cranes, and a pilgrimage to see them had been arranged for me by Ugyen Rinzin, the owner of Bhutan's top travel agency. Rare black-necked Tibetan cranes, Ugyen told me on the phone in hushed Buddhist tones, overwinter in Bhutan's central valleys, arriving in thrilling numbers each November, a species in serious decline virtually everywhere else. Happily, it is the kingdom's Buddhist traditions that have proven to be its conservation trump card. "Respect for the natural world is a central tenet of Buddhism," states the preamble to the 1990 Paro Resolution on Environment and Sustainable Development. "Man is just a sentient being among other forms of existence," noted one of Bhutan's UN representatives in his keynote speech at a UN meeting. "The assumption that man is on top of the chain of beings is misplaced, considering the mysterious web of interdependent relationships that is now being confirmed through scientific studies. Reality," he concluded, "is not hierarchical but a whole, circular, enclosed system. Sustainable development is, therefore, in the interest of every being, every day, not just in the interest of future generations."

A Canadian forestry consultant I ran into on my trip put it this way: "I would say that Bhutan is the one country on earth that's on the threshold of learning to do it right."

That first morning dawn broke in a glossy magenta yak-tail pattern flaring sideways across the sky. By nine my driver and guide arrived in the sparkling Land Cruiser that Ugyen had arranged for me. Soon we were wending our way around paper clip turns on the road to a valley called Bumthang. Every few moments, another sector of dale opened up as if we were trespassing through a system of colossal geodes. Signs of the Buddha were everywhere. We constantly passed roadside boulders painted gay colors and inscribed with prayerful words written in Dzongkha, Bhutan's lovely lingua franca since it first opened to the West in the 1960s. And always there were prayer flags, long banners in five colors representing each of the five elements (air, water, earth, fire, and sky) attached lengthwise to tall posts from which they strobed in the ever-present mountain zephyrs. It was hard to imagine a place of greater peace.

The next afternoon, my guide, "T. G.," by way of complicated past-life familial configuration, arranged for us to attend a special ceremony performed by the lama of Bumthang's famed seventeenth-century Kurjey Lhakhang Dzong, or temple. T. G. and I sat on cushions on the floor. Two lamas were perched on cushions to our right at the back of the beautiful, ornate room. To the front, a younger assistant tended the altar, lighting red incense and butter lamps, and pouring what appeared to be some sort of Buddhist holy water into silver chalices. Soon the top lamas began chanting, reading from narrow, well-worn pages, their words tumbling out in an astonishingly swift stream. The stream became a single sound that rose and lowered then rose again, broken only be the occasional beat of a drum. Very shortly, my mind took flight too.

Afterward, T. G. informed me that the lamas had asked the Buddhist deities to make Bhutan's wildlife reveal itself to us, and to protect me when I began my long journey home. Half an hour after we left Bumthang, a strange black-and-rust-colored, mooselike animal crossed the road right in front of our truck while Mount Jhomolhari gleamed in the middle distance.

"Jura!" breathed T. G., meaning one of Bhutan's rarely seen native ruminants.

Soon after, we saw a kestrel hunting from a power line. Then a Himalayan pied kingfisher, a crimson-breasted pied woodpecker, and a little wallcreeper. Our coup de grace was a whole flock of cuckoo doves preening in the understory around a roadside creek, dazzling us with their fabulous long gray-barred tails. I said a quiet prayer of thanks to the nature gods and to the kindly lama who had so successfully intervened on our behalf.

T. G. smiled. "Prayer is everywhere, you know," he said. "In prayer flags, in every drop of rain, in every leaf—even the air is filled with prayer in Bhutan."

By 5:30 the next morning we were picking our way down a yak trail through the forest behind the Gangtey guesthouse, an exhausting activity at nine thousand feet. We crossed the frosted flats of Phobjikha Valley, winter home of some three hundred black-necked cranes. Our destination was a distant wooden hut and bird blind, the only structure on this governmentally protected marshland.

We heard them before we saw them. Their cries hovered in our ears like clarinet notes from outer space. The cranes.

Black-necked cranes were hunted in Bhutan until around 1980, when killing one was made an offense punishable by life imprisonment. By the time we arrived at the blind, it was already filled with birdwatchers from all over the world. The crane count, so far, was 129.

Nothing can communicate the drama of seeing black-necked cranes in the wild—their sheer size, at four feet tall with an eight-foot wing span, and their elegant yellow eye circles, flamboyant black tertial bustles, and especially the hopping open-winged jig they do. Rumor had it that they were going to take off any moment, but they stayed for hours and called and huffed and fluffed and called and danced and danced and danced. Eventually they took to the air in threes, blessing us with their strange symphonic absolutions as they became small black crosses in the sky. Standing there on that eons-old glacial moraine, with the first twists of winter wood smoke curling heavenward from distant farmhouses, I wanted with all my heart to believe that the circle of the black-necked cranes would remain unbroken. For what, I thought, is migration but the eternal path of nature made visible to us by animals that faithfully follow its lead. The difference is that in Bhutan this path is a holy thing, the Wheel of Dharma itself,

Ugyen Rinzin, Bhutan

a symbol of the fundamental teachings of Buddhism—and of Albert Schweitzer—and its inherent reverence for all life.

"This is why holy people instinctively love animals," the Holy Pig Farmer confirmed when I called to tell him about my Himalayan adventure. At the Black-Necked Crane Festival in the Phobjikha Valley, Ugyen Rinzin had explained that Bhutan's fierce dance masks, which look to the western eye to be the snarling faces of great mythic beasts, "actually represent the demons that dwell between the worlds. When people die, their souls must confront these demons, and the dances are designed to familiarize people with these monsters so that they will not become frightened and lose their way."

Demons? Did he say *Demons*?

"Of course," Ugyen confirmed.

It was the first time in my experience that anyone outside of the Christian Gospels themselves had confirmed the existence of demons. The fierce and noble faces of Bhutanese dance masks now guard either side of the door to my work studio, and a small collection of handsome Bhutanese Dharma objects now graces my private altar, and always will.

24

Val Speaks

January 2000

With the prayerful winds of the Himalayas at my back, the regular heart-beat of my spiritual life marched me right into the new century. Despite my ever more global mystical encounters, the most remarkable evidence of the Divine continued to show up in my own room.

Late in the night of January 19, 2000, I was visited upon by a most unusual Red One. It was a female energy (though, as with the first lovely Red One, I can't explain how I knew). But its shape was far less defined compared to the others, not a specific form but sort of blobby, like an amoeba, and not an intense red, either, but an anemic rose. For some reason, it occurred to me that I had never asked a Red One how it was doing, despite the fact that they were always checking in on me, so this time I did.

"What's your name?" I mentally asked this odd pink entity.

Instantly, I "heard" a creaky old-person's voice reply: "Very well, thank you."

Hmmm. Maybe I wasn't projecting clearly enough?

"So, you're doing well?" I thought, trying to call forth more effort.

"My name? Oh, I'm the Spinster."

The Spinster?

"You know," I offered, "I can't see you as clearly as I see the others."

"Oh, that's all right, dearie," The Spinster replied, "I don't see so well, myself. Don't hear so well either!"

And with that, she vanished.

I confess to giving into a gaggle of giggles. Val Brooks laughed out loud, too, when I told her about The Spinster at lunch the next day, a rare Thursday meeting thanks to a glitch in her usual Tuesday schedule.

"They're sending you old angels!" Val hooted. "You must be doing a lot better!"

We both found this rather hilarious. When Val finally wiped her eyes she noticed that I was rubbing my ring finger again. For months I'd been feeling what I could only describe as a phantom ring on my left hand, heavy and substantial . . . and weird, because it wasn't there!

"The Phantom Ring?" she asked.

STONE SOUP © 2009 JAN ELIOT

I nodded.

"Just a sign of rings to come, sweetie!" Not a statement to be taken lightly from someone who wears a ring on almost every finger.

But the gaiety subsided when I returned to my apartment. An upsetting message awaited on my answering machine. It was from my fellow conservationist and fly-fishing buddy from Vashon Island, Danny O'Keefe, the composer of the old hit "Good Time Charlie's Got the Blues."

"I have some sad news," he said in a voice filled indeed with the blues. "Hazel Wolf passed away last night."

Hazel? Last night?! Oh my goodness—The Spinster!

Hazel Wolf was my conservation hero. She'd been the secretary of the Seattle chapter of the National Audubon Society for thirty years, and a nonstop activist for peace and social justice. She could charm the most rabid anti-environmentalist conservative, and usually got him or her to join the National Audubon Society! She had, in fact, single-handedly recruited more new members than anyone in the group's long history. I'd written about her, shuttled her to meetings, contributed to the environmental newsletter she edited for decades, and taken her to lunch whenever I could if only to ask her again to describe her phenomenally joyful life philosophy.

I took Hazel to lunch a few days after President Bush Sr. had plunged us into the Gulf War. The horror of it all ruined my appetite. Hazel, however, was thoroughly enjoying her spicy Thai noodles.

"How do you do it?" I asked her. "How can you be happy—much less hungry—with this terrible thing going on?"

Hazel stopped mid-bite, lowered her chopsticks, and regarded me with bird-bright eyes. The little tufts of white hair standing up all over her head actually made her look like a baby bird. But her words were those of a wise old teacher. "You do what you can," she told me sweetly. "That's all you can do, and then you enjoy your life because worrying never helps anything at all." I could almost hear her silently adding: "And it makes you very dull lunch company!" I had even been resoundingly out-kayaked by Hazel when she was well into her nineties. Now she was gone. Tears stung my eyes.

Then it came to me: "Wait a minute! It's the new century! Hazel made it!"

Born in 1898, she was, by her own gleeful decree, "older than electricity." She had personally known seven generations of her own family, and her goal was to live in three centuries. Darn if she hadn't done it. Of course she did. She was Hazel Wolf, and Hazel Wolf could and would and did do anything! How I wish I'd known I would see her again after her death—how she would have scoffed at the idea. Hazel Wolf was the most earth-bound atheist I'd ever met.

"That's why I love atheists," the Holy Pig Farmer told me when I called him with the news. "Because they're like Hazel. She was a holy woman."

"Hazel?"

"Oh, yes. We can tell from everything you say about her. She cared about people, especially the poor. She cared about animals."

I could hear Lory's cows mooing.

"She was in every way Christ-like."

"Do you think people like Hazel are turned off by religion," I asked, "because of all the fighting and fussing? All the hypocrisy? And the intolerance when churches should be the most tolerant places of all?"

"I think," Lory answered quietly, "if people like Hazel had attended churches that taught who Jesus really is, his goodness and joy, and his unconditional adoration of us all, then they wouldn't have become atheists. So many churchgoers are taught these fearful, wrathful images of God by unhealed ministers and priests and nuns, and it's wise that people reject those images. But by her happiness and service and love and compassion, you can tell that Hazel was a very holy woman. God blessed and directed her life.

"How do you know if someone's holy?" he suddenly asked me.

"I don't know."

"Because the person is happy and kind. Now there's holiness inside every person, every person is holy. Everything Jesus taught is how we can wake up to that. Everything the Buddha taught is how we can wake up to that. Everything Hindus teach is how we can wake up to that."

"What about Islam?" I asked.

"Islam is interesting. My perception is that the energy of God is like a diamond with many facets, and every surface—every religion—is part of a divine reflection. Holy people exist in every religion. You will meet Muslims who are absolutely holy; in Islam you'll find people who are filled with anger and bitterness and terror. Same with Christianity. But every religion offers a pathway to God, and the big mistake is when religions say, 'No, this is the only way to salvation, this is the only way.'"

Lory was still for a long moment.

"But, you know, the kingdom of heaven has a million doors, and the path you're on right now, Jessica, leads to one of those doors—it's your door."

That year I spent Easter break with my parents. Mostly because my busy baby sister, Heather, had decided to pay them a rare visit too. I think you have to have sisters to know the sweet domestic nothingness of just being in the house together, cooking, or watching old movies on TV. It's a girl thing. A sister thing. And it always reminded me that I didn't have little girls of my own.

Mother had found a vintage *Blondie* movie, and we sat there roaring at Dagwood's antics and the silly jokes, with Heather leaning on Mother's right shoulder and me leaning on her left. How few simple feminine familial moments like this do busy career women have these days? Hazel Wolf didn't even want any, and raised her only child—a daughter—in boarding houses, mostly because she hated cooking and loved living with other people.

But I was starved for this domesticity. Starved! All of a sudden, it all came into sharp focus: Blondie standing there in her old-fashioned kitchen, a mixing bowl on one hip and Baby Dumpling on the other, the very portrait of Home Sweet Home. A scorching pain slowly rose up from the depths of my woman's soul like rising bread dough. Tears flung themselves on my cheeks like splattered bacon grease, and four little oven-hot word biscuits popped out of my open mouth:

"I wanna be Blondie!!!"

...to which my deliberately childless happily-married-to-a-rocket-scientist superstar–Silicon Valley attorney little sister coolly replied:

"What ... and marry an idiot?"

It *was* funny. But something had broken and its truth had spilled across the floor of my heart like a dropped egg. I was, at least, on record with myself: I really did want a husband and a home and, somehow, a family of my own. I did. I did, indeed.

On Easter morning I dutifully drove back into town to go to the church whose hopefulness that time of year I loved, and then I drove all the way back upriver to help Mother and Heather with Easter supper. The phone rang. I managed to answer it with a mixing bowl on one hip, and *The Joy of Cooking* cookbook that weighed as much as a baby on the other. It was Alan, my mother's antique dealer friend, calling with the good news that after four years of failed attempts he had finally sold my old evil vanity. That morning. That very morning. On Easter Sunday.

Soon after my Blondie Attack, the desire to own my own home eclipsed my fear of living alone. I was overcome with House Buying Fever.

"I thought you were getting to that point," Rande told me. "But you had to get there on your own—I couldn't help you."

Within a month I'd found a dainty light-flooded house on a hill with a transcendental view of the western mountains. I bought a wiry ranch kitten supposedly related to the coastal bobcat and named him Willie, and a rascally brown schipperke puppy I called Poiroux—Roux for short. My happy little family soon was thriving in my pretty hillside home, whose quietude I loved, just like Deepak said I would.

25

THE ELEPHANT GOD

December 2000

After church one Sunday I took myself out to lunch, and who should pull a chair up to my table but a scruffy fellow from my old apartment building. Everyone seemed to call him "The Con Man," though I had no idea why. To me he was just one of those weird little pigpen guys nobody likes much. But he was quite the religious scholar, and I enjoyed listening to his freewheeling dissertations. He held a flyer in front of my face. Some white-guy guru was giving yet another public talk. The Con Man asked if I'd like to attend it with him.

"Oh, no, thanks," I said and then absently glanced again at the photograph. Sparks flashed in the guru's gaze. I blinked. And looked again. Again, something like sunlight on water glittered in the man's eyes.

"Who is that guy?" I asked The Con Man.

"Oh, he's the husband of a woman who got enlightened in India, and now he is too." *How convenient*, I thought with my usual allergy to America's silly spiritual infatuation with such a backward place. However. That night I was awakened by a vision unlike anything I'd ever experienced: in my mind I was standing in the doorway of a second-story shop in some kind of little boutique mall, looking out at the band of blue sky above the roofline across the way. Mysterious little rainbows were looping up above the roofs, apparently from something I couldn't see yet. Very slowly, the source of the rainbows rose into view: that Indian god with an elephant head! He was literally shedding prisms.

The magical Hindu god sat cross-legged on a carpet. Sweet, whiny Indian music was playing from an unseen place, and the little deity was wagging his funny elephant head from side to side. A bright intelligence glittered in his eyes, which made the apparition seem all the more alive. This elephant god *was* alive. He was as real as the Red Ones, and as real as the vision of my father's face in the sky. In fact, his image had exactly the same carved-from-light qualities, and it radiated the same blissful goodness. I was enthralled.

The vision slowly lowered itself back behind the rooftop, and at the same time a man approached from my left. It was Guido Rahr, my long-lost fishing buddy and fly-fishing coach! Guido strode right up to me with that natural authority of his, took me in his arms, and kissed me passionately. "NO!" my mind screamed. "This is wrong! Guido's my brother!" But then I realized that Guido had morphed into a different man, taller but with the same intensity of spirit, the same almost British manners, the same athletic build and fast-forward energy and natural joie de vivre. He was just as handsome, too, I noted.

Instantly, I was rapturously in love ... I just had no idea with whom! But the feeling was so real (and he felt so real!) that I knew that he existed. And somehow would find me someday. So sure was I of this arguably illogical recognition that I bought my phantom lover a Christmas present that year: a box of "Lightfoot's Pure Pine Gentlemen's Athletic Soap" I'd happened to run across while shopping for my sisters' gifts. It was, I knew, just

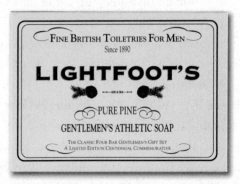

Actual box of soap Jessica bought for her unknown future beau

my guy's style. I wrapped the box with a gold ribbon and kept it in my lingerie drawer, only partly for its wonderful gentlemanly fragrance.

As soon as I woke up the morning after the elephant-god vision, I called The Con Man to ask him what this charming Hindu diety symbolized. True to form, The Con Man just laughed his unattractive hyena laugh and said, "Oh, that's Ganesh. Look him up on the Internet."

What I found was astounding. According to a super-beloved late-nineteenth-century Indian medical doctor-turned-Swami named "His Holiness Sri Swami Sivananda Saraswati Maharaj" (but you can call him Al), Lord Ganesha is the "embodiment of wisdom and bliss." Not only that, he presides over the "muladhara chakra," which is the psychic center of the body where the kundalini shakti dwells ... the very same "spark of life" Swami Satchadinanda had blasted into those fruit-and-nut balls at that New Year's Eve guru gathering my old boyfriend had dragged me to in 1983! "Lord Ganesha is," Swami Sivananda insisted, "also the Lord who removes all obstacles on the path of the spiritual aspirant, and bestows upon him worldly as well as spiritual success."

I wondered if Ganesha could get salad dressing stains out of silk blouses too.

That bit of cheekiness was rewarded by the next revelation: that the elephant god also represents the "complete conquest of egoism," as symbolized by the fact that he runs around town riding a lowly mouse ... which sounded an awful lot like Jesus riding into Jerusalem on a donkey. Hmmmm ...

"Take fresh spiritual resolves," the good Swami went on to implore us, "and pray to Lord Ganesha for inner spiritual strength to attain success in all your undertakings. May He remove all the obstacles that stand in your spiritual path!"

Holy Moly.

When I called Val Brooks to tell her about this latest vision, she squealed with delight.

"Oh, Ganesh! He's my favorite! I have a Ganesh statue on my desk!"

Wonder of wonders. I had no idea that Val had even heard of the elephant god. But then, I'd continued to notice that a lot of people who seem completely "normal" have all sorts of wild private spiritual lives. Once I asked my church friend and fellow clanswoman Celeste Maxwell Rose how long she'd been a Presbyterian and she smiled and said: "Oh I'm actually a devotee of Yogananda." Another church friend, Yvonne Young, I learned, had spent a whole week in Southern France at Plum Village, spiritual retreat of the Vietnamese Zen Buddhist master Thich Nhat Hanh. You just have no way of knowing what people are actually up to spiritually these days. But almost everyone sure seems to be up to something!

At our next literary luncheon Val presented me with my own little golden statue of Ganesh and said:

"I think it's time for you to go to India."

Ganesh statue Val Brooks gave Jessica

26

DANCING WITH STEPHEN HAWKING

January 2001

As you might expect, with Lord Ganesha the Obstacle Obliterator at the wheel, it only took a week for the editor of a woman's golf magazine to call and ask if I had any "spiritual golf story ideas possibly based in India."

In one of his spiritual rants, The Con Man had told me about an eighty-plus-year-old golfer-turned-spiritual teacher in Mumbai who used to run the Bank of India before he got enlightened and retired. Or something like that. Apparently The Mystic Golfer had always been drawn to the spiritual and had eventually lost his mind (the small one) while translating some of his own guru's teachings from the man's native dialect into Sanskrit. The story goes that suddenly he knew what his teacher was going to say before he said it, something all wives do with their husbands every day. Nonetheless, this is a big deal for a guy, apparently, so The Mystic Golfer's teacher confirmed his pupil's enlightenment—"verified" is the word used in these circles—and upon his retirement The Mystic Golfer became a bona fide spiritual teacher himself. But of course.

Anyway, he was—or used to be—a serious golfer, and my editor thought that he probably had some interesting golf tips. So, in the first week of January, in the second year of the new century, I found myself winging east on a plane packed with Indian businessmen in crisp white shirts seated beside wives scented sweetly of curry and anise whose brightly colored saris made my own "chic" gray-and-black look like so much dryer lint.

That was my introduction to the sensory glories of Indian culture, a debut made all the more mysterious by the churning, swirling, enduring energies of Mumbai.

It's such a long haul from America's west coast to India's that you arrive already in an altered state. The rising flood of fellow passengers who appeared to represent most of Mumbai's twenty million residents pushed through the city's rabbit warren of an airport toward slowly snaking lines of most of the city's fifty thousand taxicabs. It was enough to trigger an out-of-body experience ... or make you want one. But the golf magazine that had commissioned me was topflight (ha ha), and I was booked at the superlative Oberoi Hotel Mumbai.

The place was such a wonder of cool granite civility I failed to notice the announcement that a string theory conference called "Strings 2001" was in progress. A sweet young woman escorted me directly to my beautiful room on what she called the "Ladies Only Floor." Moments later a man appeared at my door. "To help with the Googley," he explained sheepishly. He had my laptop Googling like a champ in no time. I showered off the grime of international travel, ordered a supper of fragrant fruited rice, scorchingly good not-for-wimps curry, and some kind of divine little dessert involving pistachios and rose water that I considered saving as a temple offering. All I can say is that what we call "Indian food" at home is to Mumbai what Taco Bell is to Guadalajara. Deeply contented, I collapsed in my good, clean bed, blithely unaware that some of the brainiest physicists of our time were sleeping under the same roof.

With the coming dawn came the realization that the Oberoi Mumbai is actually on the Arabian Sea. And I had quite the water view. But it was an Impressionist's vista at best thanks to the ever-present Mumbai Mist. The city is an amalgam of seven islands knitted together by four rivers and a lotus flower of creeks. Add to these ubiquitous aquatics winter temperatures of at least ninety degrees, and you can watch the resulting humidity rise cobra-like off the Arabian Sea each morning and slither slowly into town.

The effect is, to say the least, disorienting.

Once outside, I was further spun round by the turning tones of sitar music and ever-present strands of incense smoke that twist out of every Indian home, shop, and temple at any given moment of the day. The plumerial sweetness of India's champa flowers wrapped its long golden fingers around the dirt-and-sugar resin of sandalwood, orbited the cool menthols of camphor, then fell into the warm arms of saffron, clove, and musk. I felt as though I were breathing in the Garden of Eden. It was all I could do not to swoon. At least, I thought, I wasn't swooning from the poverty as I had imagined I would.

There were very poor people everywhere, but they weren't lying around the streets in abject dereliction as the poorest of the poor are left to do back home. They were busy. Very busy. Everyone in Mumbai seemed to have something important to do, whether it was selling spicy potato vada pav or sweeping the streets with hand brooms they made themselves or creating beautiful marigold puja offerings for the citizenry's constant temple visits. The energy of industry animated the city, and there was a sense that all this activity was both ancient and orchestrated, as if it were saying: "Who are you to think India doesn't know what it's doing?" At least this side of the slums, anyway. The whole thing reeled with color, too, and, inevitably, a cow wandered through it.

Overwhelmed and overheated, I staggered back to the hotel and was greatly relieved to find my courtly, mustachioed driver, Anand, waiting for me in a mercifully air-conditioned Mercedes. Soon we were off to The Mystic Golfer's home somewhere in upscale Mumbai.

But the city's traffic swirls much like its viper vapor does. And its fifty thousand motor vehicles hug the deep arc of the inner harbor so tightly they throw metal crochet all over the curvy hips of Back Bay and Chowpatty—not to be confused with "Cow Patty," although given the protected status of cows in India you may have a point—Beach. To my horror, more sitar music soon drilled the quiet of our car, along with a calliope's worth of bowed and plucked notes wincing forth from the sarod, sursringar, sarangi, and other instruments of Hindustani torture, including some kind of Indian violin.

Anand smiled. "God music," he said, wagging his head just like Lord Ganesha did. Hoh boy.

A high vivid feminine voice undulated out from Anand's cassette player, and true to his promise, the melody bespoke of a heavenly glamour. After about five minutes of this you begin to do an involuntary backseat hula and make "Happy Talking" gestures with your lovely hands as they fly like a bird over the ocean ... or, at least, Cow Patty Beach.

By then Anand radiated joy. His head woggled, his smile boggled, his fingers toggled the glossy black knuckles of the steering wheel. If he didn't look so much like Inspector Clouseau in glasses I might have taken his choice of mantra a lot more seriously. Clearly, he loved his God music very, very much. He played it every time I was in his car. In fact, that's all he played. Ever. He played it when he picked me up to take me to see The Mystic Golfer each morning, and he played it every time he delivered me back to the hotel each afternoon. I considered that this happy eternal celestial sound loop might have been the only music Anand owned. I suspect, however, it was the only music he liked. It was, I am sure, Anand's daily spiritual practice, as it did go on ... Anand ... Anand. After listening to it for one week straight, I can still hum the entire melody nearly a decade later, and do a semi-respectable imitation of the lyrics, which, to the Western ear, sound sort of like the Dixie Cups' old hit "Iko Iko," albeit slowed waaayyy down and sung by a very talented killer bee: "Jockomo feena-AH-ah-NAAHHhHhHhhH-nayyyyyyy. Jockomo feenaaaaHHhHHahHAaaaa nayyy." I am quite sure that when I die the coroner will find the words to Anand's goddamned God music etched on the inside of my skull ... in Sanskrit. With Anand's God music wending through my mind there in Mumbai's twirling traffic, whirling incense, and the curling blue cobra fog of the Arabian Sea, is it any wonder that when I finally met The Mystic Golfer he found me, well, rather vacant?

In the old tradition of Indian ashrams, The Mystic Golfer opens his home to all interested spiritual seekers from ten to noon every day. I was surprised to find maybe a dozen people—mostly Americans, a few Europeans—milling around his front steps awaiting show time. Finally someone opened the door, and this gathering of kind, selfless seekers took off up the stairs with the competitive zeal of a bunch of NBA stars. I found it rather unseemly and chose to walk at a not uncool pace miles behind everyone else ... and promptly got lost.

"This way, Miss," offered a helper person with a head waggle strong enough to topple a turban, had he been wearing one, which makes you wonder how these two aspects of Indian style could have possibly evolved together. Mr. Waggle ushered me back through a living room-cum-sun-room and speared an open palm through the open doorway of a small side room, which I soon saw was packed with my fellow spiritual buddies, all seated on the floor at the sandaled feet of the diminutive Mystic Golfer who was holding court in a comfortable armchair in the corner. The only available seating option left was an open wooden chair directly across from The Teacher, which one would have thought would cause a fistfight among the good, gentle seekers. The Mystic Golfer motioned for me to sit there.

"That's the Hot Seat," whispered a smiling woman to my left. "For newcomers. But he'll only grill you for a few minutes."

Uh-oh.

I learned later that everyone else in the room had been hanging with The Mystic Golfer for days, if not weeks. Since I was the new kid on the ego-chopping block, I was, you'll forgive the phrase, spiritual fresh meat. This is what spiritual students come to India to do. That's the teacher-student custom. The idea is that by being in the presence of an enlightened master to whom you feel yourself drawn (or, perhaps, to whom a golf editor might send you), her or his intense consciousness will, if you're lucky, set your own kindling on fire. To paraphrase modern master Eckhart Tolle: when a green log that's barely burning plops down beside a seasoned log that's burning like a house afire, the green log has a much better chance of going up in holy smoke. The Mystic Golfer's incendiary trigger of choice was, I soon learned, the mental laser. In a nanosecond he somehow locked his mind to mine ... and began lighting matches in the dark.

If you simply observed The Mystic Golfer and didn't get drawn into Never-Never Land by looking into his eyes, you could easily imagine the man in a sleek black suit, sitting in a big fancy back office from which he basically ran the biggest bank on the subcontinent. Today he was wearing loose cotton guru-style pants and a pressed white tunic top, but his silver hair was still parted and combed with executive precision and he spoke the English of commerce—clipped and precise. He was not an imposing figure, being no more than five feet four and fine-boned as a bird, but he radiated power. He reminded me, in fact, of a kestrel, small but command-ing, his mind hovering above us all, his hunter's eyes missing nothing. They were, by the way, black as outer space and glittery as stars. If you dared to look deeply you could see whole galaxies in there. Earthwise, the man, in other words, was a goner.

I had seen this before. Swami Satchidananda's eyes were like this. They tell you that the man within is there, and the man without is not. Here, and not here. The concept is that something or someone has blasted the for-merly small mind of the now fully enlightened out into hyperspace ... or wherever it goes when it's gone. And that is the goal spiritual teachers are forever trying to pound into our small minds: that the spirit that inhabits each human body in fact extends out into infinity. Deepak Chopra puts it most eloquently: "Right now you are at the center of the universe because infinity extends in all directions ... you are not a local event."

And what, pray tell, would it feel like to be aware of that?

It would feel the way The Mystic Golfer's eyes looked. And while those eyes shone light into every hidden corner of my small mind, a stream of words flowed from the mouth below them. But I heard hardly a one. Because his laser gaze vaporized anything he said the moment he said it. This was not about words. This was not a conversation. This was the Tele-pathic Indian Inquisition. Are you now, or have you ever been, aware? How aware are you, exactly? How aware could you be? And what on earth is blocking your chances of being completely aware of the daunting truth that the entire frigging universe is pulsing away at the deepest core of you? The thing went on for one solid hour and for one solid hour I said virtually nothing, and just sat there ... and burned.

I can tell you, the Hot Seat can get pretty hot.

Finally it was done. The Mind-Lock released, and without my having given him any information about myself at all, The Mystic Golfer issued his prognosis. I had to look out for two dangerous tendencies. Two spiritual Achilles' heels. Two stumbling blocks apparently guaranteed to trip me up on the race to Eternity.

"First, you take things too personally," said The Teacher. "Taking offense is all ego, nothing more. Second, you have to give up always wanting to go first class. My wife and I," The Mystic Golfer went on, "we have enough money that if our refrigerator breaks, we can afford to go out and buy a new one. But can we pay for first-class tickets to travel the world? No."

How offensive! Not to mention presumptuous. Why, I never pay for first-class anything—the magazines I write for do. (The upscale ones, any-way—conservation work is all sub–cattle car at best, of course.) I started to defend myself but stopped short and sat quietly thinking about this as someone else asked a question and the session moved on. Maybe The Mystic Golfer had tapped into the eternal conflict between my love of exquisite things and the uneven arrival of my paychecks? But wait, I thought. I always manage. You develop an eye for great deals and you pay for things in installments that cost less than what most people spend to go out to dinner. And what was so terrible about loving objets d'art anyhow? Maybe this was simply a difference in personal values?

Frank Lloyd Wright once famously said: "Give me the luxuries of life and I will gladly do without the necessities," and whenever I hear this I always add: "And if we were French, the luxuries would *be* the necessi-ties!" Because the French absolutely worship the things the United States, especially, tends to consider "luxuries" if not downright frivolities: art, architecture, design, dance, literature, food, wine, fashion, hand-painted china, poodles, perfume, perfumed poodles, even fine chocolate, speaking of objets d'art! Once when France was in a particularly bad national budget crisis the government issued an official statement saying that it would *not* cut funding for the arts. Can you imagine?!

As for little miss Louisiana-French-heritage-me, I was once driving to my bank to deposit a long-awaited check from a big magazine feature I'd worked on for months when an antique silver tea service sitting in the win-dow of a shop caught my eye. I stopped to have a look. Well, whattya know: the price was exactly, to the penny, the amount of my check. Of course I could have saved that money. Or been ahead on my rent for once

... But to my credit, it is a fabulous tea set. And it will last the rest of my life—you only need one. I share it with others, too, because I love French salon-style tea parties and use my good silver tea service at every one, much to the delight of friends and family. When my elegant ninety-year-old fly-fishing coach, Dr. H. Lenox H. Dick, came to dinner one night, he took one look at my Victorian tea service and pronounced it "museum quality" ... and being a true Philadelphia Blue Blood, he oughtta know!

As anyone who watches *Antiques Road Show* also knows, a silver tea set like mine will only go up in value ... unlike, say, The Mystic Golfer's stocks and bonds, which are probably lower than the Paris Métro right about now. In fact my entire hard-won collection of antiques is looking pretty good these days, thank you very much. And I never stiffed anyone on my rent, either.

But the bottom line was higher than any economic discourse: these beautiful old things I loved so much were made by someone's hands. The beauty that is the signature of their construction and the freshness of their design, from the elfin flourish in etched silver to the welcoming pineapple pedestal of a tea table: these are the skillful details of inspiration working through the artists' touch. And we get to touch them back. Even now, sometimes centuries later, tracing a finger where fingers labored not against a clock, but in the long slow heart of creativity, you can feel the love there still. And isn't it, really, divine, and, therefore, the opposite of idolatry?

Well, I thought peevishly, maybe The Mystic Golfer had just registered my stubborn aesthetics-or-die motto as, perhaps, a lack of ... je ne sais quoi. Oh, okay, je do sais quoi: maybe as a certain adolescent lack of restraint that isn't very helpful on the path to perfect humble inner peace. I mean, the Buddha was forever telling everyone that their desires would be their undoing. And look at Gandhi. He scaled it down to a diaper and a bowl, and I bet he even renounced refrigerators. Though by the looks of it he would have done better to renounce sugar—the guy's teeth were a mess, and clearly, he renounced dentists.

Well, all right. So maybe I do have a little work to do in the Desire Restraint Department. But what, really, is so bad about taking things personally? Sensitivity is the natural hallmark of all sensitive people. And I happen to believe it walks hand in hand with empathy, and therefore compassion, both of which are probably total nonstarters for cold, calculating big-time financial types like The Mystic Golfer. Come to think of it, hadn't he zeroed in on the two things that probably set big-time financial types' predatory teeth on edge: not being miserly with one's money and having a heart like . . . a tea party!

Maybe, I thought, Monsieur Golfer and I just have a personality conflict?

"You could be right," agreed a woman named Suzie during a break time. She was, she said, a longtime Mystic Golfer devotee and knew him well. "Even though he's enlightened, his personality is still intact, and some people don't like it. He can be really insensitive." She smiled prettily. "He was a banker, after all."

Nonetheless, I continued to endure the dual assaults of Anand's God music and The Mystic Golfer's corporate cool in order to sit with "a true spiritual master" each morning, even though he seemed to have little to say about golf. And, I confess, each afternoon I left The Mystic Golfer's home feeling euphoric.

"You're glowing," my new friend Suzie acknowledged several times. At the end of one session she invited me to meet her and friends at an Indian music concert that night. (Oh no! More God music!) The venue was spectacular: a huge rectangular plein air lake flanked on three sides by tiered seating with a thrust stage protruding into the water on the fourth side. I sat in happy silence watching the moonlight shimmy on the lake while Suzie and her friends chatted quietly. Then I sensed a new presence. And I turned to find that a middle-aged Indian couple had manifested in the empty seats to my left and were staring at me with a strange smiling intensity.

"Yes?" I asked, alarmed.

"We haf chosen YOU to present the flowers to the musicians after the concert!" the woman declared triumphantly. "It won't be difficult—you just come over behind the stage there," she pointed, "and we will meet you with the flowers. Will you do eet?"

"But ... but ... " I sputtered. "Why me?"

"Because," the man answered gently, "your light ees wery bright. We could see it from thee other side of thee lake!"

So there truly must be authentic spiritual advantage to spending time in the presence of an enlightened one, even if the guru's personality, as my photographer friend Art Wolfe might say, sucked raw dogs.

The Mystic Golfer was enlightening about this whole business of enlightenment too. One morning someone asked him if little things still annoy him now that he's enlightened. "Oh, well," he said, "yes they do. You begin to react, but ..." he waved his hand as if shooing a fly, "then you think, 'so what?'"

And he could be funny. When someone else asked him if he believed in free will he replied: "I used to believe we do not have free will. But then I realized that we do indeed have free will as far as the will to try to make things happen. However, of all the things we try to make happen, the ones that actually do happen, that is God's will. So, ultimately, your free will is worthless."

I was thinking—and laughing—about that one again when I got in from dinner with my new spiritual buddies one evening. The Oberoi lobby was packed, so I took a detour to the elevator and happened to pass a side room where a cocktail party was in full swing, complete with some darn good R & B. Drawn in by the music, I carefully poked my head around the corner only to find the biggest collection of the dweebiest looking guys I'd ever seen in one room. Talk about your glasses-and-plastic-pocket-protector crowd.

"Cambridge?" asked a grinning endearingly beluga-headed fellow leaning against the entryway.

"Uh ... U of O," I replied.

He brightened. "Oxford, then?"

I shook my head.

"Oregon. You know, go Ducks!"

"Ah, zoology?"

"Golf, actually."

He strained to hear over the music.

"Gödel, was it?"

"In Gödel we trust!" I replied. "Or trusted," I added, remembering something I'd just read in the *International Herald Tribune* about new work by astrophysicist Stephen Hawking on, you know, little stuff like why the universe exists, which is one of the most honorable uses of the masculine Y chromosome I've ever heard of. Hawking was pirouetting far above theoretical mathematician Kurt Gödel's old Incompleteness Theorem that proved back in the thirties that a self-contained universe is mathematically impossible. Hawking's stated goal was nothing less than "a complete understanding of the events around us, and of our own existence." Now he was exploring the thrilling idea that by combining quantum mechanics with Einstein's relativity, you're cooking with ... multidimensional space. Et voilà! The ingredients for a unified theory that could explain everything in the whole universe, from galaxies to people and, as far as I was concerned, Red Ones and Gray Ones too. The newest idea back then was that electrons, once thought to be static dots, are actually tiny loops of oscillating string, hence the name string theory.

"Say!" I said to Monsieur Beluga, "are you here for the string theory conference?"

He frowned.

"Of course. Aren't you?"

"Oh, gosh," I replied with a laugh, "I'm just another quantum physics peabrain!" Meaning that as a devotee of modern physics I knew only too well how infinitesimal my peabrain knowledge actually was.

"Ah, 'P-branes,' he repeated. "Good, good. Superstring theory, then."

Horrified, I realized he thought I was a physicist working on P-branes, which are a big part of string theory.

"Heavens, no!" I replied. "I *am* a peabrain ... I don't work with P-branes!"

I'd been a very amateur fan of theoretical physics for years at this point and knew that the "P" in P-branes refers to the varying number of spatial dimensions on any given "brane"—short for "membrane," which is string theory's beautiful visual model. Superstring theory takes another quantum leap (ha!) and attempts to explain all the forces of nature and every type of particle in theoretical physics in one single power-punch of a theory. The basic idea is that reality-as-we-know-it boils down to, yes, strings that vibrate at varying frequencies. And the membrane model gives us peabrains a picture of how oscillating "strings" just might look as they sweep into spacetime and create the universe. In the end, it pretty much looks like the entire universe is really just a giant endless looping string concerto.

A shriek of recognition went off inside my head: Oh my God, Anand was right! It *is* all God music!

At that exact moment, someone turned down the lights, and notes from the oscillating strings of the Indian sitar and its family of fellow whiners overcame the Western rhythms and swept out across that small universe of partying physicists—and one peabrain whom Mr. Beluga shyly asked to dance. He himself couldn't, of course, and neither could any of his fellow physicists, all of whom were only capable of bouncing up and down like excited electrons. But who cared! How often does a peabrain get to dance with a P-brane to God music in honest-to-God India at a real, live string theory conference? Does it get any better than that?

Actually, yes.

Out of the corner of my eye I noticed something oscillating horizontally instead of vertically. When I turned to see what it was, my knees buckled. There, frozen in space-time by Lou Gehrig's Disease but vibrating at the speed of genius even while strapped into his electric wheelchair, was none other than my superstring superhero, Stephen Hawking his holy, rolly self! And he was coming our way!

Sure enough, Hawking wheeled smack into the middle of the dance floor and with a renegade's grin began spinning around in endlessly looping circles, the clear and present nucleus in this sea of lesser electrons who spontaneously oscillated faster and faster, glasses bouncing, pocket protectors flying, until you could literally feel the singing web of strings that connected us all. Not a bad night for an astrophysicist looking for a theoretical backstage pass into the mind of God.

27

HILL GAYA RE APUN

January 2001

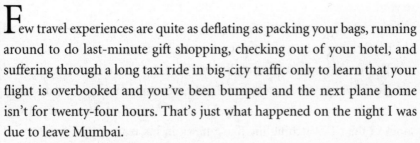

Few travel experiences are quite as deflating as packing your bags, running around to do last-minute gift shopping, checking out of your hotel, and suffering through a long taxi ride in big-city traffic only to learn that your flight is overbooked and you've been bumped and the next plane home isn't for twenty-four hours. That's just what happened on the night I was due to leave Mumbai.

Collapsed in the backseat of yet another sweltering cab (where is Anand and his air-conditioned Mercedes when you need him!), I comforted myself with the thought that I would, at least, see The Mystic Golfer again one more time. And so it was that the next morning Anand shuttled me back to my teacher-du-jour's manicured neighborhood for one last session at the feet of the master.

I hadn't said anything at all since my stint on the Hot Seat, even though The Mystic Golfer passed a microphone around for questions at each session, but I thought maybe I'd better use this gift of an extra morning wisely and, you know, SAY something! "Okay," I told myself, "if it feels right, I'll tell him about seeing my father's face in the sky." But I wasn't going to force it like The Mystic Golfer's regulars who were forever fighting over the microphone, which seemed more like greedy monkey behavior than that of spiritually minded folks, the latter being something I wasn't much more comfortable with than the former but at least they have better manners.

Sure enough, close to the end of the session the woman next to me motioned for the microphone and asked a question that needed only a short answer. There was an expectant pause, and almost on automatic pilot I reached over and took the microphone and with shy excitement recounted to The Mystic Golfer and everyone else in the little room the experience of seeing my father's face bloom in the sky like God Himself nearly a decade earlier. Everyone seemed as thrilled as I was by this event … except The Mystic Golfer. To my horror, with a dismissive wave of his hand and a bitter-cucumber scowl, he said in a mocking voice: " 'Oh, *my* spiritual experience is more brilliant than *your* spiritual experience …'" Then he caught himself and added with an audible sigh: "So, what does this … experience … mean to you?"

Too late. I already felt like an abandoned puppy in the snow that had just been run over by a ten-ton truck with chains on.

The session was now officially over and my shock/hurt/humiliation/indignation/rage was so complete that I barely made it into Anand's back-seat before erupting into unstoppable tears. Anand, of course, was more shocked than I. Watching me like a hawk in his rearview mirror, he said over and over: "What happen, Miss? Someting wrong? Family okay? What ees eet, Miss?"

Between sobs I managed to gulp out the whole story. His eyes widened with gleeful amazement at the early plot twists.

"Up in the sky? You see father?"

"Yes."

"Father he ees dead, yes?"

"Yes."

"But you see father face? UP in the sky?"

"Yes!"

"Wayyyy up in the sky?" Anand said excitedly, and I swear to God he pointed heavenward and jammed his finger into the roof of his car just like Inspector Clouseau.

"You sister she see also? Up in the SKY? She okay? No-ting bad wit sister?"

"Yes, yes ... no, no ... she's fine."

It really was hard to talk because this meltdown was totally bindaas (Mumbai slang for, well, "totally"). Truly, I had no idea why The Mystic Golfer's reaction upset me so deeply ... other than, you know, maybe the betrayal of absolute spiritual trust. When I finished telling Anand what The Mystic Golfer had said, his eyes had cooled and narrowed.

"Hoooonie," Anand whistled. "Teacher say this? Hill gaya re apun," which, in the Mumbai slang he probably learned from his kids, means roughly: "The hell you say." Or, to be more specific: "I am completely and utterly disappointed that someone of such high spiritual standing, in India no less, could show such disregard for a genuine heaven-on-earth miracle and have so little compassion for a completely innocent spiritual semi-seeker who was in no way bragging or trying to be holier than thou or show anyone up, especially a spiritual teacher for chrissake, and who, in fact, was just trying to offer some authentic spiritual testimony to your boring little Praise-Sahib morning meetings, you Mumbai bindaas banker loser!"

Anand regarded me for a moment over his Inspector Clouseau moustache. Then his voice fell into coiled cobra register.

"Miss," he literally hissed, "I tink maybe your teacher have the jealousy."

"Well," I sniffed, "I guess that's better than having the Googley."

"Googley, Miss?"

"Oh, nothing. I'm just glad I didn't tell him about my Ganesh vision."

"Lord Ganesha?" he echoed.

I sniffled and nodded.

Anand's eyes looked as though they were going to pop out of their sockets and play hockey on the thick lenses of his glasses.

"You see Lord Ganesha?"

"Well ... yeah," I told him.

"Den ... you have ... the Darshan!"

I told him all about my realer-than-real Ganesh sighting, or Darshan, which I learned much later is a Sanskrit word for "vision" or "apparition" in which the spiritual student is quite literally graced by a visual visitation from one of India's major deities, each of whom, by the way, represents a specific aspect of the one God, or, in my favorite Hindu translation, the Supreme Personality. If a student is fortunate enough to receive Darshan and if she (or he) is very, very good—meaning falls in love with the deity that has revealed herself or himself to her, and treats this extra-special spiritual coach with the purity and devotion he or she deserves—then the visiting deity becomes the student's private portal to the Divine, not to mention giving the phrase "help from above" some serious new chops. This can't help but amp up the student's ETA at the waiting gates of Self-realization, meaning that the days of your screaming rock star ego are numbered and the Real You is in line for a very big promotion into the Jazz Holy Hall of Fame. To have been visited upon by the Hindu god of the Removal of Spiritual Obstacles, then, has potent spiritual implica-tions one does not need to explain to someone who listens to God music all day long.

Anand had become very still. I had, at last, stopped blubbering.

"You know, Miss. Lord Ganesha is one toot." Anand made a swooping gesture from his mouth up into the air in front of his forehead.

"Lord Ganesha only has one . . . tusk?" I guessed.

Anand wagged his head in the Indian sideways yes nod and then made a break-in-half gesture complete with cracking sound effects.

"Lord Ganesha . . . broke a tusk??"

Anand kept wagging. Playing Indian spiritual charades was cheering me up.

"Dis bad toot, it for making wictory to feelings and make de wis-dom. Dis crying you have because bad spiritual teacher? Lord Ganesha take away!"

Anand's sweeping gesture had a four-foot wingspan.

"Are you saying that Lord Ganesha broke a tusk in the . . . uh . . . fight over emotional control?" *And how,* I thought, *do we know he didn't break it by spearing a completely annoying banker?*

"Yes, yes!" Anand sang. "Fight for de wisdom!"

"So, Lord Ganesha can . . . take away taking things too personally and being too emotional?"

"Take ALL away! All, all. Wery necessitary to spiritual dewelopment. Wery wery."

I couldn't believe it. This had to be one of the biggest cosmic setups on record. My hotel driver was giving me the same spiritual advice as the supercompetitive former head of the Bank of India who thought he was exercising his free will to take me down a spiritual notch or two when his classic upper management insensitivity actually had played right into God's hands by catapulting me into the number-one spiritual obstacle he, himself, had warned me about, which made me break down in front of my driver so he could tell me why I had the vision of Ganesh, thereby reinforcing The Mystic Golfer's original spiritual counsel about getting over taking things too personally. And all of it happened because the airline managers in the financial capital of India can't count, probably because they were trained by the bindaas banker his holy golfing self. And God only knows why the woman beside me at my last Mystic Golfer session decided to ask that lame-o last-minute question. Of course God does.

Happy to see his charge smiling again, Anand slapped the top of the empty passenger seat beside him.

"We go now Lord Ganesha temple," he announced. "Much much famous temple in alllll Mumbai. Shri Siddhivinayak. We make puja to Lord Ganesha, nice lotus flower, nice coconut, nice nice. And ..." he added with a Clouseau wink, "Nice God music!"

As the familiar windy winding whine of Anand's favorite song filled the car, it also filled me with new joy. I was hearing it—really hearing it—for the first time. At once emptied and filled, I leaned back against the smooth, cool leather, said a silent Hinduesque prayer for the cow that gave its hide for such luxury, closed my mascara-smeared eyes, and understood why scholars of sacred Indian music say the thread that binds it all is "God-intoxication." How on earth did an ordinary-Joe hotel driver end up being so spiritually advanced? Only in India.

"Anand," I said, peering at him in the rear-view mirror, "what does your name mean anyway?"

He grinned back.

"Anand?" he answered. "It mean ... bliss."

We were back downtown again and one of Mumbai's unbelievably long red lights gave us a welcome break from its spinning traffic. A tap at my window put me nose to nose with a cow-eyed little boy no more than nine years old. He was holding a book, its cover pressed hard against the window glass. Anand began to wave the child away, but I stopped him. The book the boy was trying to sell me was none other than a copyright-impaired Indian black market copy of Deepak Chopra's *How to Know God.* I rolled down my window.

"Have you read it?" I stupidly asked the child. His huge tea-colored eyes widened with incomprehension. Anand translated for him, and with a mini–head waggle the boy rattled back something in Hindi.

"He say," Anand reported slowly, "he cannot read."

The light turned green, but Anand endured a chorus of honking horns while I dug out a fistful of rupees and pressed them into the boy's small hand in exchange for the book I knew held the literary Akashic Record of my father's last hurrah. Then I made a silent promise to do everything I possibly could to bring my parents' educational work back to the street children of India.

28

AVATAR OF THE HEART

February 2001

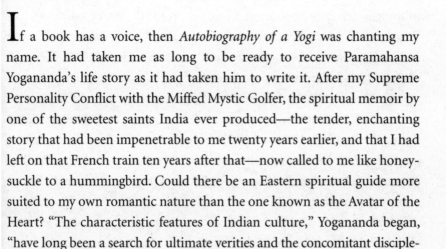

If a book has a voice, then *Autobiography of a Yogi* was chanting my name. It had taken me as long to be ready to receive Paramahansa Yogananda's life story as it had taken him to write it. After my Supreme Personality Conflict with the Miffed Mystic Golfer, the spiritual memoir by one of the sweetest saints India ever produced—the tender, enchanting story that had been impenetrable to me twenty years earlier, and that I had left on that French train ten years after that—now called to me like honeysuckle to a hummingbird. Could there be an Eastern spiritual guide more suited to my own romantic nature than the one known as the Avatar of the Heart? "The characteristic features of Indian culture," Yogananda began, "have long been a search for ultimate verities and the concomitant disciple-guru relationship." From that moment on, I was his.

I read *Autobiography of a Yogi* like a person—or a hummingbird—dying of thirst. Here at last was a chronicle by a recognized master of a genuinely mystical life. And here was someone who had never wanted anything in life but to know God, insisting that his readers make their own spiritual development the number-one goal of their life, much as Jesus said: "Seek ye first the kingdom of heaven." Here was a proven and beloved authority who also "saw" entities from other dimensions, or from other parts of the light spectrum, and who "heard" God speak to him and knew there were angelic beings on hand to help out—real ones, not Hallmark wannabes. Yogananda personally experienced the living Christ many times, and—miracle of miracles—he saw Christ as an "opalescent blue light," just like Aunt Katy's "blue window." He even spent an entire year of his life traveling the globe to personally visit the most hallowed saints and spiritual masters in order to include them in his opus.

I was absolutely thrilled to read on page 475 that on this trip Yogananda had had a Darshan eerily similar to my own, and in his Mumbai (then Bombay) hotel room, no less. In 1936, the "glorious form" of the Indian deity Krishna, god of love and divine ecstasy, "appeared in a shimmering blaze … over the roof of a high building across the street," just as Ganesh had appeared to me above the roofline of the shop across the way from where I was standing in my own vision. Krishna's visit in fact heralded the imminent arrival of the most powerful spiritual and ecstatic event of Yogananda's astonishing life: the resurrection of his longtime beloved Indian guru, Sri Yukteswar, in the flesh, as much as flesh is flesh, being, of course, the visible creation of singing cosmic strings and light. For the ensuing two hours Sri Yukteswar presented his star student with a discourse on the true and implicitly mystical nature of the universe, and of life on Planet Earth. My long-ago beau was right: nowhere in contemporary spiritual nonfiction is there a more complete—or hair-raising!—Eastern reflection on the Great Questions: Who are we? Why are we here? And where the hell— or heaven—are we?!

Autobiography of a Yogi also made possible—if spooky—sense of an old family mystery. When I was eleven years old and a piano student of little promise, one day I composed a song. It came from nowhere and was hauntingly beautiful, with a syncopated rhythm so unusual my piano teacher never could get it on paper, try as he might. I wrote lyrics for it, too, inexplicably all about the happy coming together of the East and the West, and to that end I named the song "Jade and Gold," the latter representing "The West" to a California girl who grew up hearing about the Gold Rush. Yogananda knew that his karmic assignment was to bring the East to the West, so much so that in 1924 he founded a magazine he named *East/West.*

Decades later, very nearly on my birthday, he consecrated his Self-Realization Fellowship Lake Shrine and Gandhi World Peace Memorial in Pacific Palisades on Santa Monica Bay between the California beach towns where Rande and I grew up. I like to think that my little song—the only one I ever wrote—is in some way a tribute to the kindly yogi whose autobiographical opus remains the most profound spiritual confirmation that anyone drawn to the subtler realms could hope for. Reading it told me that here, at last, was someone who understood.

Thank God.

Jessica's copy of Autobiography of a Yogi

29

MILK TEETH MIRACLE

June 2001

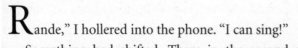

R ande," I hollered into the phone. "I can sing!"

Something had shifted. There in the second summer of the new century, my heart had become a lighthouse, its light sweeping out in all directions, connecting me to everyone and everything in the whole wide world ... even just sitting in my living room at home. And, as if to confirm the Buddhist belief that the heart instructs the voice, my normally wimpy singing voice had magically matured. I had been driving by myself, I told Rande, singing along with the classical music station, and for no apparent reason my voice suddenly opened up and had depth and timbre and even a little power. I could sing!

Rande, whose natural singing voice has always sounded like a fine 1940s torch singer, laughed. "Maybe we can finally sing 'The Boogie-Woogie Bugle Boy' as a duet," she said.

At church that Sunday, I told a friend who was a fabulous soprano and choir member about my newfound voice, and she talked me into joining the choir on the spot, despite the fact that I couldn't read music. At my very first choir rehearsal, whom should the director seat me in front of but the beautiful tall man in the bow tie whose overwhelming bass voice had about bowled me over at church three years earlier. And there he was, booming into my ears again.

I soon learned that his name was Tom Andersen and he was an attorney. "And he is divorced now," my soprano friend added. But I was more interested in some legal advice about a dumb magazine whose editor had refused to pay me even after publishing a story of mine. I decided to ask Mr. Andersen about it at the choir party that weekend (leave it to me to join a choir the week before it adjourns for the summer!).

Wanting to appear professional, I intended to present Mr. Andersen with one of my business cards, but I seemed to be completely out of them. Just before the party a mad search of every drawer, every purse, even every luggage tag turned up nothing. Standing in the middle of my room, wondering what to do, I looked down to see Roux waddling in with a small rectangle of paper in his mouth. No, I thought. It can't be.

It was.

Somehow, the puppy had found one of my business cards—surely the last one on the planet, albeit crumpled and dirty and not very professional looking at all. This from a puppy that wasn't even house-trained much less able to take telepathic Lassie-style commands. The event was far too much of a miracle to give its evidence to a perfect (-looking, anyway) stranger. Either I had a very psychic little doggie on my hands, or this was yet another case of everyday divine intervention.

Actual business card delivered by the puppy Roux

Mr. Andersen did indeed offer me excellent legal advice, and I noted that he took a stack of the cookies I'd baked for the party home with him.

Choir started up again in September just after the tragedy of 9/11, an event that I think made all of us glad to be together and singing. Mr. Andersen and I continued noticing each other at rehearsals and at church until each of us began to beam like Christmas lights when the other walked into the room.

When I mentioned him to my wise and talented neighbor Laura one afternoon, she said his name sounded familiar. "I think Ken knows him," she added, meaning her husband, Ken Butters, one of the best orthopedic surgeons in the Northwest, who happened to come home soon after. "Tom Andersen?" he said. "Workers comp attorney. Fabulous guy! You should go for it."

At choir rehearsal on January 16, 2002, I broke my Daughter-of-a-Southern-Mother rule of never making the first move and asked Mr. Andersen over for supper. What I actually said was: "If I invited you to dinner, would you accept?" thereby avoiding any further embarrassment in an already overwhelmingly embarrassing situation. But he just grinned and said: "You must be awfully shy—you can't even look me in the eye!" Damn lawyers.

On Thursday, January 24, Mr. Andersen arrived by bicycle and appeared at my doorstep holding a bouquet of Peruvian lilies that were listing like someone had recently tried to decapitate them. "I just want you to know that they were perfect until I swung my leg over my bicycle and almost cut them in half!" he boomed, thrilling me with his flawless grammar.

"I'd know that voice anywhere!" hollered another voice in the dark, followed by the lanky figure of my neighbor Ken loping up my front steps to pump Mr. Andersen's hand while Laura whispered loudly at him from below to stop it and come back down because this was a date! Damn doctors.

Mr. Andersen and I had a marvelous time and quickly learned that along with our love of sacred music we had everything that counted in common: progressive politics (his family marched in civil rights protests for weekend activities) and travel—especially to Europe (as a teenager, he lived with his family in Europe for four months not too many years before I spent my junior year of college in France: he became an Anglophile, I a

Francophile). We found that we both put family and friends first and love to host large gatherings, and we even share a Victorian fondness for fine old things (he collects antique maps; I collect antiques) and we both adore dictionaries! When he told me he was a longtime subscriber to the *New Yorker,* that did it. Almost unbelievably, we discovered that his Midwestern parents had moved to Vashon Island the same time I did at the beginning of 1990. Mr. Andersen had visited his parents there regularly over the years and had, we reckoned, ridden his bicycle by my old log cabin dozens of times ... probably when I was inside reading the *New Yorker.*

At church that Sunday, on January 27, I noted the unmistakable light of love in Mr. Andersen's eyes ... then panicked and promptly left for lunch, a movie, and then dinner with various girlfriends. When I got home, my neighbor Laura called to report that Mr. Andersen had stood in front of my house waiting for me for four hours, calmly reading the *New York Times* in the snow. This explained why I'd found his business card wedged into my front door with a note scribbled on the back saying that he would "like to continue our conversation." He was back on my doorstep the following evening, and I was falling hard and I knew it.

While I was sitting beside him on my sofa, the powerful magnetic pull in his direction suddenly felt like a terrifying undertow. All of the horror of the Harrison Years washed over me and I leapt to my feet, put my hands on my hips, and gave Mr. Andersen what we have come to call "The Speech."

"Listen!" I said in a shaky voice. "Maybe you're just messing around here ... but I'm not! I don't know what you want in your life and I don't know if you're The One ... but ... you could be and you need to know that I want a real partner this time, and a home and a family! And if you don't want those things then I will ONLY be your friend! And ... I also want a diamond!" I threw that in for good measure, though I had no idea why because, at the time, I didn't even know I wanted a diamond.

I did know that I felt like adding: "I Wanna Be Blondieeeee!!!" Fortunately, I didn't.

Lucky for me, Mr. Andersen just grinned and said: "Well, then, we'd better start talking." Months later he told me my little speech was the smartest thing I could have done, because, he said, it instantly told him I valued myself and, therefore, so did he. Of course it helped that the things I wanted were exactly the same things he wanted, and how else would I ever have found that out ... before it was too late!

In short order Mr. Andersen introduced me to his two beautiful, regal, brilliant, talented grown sons, Ben and Eli, both taller than he is and just as hilarious (it runs in the Andersen clan). I knew without a doubt that here were the Three Kings from Chris Goldsmith's reading nearly four years earlier.

We three kings (and one small queen) of Oregon are

On Valentine's Day I presented Mr. Andersen with the business card, now framed, that my puppy had magically manifested before the choir party the previous year, his little milk teeth puncture holes still visible. I also gave Mr. Andersen the box of Lightfoot's Pure Pine Gentlemen's Athletic Soap I'd bought for my phantom future true love the Christmas before.

In March, we flew to Minneapolis so I could meet Tom's parents, Hank and Mary Andersen, who had recently moved there from Vashon. When they opened the front door of their chic downtown condo, I took one look at Tom's handsome father and was seized by the clear memory of having a stranger-to-stranger conversation with him in the rain at a nursery on the island a dozen years earlier.

"You were wearing a brown corduroy jacket!" I said, "and a sort of wool Sherlock Holmes hat ... with earflaps!!"

At that, my future father-in-law walked over to the hall closet and returned waving the very hat I had described.

"You mean this?" he asked.

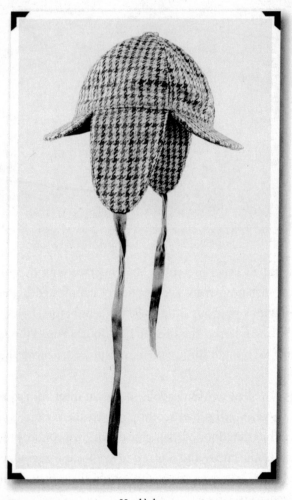

Hank's hat

30

THE CHRISTMAS SOLDIER

March 2002

I soon learned that Tom's parents love spirited conversation as much as he and I do, something my own dear quiet parents didn't really share. Tom's mother, Mary Andersen, is a fiercely fabulous punster, and his father, Hank, is a people-person extraordinaire! In his day, Hank was a much-loved Presbyterian minister, and it soon became clear that his mind was as anchored in the Divine as the Holy Pig Farmer's. His enlightenment—though like Lory, he was far too humble ever to call it that—was the result of a life-changing experience in World War II.

On Christmas Eve in 1944, a German submarine torpedoed the *Leopoldville*, a Belgian troopship carrying Hank and some two thousand other soldiers from England to Cherbourg, France, to join the Battle of the Bulge. Sitting in his elegant living room, Hank told me the story.

"Now don't go overboard," warned Mary, who had listened to her husband tell this tale for half a century.

Hank was a nineteen-year-old sergeant at the time, and moments before the torpedo hit he invited his own men and anyone else interested to climb out of the miserable hold and sing Christmas carols. Those who thought singing Christmas carols was uncool—or were, sadly, too seasick to sing—perished. With an official tally of 763 casualties, the sinking of the *Leopoldville* only five and a half miles off the coast of France represented the largest troopship loss of the war. Many of the survivors were among the soldiers who had accompanied Hank above decks to sing Christmas carols, and had managed to successfully leap from the sinking ship down onto rescue boats bucking in the rough winter seas.

The next morning, Hank woke up in the bombed-out Cherbourg maritime station, looked up at the blue sky, and "thought I had died and gone to heaven." Traumatized beyond words, all he could do was sit listlessly with the other survivors who had been taken there. "We were," Hank says, "like zombies."

The U.S. Army was segregated back then, and the African American soldiers served as supply managers called quartermasters. When they heard about the boys from the *Leopoldville*, they sent trucks to collect them and bring them back to their camp and then fed them their own Christmas supper. While the boys ate, the black soldiers stood around them in a circle and sang Christmas carols and spirituals to them.

"And the horror of the war lifted off of me like a veil," Hank told me. "I actually saw Jesus walking among us and healing us, though none of the other survivors I spoke with later experienced this." Hank's voice choked. "I went from hell to heaven in an instant, and I never left."

The next morning Tom, his parents, and I walked to Westminster Presbyterian Church a block away, where Tom's brother, Tim Hart-Andersen, served—and still does—as minister. A beautiful Romanesque edifice built of famed Minnesota blue limestone, Westminster practically vibrated with its own vitality. And even on an ordinary Sunday in winter, the pews were filled, and not only with octogenarians either. *Now this*, I thought, *is what a modern progressive church should be.* At lunch after the service, when I mentioned Hank's Christmas story to Tim, he told me about his friend Rabbi Joseph Edelheit, a PhD from the University of Chicago Divinity School who wrote his doctorate on the New Testament. "He speaks on the New Testament from a Jewish perspective, all the time," Tim said. "And he loves to sing Christmas carols. How about that for enlightened?"

And how about that for a spiritually enriched future brother-in-law! The following December, Hank submitted a written version of his World War II Christmas experience to the *Minneapolis Star Tribune*, which had called for holiday stories from its readers. His submission attracted the attention of a *Tribune* staff writer named Gayle Rosenblum, whose deceased father had also survived the sinking of the *Leopoldville* but had never shared the details of the event with his daughter. Gayle visited Hank and Mary at their apartment in order to learn more. Her report ran as the front-page feature of the *Tribune's* December 22, 2002, Sunday edition, filled with photos of Hank as he retold his story. It turned out that Gayle's father had been a Jewish cantor, and together she and Hank divined that he had survived the sinking of the *Leopoldville* because he loved to sing— he must have joined Hank's impromptu above-decks choir. Gayle wrote that Hank's story solved another mystery: why she had been teased her whole life for being "a Jewish girl who loved Christmas music."

31

HEART CLOUD

September 2002

Lucky for me, with a father like Hank Andersen and a mother as tolerant as Mary Andersen, Tom understood and accepted my colorful spiritual life as if it were the most natural thing in the world … which to me, of course, it was. He even seemed a little proud of it. "You need to read C. S. Lewis's *Space Trilogy*," he told me one day, then lent me his copies. Lewis, I soon learned, described the light beings I'd seen for years so perfectly that I'm quite sure he must have seen them himself.

And how I appreciated Tom! His joie de vivre, his enthusiasm for just about anything, his brains and strength and candor and patience and hilarity and be-still-my-heart, drop-dead good looks, but most of all, his devotion to his parents and his siblings and his fine young sons and now, hallelujah!, to me. How on earth was I lucky enough to end up sitting in front of this guy in a choir, of all places? How could my simple prayer for a real partner and a new family have been answered so perfectly and completely in such record time? How, indeed.

Our love affair bloomed at warp speed, with Tom doing everything right—full commitment, full joy, honoring me and himself and us at every turn. It was as if God invented the man specifically to erase every wrong and selfish thing Harrison had ever done. I'd never had so much fun! Then at dinner out one pretty Saturday night in May, Tom presented me with an astounding three-diamond engagement ring. The moment he placed it on my finger—with everyone in the restaurant cheering!—I realized it was The Phantom Ring I'd felt on my left hand for years.

That week we put my little house on the market. But after six months it hadn't sold, in a neighborhood where buyers fight like pit bulls over far less charming homes. By October, two weeks before the wedding, my wonderful house *still* hadn't sold. We were investing all our finances into remodeling Tom's house, and the ongoing mortgage demands of my own were compounded by the fact that my travel writing career had been in a free fall since 9/11. Driving to my house from Tom's one Indian summer afternoon, I finally had it out with God for the first time. Weeping and gnashing of teeth doesn't begin to describe it.

"WHY are you doing this to me!" I cried out like Job. "I LOVE you. I've devoted my life to you! You know I love you. And I thought you loved me!! How can you treat me this way! You're supposed to LOVE me! The Holy Pig Farmer told me I am YOUR holy child!!!"

At that point I saw a strange little wispy cloud bouncing into the piece of sky above me. There were only a few other clouds around at the time, and they were all behaving normally, remaining perfectly still in the windless sky … except for this one little dancing wisp. Its behavior was so bizarre that I completely forgot my hysterics in order to watch it. When the little cloud reached the plane of blue directly in front of me, it began moving in a circle, like a cartoon cloud some artist was having fun with. Then it formed itself into the shape of a perfect heart … and stopped. The heart cloud hung in the sky in front of me long enough for me to consider running into my house to grab my camera. But the moment I had that thought, the cloud pulled apart and vanished.

My house sold at full price in two weeks flat.

32

Blessed Assurance

October 2002

The afternoon of October 12, 2002, on a day like spun gold, Tom and I were married at Central Presbyterian Church, where we met.

Rande and my sister Valerie were my lovely maids of honor. Rande had a great time telling everyone that I "had to marry an Andersen so we'd finally be sisters," even though her husband's surname is spelled, as Tom puts it, "the wrong way": Anderson. Ben and Eli stood up for their dad with their usual bemused nobility. My cute teenage nephew Jesse escorted his grandmother, my beautiful mother, a vision in an all-apricot ensemble, to her seat beside my ever-fashionable brothers-in-law Scott Wilson and John Beal, the latter smiling beside my chic baby sister Heather in a rare family appearance that pleased me more than John could have known.

With admirable solemnity, my nine-year-old niece, Amber, served as one of our three adorable petal-flinging flower girls along with Grace Whitmore and Sarah Deal, two of Central's precious few children. When my mother-in-law-to-be learned that Sarah's hammer-thrower father Lance was an usher, she announced: "I wouldn't trust him as far as he could throw me!" Valerie's husband, Scott, and Tom's cheery best friends Keith Rogers and Scott Palmer were our other ushers, and the latter two both reported that they'd never seen their law school buddy so happy. This was something I'd been hearing for months from virtually everyone who knew Tom. A sweet elderly lady of the church had pointedly taken me aside to say that she'd known him very well for twenty-five years. "You've opened his heart," she told me. "Tom used to be a little, you know, severe," echoed his fellow choir bass Rich Litchfield. "Now's he's just tickled all the time." Rich, it should be noted, takes credit to this day for getting us together, claiming that he told me to stop wearing my "modest clothes and show off a little." Which I never did, of course. Tom, however, insists that the point of no return for him was when our choir rehearsed the lilting old hymn "Blessed Assurance," which had won new fans in the mid-eighties in the Academy Award–winning films *Places in the Heart* and *The Trip to Bountiful.* "When our director told us to sway to the music," Tom reports, "and you did . . . well, let's just say I lost my place in the music from then on."

My gorgeous new Amazonian sisters-in-law, Barb Andersen Chandler and Jennifer Andersen Popp, sat between their übercool husbands, John and Rhys, and their mom, Mary, and a handsomer—or taller!—block of family support would have been hard to imagine. My fly-fishing brothers—Greg Tatman and Guido Rahr—were there, as were my "surrogate fishing fathers," Roger Bachman and Len Dick. Their grinning approval, along with that of my fellow Red Moons writers and Val Brooks's gleaming Marilyn Monroe smile, kept my knees steady as my stepfather Bob walked me down the aisle. Tom took my arm when I arrived quaking by his side and regarded me with teary-eyed love. The light under which we stood was so bright it highlighted features of his face in new ways that inspired me to new heights of romance and the declaration: "You have really long eyelashes."

Ben and Eli were in charge of our wedding rings and came through like the champs that they are, and the ceremony was presided over by my new father-in-law, the Reverend Hank Andersen, and my new brother-in-law, the Reverend Tim Hart-Andersen. My other new sister-in-law, Tim's knockout wife the Reverend Beth Hart-Andersen, offered a lovely nuptial prayer, and it was clear to everyone in the sanctuary that I had hit the spiritual jackpot.

Our choir, of course, sang like angels during the wedding, including a rousing rendition of "Blessed Assurance."

When Tom and I left the sanctuary, we were encircled by fluttering white homing pigeons that everyone thought were white doves (but doves fly away). The pristine little birds were released from small wooden cages when we stepped outside the church, my *petit surpris* for Tom. When our photographer presented us with our wedding photos later, we both stopped short at one in particular: a picture of the happy bride and groom in the background, Tom's face agog with open-mouthed glee, and a bird hovering large and open-winged above our heads like a white angel. When Hank saw the photo, he gasped and looked at us and whispered: "The Holy Spirit!"

Tom and Jessica's wedding day, October 12, 2002

The Holy Pig Farmer wasn't able to come to the wedding, but he did give us a proper benediction:

"Love is very much part of the answer," he told us on the phone, "but it doesn't stop there. There are three things that are required. Very simple, but very profound. First is to be who you are. Second is to fall in love. And the third is to adore. Now, most people can't do all three. If you fall in love, you fall in love with the entire world, and with heaven, because the universe is holographic. But then, the next one is to adore, which is a deep and profound reverence and gratitude for the being with whom you've fallen in love. Now, since the world is holographic, that means that if I fall in love with someone, I've just fallen in love with the entire world … and with heaven. And that experience can only lead to adoration. When you adore, you begin to be aware that you are a part of everything, every plant, animal, star, it's part of you, there's just the One. We live in this divine energy that's so incredibly creative and magnificent. Yogananda knew that everything is God energy—it's throughout his whole book; the words themselves are imbued with God energy. Everywhere you are, you are on the God Path, and all you have to do is just know this. Then the veil is lifted and all is well, all is well, all is well."

Or, as Amber put it when my new husband and I climbed into our getaway car with my new stepson Eli at the wheel ready for a hair-raising dash about town:

"She's got a veil, and she knows how to use it!"

Part V

Midnight Talks with the Daughters of Islam

© *Cedric Angeles Intersection Photos*

I believe that the more time we spend choosing to run the deep inner peace circuitry of our right hemispheres, the more peace we will project into the world, and the more peaceful our planet will become.

JILL BOLTE TAYLOR

NEUROANATOMIST AND AUTHOR, *MY STROKE OF INSIGHT*

The ultimate goal of Islam is peace.

HEYAM ALI MUSTAFA

33

THE SQUIRREL AND YOGANANDA

May 2003

Six months after I moved into Tom's house, I was working at my computer when I heard a sickening thud. A little squirrel had tried to leap from our big maple tree across our back patio to the roof and missed. Now she was crawling around on the patio stones in terrible frantic circles, her back legs paralyzed and splayed out behind her. I couldn't bear it. For the next hour I focused every bit of willpower I had on the injured squirrel, and called on Jesus and the Buddha, everyone!, but especially, for some reason, on Yogananda, and begged them—tearfully and loudly!—to heal her. I don't know how I knew she was a girl squirrel, I just knew, in the same way I had known the first Red One and The Spinster were female energies. By the time I'd prayed for the squirrel for an hour, she had become nothing but molecules spiraling around on the patio in front of me.

Then all of a sudden, the little thing assumed squirrel position and stood up on her back legs. They worked! When she disappeared over a little ledge by the patio, I carefully crept outside. I was half afraid I'd find her in a heartbreaking heap down below but then I spotted her gingerly climbing up the maple tree. She was okay! She would live! We had healed her!! I called Lory to tell him all about it.

"*You* healed her," he assured me. "Nature can teach you all kinds of startling lessons. When we join with another, we become naturally miracle-minded," he said. "A miracle isn't a change in the material world; a miracle means you're looking at the world through the eyes of Christ . . . but you cannot will that power—it's a gift. When you healed the squirrel you experienced the miracle. It was a gift."

To receive the gift doesn't even require a belief in God, Lory insisted.

"People ask me if I believe in God. My answer is: if it's ninety degrees out and it's sunny, do I need to believe it's warm? See, miracles are natural. They occur all the time. Seeing a miracle requires only a little willingness to see the world with the eyes of Christ."

I was about to tell Lory about a documentary film I'd seen on the life of psychologist Carl Jung. Someone asked him on camera if he believed in God and he shook his head. "No," he said. "I don't believe, I know." But Lory began talking first.

"My goodness," he said. "A golden eagle just landed in my field. There's another one. And another one. More are coming."

He started to laugh. "Well, my goodness. There are about a dozen golden eagles in my field right now. Huge golden eagles, not bald eagles. I've never seen that many of them together before. Here comes another one, right now, as we speak. And another. Two, no three more. My goodness."

By the time we hung up, fully seventeen golden eagles had landed in Lory's pasture.

The following morning, soon after I began working at my computer again, I looked up to see the squirrel—my squirrel—crawling slowly toward my picture window. She moved a little slowly, but she seemed fine. To my complete astonishment, the little thing crept right up to my window, climbed up onto the window ledge, stood on her hind legs, put her forepaws on the windowpane, and stared at me. I could see six little pink nipples—she had babies! All of them would have died too if she had. We had saved perhaps seven lives, which certainly would have pleased my Bhutanese Buddhist friends greatly.

After that one, whenever I walked out on the patio to water the plants, my little squirrel would run like a puppy right to my feet. And if I sat down, she'd come up and put her paws on my foot or my leg and stay there with me for whole minutes.

The healed squirrel on Jessica's sweatpant leg

34

AND THE ANGELS SANG

September 2003

A month before Tom's and my first wedding anniversary, my mother's side of the family gathered at Aunt Katy's house in Fort Worth, Texas, on Labor Day weekend to celebrate Katy's eightieth birthday. Little did we know we were saying good-bye. My mother was dying.

By the time we were back home in Oregon, Mother was shuffling instead of walking. Mental confusion soon followed. This brilliant woman who had changed American education could hardly put a sentence together. And she was in great pain.

While her doctors were trying to figure out what was wrong, I convinced Bob to let me take my mother to see a gifted hands-on healer. Mother fell asleep soon after we helped her onto the massage table and the healer took my mother's feet in her hands.

"Her body is filled with ribbons of pain," the healer said; then she proceeded to "drain" the pain out of my mother's body. When the session was over and my mother woke up she was, indeed, pain-free and remained so, unheard-of for a victim of advanced cancer.

Bob agreed to take Mother to see the healer every time they drove into town for their many trips to Mother's doctors. He would run errands and I would sit on the healer's sofa across from her massage table while she worked in silence on my mother. During one session I suddenly saw that the room was crowded to bursting with angelic beings. A heavenly host, indeed! Dozens of them seemed to be crowding around my mother. When I gasped, the healer looked up from her work, smiled, and mouthed the words: "You see them too?" When mother came to, she blinked and looked around and frowned and said, "Oh, I feel as though I'm in the wrong place."

Suspecting a stroke, her doctors finally sent her to a sharp-eyed young neurologist. He suspected something else, and a mental acuity test followed.

"What state are you in?" he asked my mother.

With heartbreaking effort she slowly replied: "The state of chaos."

The neurologist sent her directly to the hospital where he prescribed a spinal tap, which he performed himself. The results were not good. Breast cancer cells from a bout with the disease years earlier were now attacking my mother's cerebral cortex. She was given only weeks to live.

At the hospital I reminded my mother that I could "see spirits" and extracted a promise from her that she would visit me after she left her body. She agreed with an "I will," in a tone filled with the energy of "duh."

On the way home from the hospital when Bob launched into a fiery diatribe about something, Mother's slow but clear voice rose from her bed in the backseat: "How ... doyou ... really ... feelabout that ... Honey?" Gallows humor.

Bob, Tom, and I remained by my mother's side day and night for the next month. Tom dutifully took time off work or drove in from upriver, which added an hour and a half to his commute. I slept clinging to him like a life jacket.

Then one night I was awakened by distant voices. I couldn't quite make out where they were coming from. Then realized I was hearing some kind of heavenly choir, and it was singing my most beloved anthem, Mozart's haunting "Agnus Dei." Leaving Tom sleeping, I rose from our bed and followed the voices to a skylight, then looked up at the night sky. It was filled with a trillion stars, more than I've ever seen anywhere, especially under the near-constant cloud cover of western Oregon. It felt as though I was looking at—and hearing—the heavens anew.

My little niece, Amber, and my honorary niece, Sarah Deal, sat with Mother and me for hours after that. They'd been friends since they were both flower girls at Tom's and my wedding the year before and often stayed together at our home when Amber was up visiting Mother and Bob on holidays. They were only ten, and it was touching to see such young girls be so still for so many hours. But then, Amber and Sarah shared the natural spiritual awareness that many children have. At one point, one of my parents' Baptist employees stopped by to convince Mother to "accept Jesus as her lord and savior," which she actually said she did. Once this fellow left, Sarah said: "He really didn't need to do that because Jesus has been standing right behind your mom's bed the whole time." Meaning, she saw him there.

For the last few days of my mother's life, I privately attempted my own hands-on healing and set my hands on the tumors growing on her neck. For two days running, I kept my fingers there, silently praying for help. Then, with no warning whatsoever, I felt something drain into my hands. It felt dense and unpleasant, and it had its own viscosity, like motor oil pouring from a can. Startled, I looked into my hand, but there was nothing physical there at all. Still, the sensation of something vile sticking to my fingers bade me run to the bathroom to wash my hands. The next morning, my mother's tumors were half the size they had been, and I prayed that this was the sign of a miracle healing to come. Alas. With Tom holding one of my mine while I held one of my mother's, and Bob on the other side of her, holding her other hand in both of his, we stayed with her until she took her last catching breath. Tom and I both watched carefully to see if we could witness her spirit leaving her body. We didn't. But there was a pronounced transformation at the instant of death, an audible gasp, a physical clutch, as if her body hadn't so much died as been shed by the powerful force that had animated it all those years. Which, of course, is exactly what had happened.

For weeks afterward, I watched for signs of Mother's spirit, but nothing appeared. The Other Realm was unusually quiet. Then one peaceful night two months later, I was awakened by a Red One. But not just any Red One. This little light was practically bouncing with joy. And its bright red edges were tinged with apricot, my mother's favorite color, the color she wore to our wedding. I knew it was she!

"You DID it! Mother, you're so beautiful! You DID it!!!" I cried out.

"What did I do now," mumbled my sleepy husband.

"Nothing! Mother's here! Wake up and look!!"

He did, but as always when I tried to show him a light being in our room, he saw nothing. But he smiled anyway and said: "Well, good for her." Then his head dropped back on the pillow. And my mother's bright little sunset-colored spirit vanished as quickly as it had come.

Only days later we learned that Aunt Katy had passed away, too, following her big sister in death as she always had in life, two souls clearly closely bound, perhaps, I often muse, as the Holy Pig Farmer said, by their shared spiritual ancestry.

35

In the Hall of the Spirit Bear

August 2004

As all first-born daughters know, losing one's mother swiftly upgrades you from child to family matriarch. Thus did my new role as wife and stepmom take on special domestic depth. Ben and Eli both lived in Eugene. Eli was finishing up his undergrad degree at the University of Oregon and Ben had been admitted to U of O Law School thanks to his near-perfect LSAT (Law School Admission Test) scores. Their mother's career had taken her out of state years earlier, and Tom's job in Salem was an hour-plus drive north. Since I've always worked out of my house, the marvelous duty of keeping the home fires burning fell to me, much to my delight. What a cool way to become Blondie! So Tom's and my married life hit the ground cooking, and we were having Ben and Eli, and often four or five of their buddies (usually as tall as they are) over for dinner sometimes several times a week. If you want good training in running a twenty-four-hour diner, marry a guy with two popular, twenty-something six feet six sons! It helped that Tom happens to make the best homemade pizza in America.

Meanwhile, work had returned to travel writers shipwrecked by 9/11. I was now balancing my usual blistering deadline schedule with our lively home life. And so it was with a sense of happy exhaustion that I accepted a magazine assignment on western Canada's "Spirit Bear"—a unique, all-white subspecies of black bear on the north coast of British Columbia based at one of the finest nature retreats on earth, King Pacific Lodge.

It was founded by Joe Morita, whose father founded Sony and who, despite his sophistication with international finance, remains a dedicated conservationist. Joe Morita also has a rare deep respect for native culture, and is known in central coastal British Columbia as the only developer who followed First Nation tradition and approached the local Tsimshian Nation's Gitga'at chief with a handsome fresh salmon before sitting down with him to negotiate terms for building King Pacific Lodge. The lodge is, in fact, a floating lodge, which in the season is affixed by cable to Princess Royal Island in the heart of the Spirit Bear rainforest habitat.

"Each time I see the white bear it's like seeing it for the first time."

Marven Robinson's peaceful voice was hard to hear over the thunder of his boat engine. Then thirty-six, he was by all accounts one of the lodge's and the region's best bear-watching guides and knew more about the Spirit Bear than any visiting PhD. A member of the Tsimshian Nation's Gitga'at band, Marven lived in Hartley Bay, a remote village of two hundred souls some four hundred air miles north of Vancouver, B.C., and a half hour by boat from King Pacific Lodge. Discerning nature lovers from all over the world come here for world-class whale watching, old growth hiking, and unspoiled catch-and-release fly-fishing, but Spirit Bear expeditions are the lodge's signature adventure. Staffers have built simple wooden viewing platforms along nearby salmon streams where guests sit, often for hours, waiting for a glimpse of pale fur. Many guests are rewarded with splashy salmon fishing sessions only inches from their feet, as Spirit Bears tend to be almost docile during the day.

"He looks at you like he thinks he's invisible," Marven told us.

As luck would have it, heavy rains the night before had pushed the rivers to unfishable levels for bears, so we headed by boat with another couple staying at the lodge to the entrance of a dip on the map called Cornwall Inlet.

"We saw the white bear there last night," Marven reported. "There's still huckleberries there now too." He shook his head. "My wife, she always tries to get me to go berry picking with her. I *hate* berry picking!"

The woman of the other couple and I both laughed, then she clapped her hands to her ears.

"Oww!" she cried.

Her ears, I saw, had turned scarlet.

"They always do this when I'm near powerful energy centers," the woman said.

Marven nodded.

"That forest there? That's a Gitga'at holy place." He seemed impressed, and so was I. It seemed I couldn't go anywhere now without some kind of spiritual drama occurring nearby. And they often involved the most unlikely candidates for such things, much like this lovely well-to-do Asian woman from Vancouver.

"Instead of Radar, we're gonna call you Radear!" Tom told her; then I gingerly asked her about her curious energy-seeking ability.

"Oh, we're completely into energy," she replied gaily. "We follow Eckhart Tolle," she said, meaning, of course, the mystical author of *The Power of Now*. "He's based in Vancouver too."

"We've even been to Brazil to see John of God," added her normal-looking khakis-and-boat-shoes businessman husband, referring to the jungle psychic healer who does surgery with rusty knives ... and apparently cures people of all sorts of ailments ... without giving them tetanus. "He was great!"

I looked at Tom. He was, I knew, thinking exactly what I was thinking: is there some sort of quiet international spiritual revolution going on or something?

A humpback whale breached just off our stern like an exclamation point. Then a raw cackle exploded from Marven's radio. It was Eddie, Marven's older brother, out fishing in the family boat with his kids.

"Heeeeeyyyyyyy Marven! What are the whales doin'?" Eddie asked.

"Up and down," Marven replied. "Up and down."

"Ooooooo-kayyyy!" said Eddie.

Marven cut the engine and we scanned the terrain off our lee side. The coastal drop-off was so deep there Marven was able to pull the boat close enough to the rocks for us to see little red fruits glowing in the green fans of the huckleberry bushes. But no white bear stopped by for lunch. Marven thought there might be some "munching on barnacles" around the corner. Barnacles? "Scrape 'em right off the rocks with their teeth," Marven told us. "I don't think many people know that."

Not unless they live in the Hall of the Spirit Bear like Marven.

Alas, no one was scarring his nose on barnacles when we rounded the next bend, and no white bear arrived to do so in the half hour we waited. After an excellent gourmet boxed lunch—another lodge specialty—we spent the rest of the afternoon bear spotting while Marven maneuvered the cabin cruiser all over middle B.C.'s crenated islands. Finally, it was time to return to the lodge.

"Tomorrow, we'll try the river," Marven promised.

Radear's earlobes turned carmine red again when we passed the Gitga'at Holy Place on the way in.

I had signed up for a massage at the lodge's tiny two-room spa, a treat I was truly looking forward to after the long day on the water. My masseuse was a tall, strong, vigorous girl named Megan, and as soon as she laid her hands on me I found myself watching a flickering Technicolor movie that was somehow being projected on the inside of my forehead ... at least that's what it felt like. The scene, of all things, was a wedding. It was taking place out-of-doors, and there seemed to be countless buckets of pink garden flowers exploding from every direction. My vantage point was directly behind the bride in a traditional white gown who was in the process of walking down the aisle with her father, who was dressed in a light gray-blue jacket and white dress shirt (I could see the collar). The only odd thing was the father's hair—it seemed very blonde and spiky.

I tried to ignore the wedding scene, but it wouldn't go away. Finally I just had to say something.

"Megan, um, are you engaged to be married anytime soon?" I asked.

"Not me!" she half-yelled with a laugh.

"Okay, how about any of your girlfriends? Anyone get engaged lately?"

"Nope," she replied.

Figuring that virtually all masseuses and masseurs are sure to be more energetically, if not spiritually, aware than most, I took a chance and told Megan what I was seeing.

"Oh!" she said. "That was my sister's wedding! We were *so* over the top with those pink flowers. But that was, like, ten years ago." The moment she said this, the scene inside my head switched … to a funeral! I was now watching a group of very sad people on what appeared to be a misty late spring Pacific Northwest day, throwing flowers onto a vanilla-cream-colored cloth of some sort laid over a casket that was being lowered into a fresh grave. I wasn't about to mention any of this to Megan.

"So," I said instead, trying to sound cheery, "I was watching your dad walk your sister down the aisle."

"That wasn't my dad," Megan replied. "That was my brother. My dad died young."

Yikes.

"Were you old enough to go to your dad's funeral?" I ventured.

"Yes, I was," she replied. Fortunately, she didn't seem upset at all, so I told her all the details.

"You know," she said, "there *was* a sort of pale yellow cloth on his casket! And, yes, we threw flowers on it as it was lowered into the ground. Wow, this is amazing."

But why was I seeing these precious familial scenes? What, really, was going on here?

That's when it hit me. Like someone who had been noodling a tough clue in a crossword puzzle and is suddenly blindsided by the answer, I understood without a doubt why I had been shown these images. Megan's father. It was all about her father.

"Megan!" I said, almost jumping off of the table. "Who walks down the aisle after the bride?"

She stopped and thought for a few moments.

"Well," she said, "no one."

"That's right! No one walks down the aisle after the bride does," I said (having recently been married myself helped my clarity on this point). "So *why* would I be 'seeing' your sister's wedding from *behind* her and your brother?"

Megan shook her head.

"BECAUSE," I cried, "I was seeing your sister's wedding from the vantage point of your dad, who was right behind them—that's the POINT.

Your dad—or God or both of them—used me to tell you that he was *there* with your sister on her wedding day!"

Megan and I were both getting all weepy at this point.

"He wants your sister to know that he was so sorry he couldn't be there in the flesh to walk her down the aisle, but he *was* there in spirit! I mean, I don't know exactly how it works, but somehow when you touched me, I connected with your energy and your family's energies—it's this Unity Consciousness thing I have—oh, never mind! The important thing is that you have to tell your sister that your dad was *there.* That's what he wants her to know!"

"I'm calling her tonight!" Megan said. And we were both so excited by the remarkable surprise we had just shared that I don't think she remembered the rest of the massage any more than I did.

When I closed my eyes to go to sleep that evening, the cool night wind stole in through our window and scented our room with the rich dark loam of ancient rainforest, and the movie screen in the front of my head lit up again, this time with the piece of coastline where the huckleberries grew. And from the far right side of the frame, what should pop in but the lion-like head of a real, live Spirit Bear.

"Tom!" I said, "We've got to have Marven take us back to the huckleberries tomorrow!"

"Snorakgaleagaggle," he muttered sweetly from the depths of Dreamland.

In the morning, Marven took us to a viewing platform on the river first, and we did see a black bear, but the elusive white bear remained elusive. At my near-nagging, he agreed at last to motor us all the way back to the Land of the Huckleberries, feeling, I'm sure, as enthusiastic for my idea as he was when his wife made him go berry picking. We idled offshore and waited. But not for long. Not five minutes after we arrived, entering from the dense forest on the right, a huge beautiful peaches-and-cream honest-to-Bakbakwalanooksiwae (the Cannibal-at-the-North-End-of-the-World and a primary figure in Northwest Coastal Indian ceremonies) coastal temperate rainforest Spirit Bear lumbered into view as if on cue. And, O, was she magnificent! O, was she worth the suspense! My, O, my, O, my. What a bear!

On our last morning at King Pacific Lodge, Tom and I were having breakfast before our floatplane would take us back down British Columbia's green-and-blue coastline, and who should dart into the dining room but Megan. She crouched down beside me, put a hand on my shoulder, and said: "I'm so glad I caught you! I called my sister and told her what happened, and you know that night you got the massage? Well, that was her tenth wedding anniversary!"

Spirit Bear, King Pacific Lodge

36

OF MICROSCOPES AND JELLYFISH

October 2004

It was October and our second wedding anniversary was a week away. Time for my one monthly girly indulgence: a pedicure.

I had told the owner of my favorite salon about the accidental psychic spa reading I'd given to Megan in British Columbia, and she had shared the news with some of her more spiritually inclined clients. Which explained why, as I approached the salon that day, a woman I'd never met in my life came running out the door calling: "Oh, you're the Spa Psychic!" She proceeded to dig a photograph out of her purse and thrust it in front of my face, saying: "Whatta think of *him*!?" I looked at the picture, and before I knew it I had blurted out: "Oh NO! He hates his mother! He'll never commit to you or anyone!!" Then I added, "Uh, I think we'd better go inside." Thus did my hope of enjoying a lovely stress-free hour of pampering evaporate once again as I found myself providing an unexpected service to someone else instead.

A deeper reading of the photograph—her on-again/off-again boyfriend it turned out—only revealed more of the same. "He's terrified of women. He'll never commit. He'll play a cat-and-mouse game with you forever." The only solace was when the imagery changed to a woman in a ponytail brilliantly and passionately playing a piano.

"Do you play the piano?" I asked the woman, and she and the salon owner burst out laughing.

"She was a concert pianist," the salon owner explained.

"Well," I told them, "all I know is that when you play the piano, that's when you're really free. I hope you play enough."

The woman left while I was still mid-pedicure, and the salon owner confided that I had "nailed" her client's boyfriend. They had been breaking up and getting back together for years, she told me. It never went anywhere and she never got the message.

"You know," I said. "I don't think she can. Or that she wants to get the message." It had come to me loud and clear that this ongoing drama was just that—a drama, starring the woman's Very Little Me, as Deepak Chopra had put it, and probably her boyfriend's Very Little Me as well. They were locked in a dance neither of them really wanted to end. *How sad*, I thought, then realized this was not the sort of thing on which I had any interest in spending my time—or my apparent gift.

But the salon owner had other clients who really did want to grow, and could. Before I knew it they were asking for readings from the Spa Psychic! Oh dear.

Finally, I agreed to give it a try and an official appointment was made. I was to give a certain client a reading while the salon owner gave her a pedicure.

An hour before the reading was scheduled I began to feel ridiculous. What the heck did I think I was doing? I stepped into the shower and made a little deal with God: "Give me an image—a clear image—that will mean something to this person, and if it does, then I'll do the reading. But if it doesn't, I'm turning on my heel and getting outta there, and that will be the end of all this!"

Immediately, what should appear on my Inner Movie Screen but … a microscope. An old-fashioned black, microscope. Okey-dokey.

Feeling like a complete fool, I walked into my friend's salon and told her my plan. She thought it was a lot funnier than I did. When her client arrived and took her place on the pedicure throne, I took a seat next to her and held her hand for extra Unity Consciousness. But the microscope image had come without any contact with her whatsoever, and, as with the client with the bad boyfriend, I'd never met this woman in my life.

I began by telling her that I'd asked for an image on her behalf; then, laughing nervously, I told her about the microscope. But the woman did not laugh. Her eyes widened and she stared at her friend the salon owner and uttered something I will never forget: "My kids don't even know about this."

"About what??" we asked.

"Well," she began, "I own a microscope."

"Are you a lab technician or something?" I asked.

She did laugh then. "No, no," she said, "I'm a businesswoman. I've had the microscope since I was in seventh grade. I keep it in my bookcase."

"But ... why?" I asked her. Why on earth would a woman who was at least fifty keep her childhood microscope?

"Because," she said with ice in her eyes, "that microscope was the first thing I had saved up enough money on my own to buy, and my mother could NOT say I couldn't have it."

"O ... kay," I replied. "I think we've got something to work with here."

At that the woman turned to the salon owner and said: "I was so sure this was going to be about my dad, but I can see why I need to deal with my mother first—she never protected me from him!"

Holy Moly.

At that point the images and information began coming in in earnest.

Still holding the woman's hand, I closed my eyes and let it come. Of all the crazy things the next picture I "saw" was ... a jellyfish! A big, thick jellyfish propelling itself across the screen of my mind in jetting pulses. I did laugh at that one.

"Okay! We've got microscopes and now we've got jellyfish. So, do jellyfish mean anything to you?"

The woman's eyes popped open.

"Well," she said slowly, "I was raised in Oregon, and we used to go to the beach in the summer. One summer when I was about seven, I was out splashing in the water and I got stung by a jellyfish, which really hurts."

"I know it does," I told her, being a former California beach girl myself.

"So I went running out of the water and ran up to my mother crying and telling her it hurt. It had stung me on the inside of my arm, a very tender place. And it really did hurt. But all my mother said was: 'You weren't stung. It doesn't hurt. And stop crying.' And I knew at that moment that she would never take care of me."

Then, as with Megan and the message of her sister's wedding, I got it.

"Your mother is ... no longer with us, is she," I told the woman, and she said that she hadn't died very long ago.

A sob seized my throat, and I knew that this entire session was about the abject grief this poor woman's mother felt for how cruelly she had treated her beautiful daughter her entire life.

"She is ... *so* sorry," I said, now weeping buckets. "I've never felt remorse like this in my life! This is your mother's grief, not mine." Then the words came. "You must ask your mother for help. She is waiting—just waiting—for you to ask for her help with *any*thing. You *must* ask her, because if you don't *she* cannot heal and *you* cannot heal. You absolutely must ask your mother for help."

Tears were in the woman's eyes now. "Well," she told us, "one of my daughters has a problem at work—a bad problem—and I actually did ask my mother for help with that. But ... moments after I did I said out loud: 'I don't know why I'm asking you for anything now that you're dead when you never did a thing for me when you were alive!'"

"And what happened?" I asked.

"Things actually did get better for my daughter," the woman said.

As quickly as the grief had come upon me, it now stopped. This thing was done.

The next time I saw the salon owner she told me that the microscope-and-jellyfish woman told her that she had gone home after our session and sobbed all night long about the pain her mother had caused her. "And she had never cried about her mother once either."

I had called the Holy Pig Farmer several times since the Wedding Reading at King Pacific Lodge but kept missing him. That afternoon he finally answered, and I told him about my new side career as a budding Spa Psychic. Of course he found this news very amusing. But then his voice quieted, and I knew he was smiling his Jesus Smile.

"You know," he reminded me, "we are here to bless the world. And that's what you're doing with your readings."

37

SQUIDS AND CHAOS MAKERS

April 2005

My unbidden deep-dive into the realm of energetic healing only went deeper. I was, by then, used to Red Ones and Gray Ones. But two new categories of icky light beings had begun to show up. (God only knows how many categories there actually are—Yogananda does say that humankind is plagued by these things.) Unlike the entities that accompanied physical malaise, the new ones seemed to be associated with emotional disturbances. They are, to say the least, as fascinating as they are creepy. And, as always, they are no match for the power of a strong will anchored in love, so don't worry. I named them the "Squids" and "Chaos Makers."

Of the two, I found Chaos Makers easier to get rid of. They are, I learned, responsible for creating the gross and twisted sort of nonsensical nightmares we all have from time to time. Visually, they are just as cuckoo as the nightmares they inspire. To this day I've never seen two that looked alike. One showed up one night as a sort of disembodied purply-blue flame like the pilot light of a gas stove, fizzing along in little seltzer bursts. Another one wobbled through the air one way while the absurd-looking pinwheel blade on its top rotated in the opposite direction. They'd actually be sort of fun if they didn't wreak such havoc on our daily lives.

Chaos Makers simply make you feel chaotic. They make you feel scattered and goofy and uncentered and weird when the usual reasons for feeling this way—too much to do in too little time, the impending arrival of your Great Aunt Belvedyne, looking for a health insurance policy that gives you hospital coverage *and* acupuncture treatments for less than $40,000 a month, or simply trying to buy a discount airline ticket online—are not in play. I have met people whose cardinal energies seem to me to be under the confounding thumb of Chaos Makers. You can see it in their eyes, which look a lot like little kaleidoscopes gone wrong.

Squids are a different kettle of fish altogether. For those with eyes to see, these guys look like oppressive sheets of opaque white anti-light whose specialty is making you feel like something is sucking the life force right out of you. Actually, something is. Really, Squids are just psychic vampires, and I believe they are, at least in some cases, associated with depression—The Noonday Demon, indeed. If a Squid is mucking up your energy field, you can count on not wanting to get out of bed in the morning. Again, the way to distinguish a Squid-induced depression from a real one (although if you work at it you can make serious spiritual progress with real depression too) is that, again, the reasons-as-usual simply aren't there: Your dog was not run over by a UPS truck. Your wife does still love you even though you forgot to put the wet clothes in the dryer two days ago and they're growing penicillin. You still have your job, and your teeth, and most of your hair. Your brain chemistry is just fine, thank you very much, and your childhood was too, except for that minor run-in with your big sister bathing you in pancake batter, which was as funny as it was depressing, so who cares! But if you still feel like you've got a thousand-pound toad sitting on your chest, as my literary hero Tim Cahill puts it, then, sorry, pardner—you've got Squids.

What to do?

Well, the first order of business is to learn how to distinguish between an authentic emotional response (meaning there is, in fact, something to respond to) and a Chaos Maker or Squid attack. Who knows why the Gray Ones plague us so—in *Autobiography of a Yogi* Yogananda says that demonic energies are all over the place, like germs, and their job, basically, is to keep us away from God until we're so uncomfortable that we turn to God (and God help us if we don't), which, the good yogi also says, is the real reason for evil in the first place.

Since I have had the lovely experience of feeling the full force of both Chaos Makers and Squids, I can tell you that if you pay attention you'll realize that what you're feeling—or think you're feeling—feels inauthentic, much like the grief of the deceased mother of the microscope-and-jellyfish woman felt when I connected with it. You feel it, but you know it's not yours.

Once you know this, then all that's left is a battle of wills.

Chaos Makers, as I mentioned, are easy. Getting them off your energy field is like escorting a spider outdoors. It usually won't go by itself, but with a little herding and the help of a paper towel or a glass jar, the thing will go. Gray Ones, of course, require that you do this work mentally, willing the thing that's pestering you to leave you alone.

Squids are more of a challenge—but don't worry; you can do it! The tricky part is that Squids are designed to zap your will, which is exactly what you need to get rid of a Gray One. But I soon learned that just as the Holy Pig Farmer teaches that it only takes a little bit of willingness to know the living spirit of Christ (or the spirit of any other great teacher), it only takes a little bit of will to begin the process of shoehorning a Squid off your back, so to speak. Just keep trying until you get one toe in the door (mentally, I mean) and then keep pushing. There's a surprise bonus awaiting you when you finally clear yourself of any Gray One: you receive the joy of being healthy and clear as well as the euphoria of having fought the good spiritual fight ... and won. Because by refusing to let these things run your life, even for a day, you are deeply aligning yourself with the divine glue of the universe (love) instead of your fear-mongering panic-inducing ego, and you are telling God-as-you-understand-Him/Her/It that you get the game here and you're playing for keeps no matter how long it takes to win. And should you ever need a little help on the battlefield, you can always sing a few bars of the No-Squids Fight Song: "I'm making my way back to you, God, with a burning love inside!"

"I don't pretend to understand all this stuff," I told Rande on one of our Spring Break Girlfriend Weekends, this time in Seattle. "But understanding them isn't the point. The point is to know that they exist, in their own weird little corner of the light spectrum, and they are programmed to try to trick us into believing that things are bad."

"I know," she said. "They redefine the term lowlife!"

"And they really can only prey on us when we—or our life circumstances—allow our own frequency to drop to, you know, their level."

Rande nodded. "I see demons in the eyes of my students every day. The depressed kids, the troublemakers, the ones who can't sit still or who catch every flu bug that comes along. And they have no idea that it's the demons that are running the show, not them. Sometimes," she added, "I talk directly to the demon. 'My, we're a difficult one, aren't we,' I told one last week. You could see it shrink back away from me."

"Yeah, they can't stand the light," I agreed. "And, you know what? I'm beginning to experience clearing others of these yucky negative entities, not just myself."

I told Rande about the angry girl I'd been tutoring as a middle-school reading volunteer.

"She walked into the classroom like a banshee. Ordering people around, cackling and yelling. I'd never seen anything like it. I was sitting at the far corner of the room, so I silently asked if God would let me clear her. That's all I asked. At home later that night I suddenly felt angry and snapped at Tom for no good reason. When I realized what was happening, I apologized and excused myself.

"I sat on our bed and tuned in, and then I knew that I'd actually taken this thing off of that girl. And I called on all my saints to get it off me. It took three blasts to get rid of it—then I was my old happy self again, even happier. The weirdest part was that when I saw this girl the next time I visited the classroom, she was totally changed—all quiet and helpful, and that awful ashen aura of hers was gone too. The light around her was almost pink . . . and the wildest part? She suddenly just loved me! Started bringing me flowers and wrote poems for me: 'Pink, pink, the beautiful color, the one that reminds me of you.'"

"I know, I know," Rande replied. "I get that *all* the time. They think you're a saint."

"If they only knew! And here's another one: I also accidentally cleared—or was used to clear—a woman I'd never met of some seriously bad energy. A friend had brought me to her book club as a local guest author. The hostess's home had a lovely feeling to it, so I was very surprised to later identify her as the source of a crippling sorrow that overtook me about an hour after the meeting. It took two full days to clear this stuff, and when it finally lifted I was euphoric, as always—you can't clear someone else without clearing yourself, right? I called my friend to tell her about it, and we decided to invite the book club hostess out for tea to see if *she'd* noticed anything.

"*We* sure noticed something when she walked into the tearoom: she looked ten years younger! And she had this little smile that she didn't have before. So I asked her if she'd noticed any changes in her life that week, and you know what she said? She said: 'Funny you should ask. Usually I'd drag myself home from work, fix supper, and fall into bed. But all this week I've had all this energy. I've done something new every night, and just feel . . . so alive!" When I told her about getting rid of all that deep grief, she got really quiet, then told us that twelve years earlier her husband had run off with her best friend. Can you believe it? I mean, if you ran off with Tom . . . what would I do? It's . . . impossible! And I believe she buried the resulting grief deep within her in order to raise her kids and soldier on at work. It was, I'm sure, the kind of stuffed emotion that can make people very sick later on, and if it only took two days of my time to give this woman back her life, so what?"

"Wow," Rande said. "So it really is like casting out demons." Then she laughed. "Whoever thought we'd end up being exorcists!"

But Rande and I were now faced with a serious dilemma. How do you teach people about these things? How do you tell them that this world really is just a big competition between good and evil, or God and ego—it sounds so simplistic. And that when we do mess up as we always do and get angry or scared or spiteful, we can just do what the Holy Pig Farmer says and "choose again, dear child, choose again."

How on earth do you convince people that they might have more control over their lives—and even their physical and emotional health—than they ever imagined? Or that prayer and meditation give you the best possible immunity from the Gray Side?

". . . especially when our whole culture is going down the toilet!" Rande added. "Kids think negativity is cool, Jess. And look how hard it is for us to stay positive all the time—and we know better! I think this is Mission Impossible. Let's just watch a movie!"

And what movie did we choose? Stephen King's *The Green Mile*, a thriller set in Louisiana in the 1930s about a seven-foot-tall African-American clairvoyant named John Coffey who heals people by siphoning their negativity right out of them. He ends up being electrocuted in an electric chair called "Old Sparky" after being wrongly accused of committing the very crime he had "seen" before it happened and had tried so hard to stop.

"Rande!" I said the first time John Coffey removed the negativity from someone in the movie. "That's it. That's exactly what it's like! Steven King knows! That's exactly how it works!"

"Well, I'm telling you we'd better not tell anyone," Rande replied with a hoot. "Or we'll both end up sitting in Old Sparky too!"

38

AIRPORT ENLIGHTENMENT

December 2006

The first Christmas without my mother had been so unbearable my family had scattered to the wind. Tom, his dear world-traveling parents, and I had escaped to a castle in Wales that year, and we found that, despite my personal grief, Christmas in another country can be a marvelous experience. And most assuredly less commercial. So a tradition began wherein we do a full-on family Christmas at home one year, then get the heck away from Bing Crosby the next, assuming I can secure a magazine assignment. Three years after Wales, we decided to try Europe's most famous Christmas city: Vienna.

The feeling began before we arrived at Portland International Airport. There had been no warning, no foreshadowing, no sense of impending spiritual fireworks. As usual, the experience came upon me the way they always do, when I'm simply busy doing some everyday thing. By the time we reached the airport security line, I was gone.

By then there was no me. Somehow, my mind fully slipped into what Eckhart Tolle calls "Being" and what neuroanatomist Jill Bolte Taylor calls "the deep inner peace circuitry of the right hemisphere of our brain."

Even the I-that-considered-itself-an-I was naught. In my own mind's experience there was no My Own Mind. There was only and precisely a sense of floating effortlessly in time and space, moving inside of perfect and immutable joy, a pleasure unlike any I'd experienced, ever. Even the presence of Christ Himself was different from this—that was He; this was inside "me," except there wasn't a me or an inside. And there are no words for the peace that accompanies this sort of full-frontal dive into what saints and sages have long called enlightenment.

How drawn everyone was to my nonself! "Here, let me help you," offered a fellow passenger, setting my laptop into a plastic tub for me, instead of the usual heedless barging ahead. A young security officer gently folded my coat into another tub for me and waved me on: "Just go right through," he said, beaming at the I-who-wasn't-there as if I were his most beloved relative. I almost feared he was about to fall at my feet in paroxysms of prostrations. But, as is the fundamental paradox of all true spiritual accomplishment, there was absolutely no self whatsoever to bask in these attentions, no self to desire it, no self even to register it as "mine," so to enjoy such adoration is, in fact, impossible, which cancels out any lurking spiritual egocentricity rather neatly. Looking at the young man, then, I did not see someone rapturously interested in "me": I only saw in him a brilliant work of the divine in a uniform. That's all God's mind allows you to see. Most promising was his own unconscious but absolute interest in the light not at the end of the tunnel, but at the very heart of it. All of us know God when we see it.

Once Tom and I were on the other side of security, my eyes met those of a pianist playing Christmas carols on the far side of the huge open room. He smiled, and abruptly slid "Walking in a Winter Wonderland" into an unfamiliar but inspired melody that surely was one of his own creations. *He knows too*, I thought, and smiled back.

Tom and I settled in at a little café table to await our flight, and I looked up and saw that the broad steel ribs of the airport ceiling were vibrating pink. The whole of reality was ablaze with the holy fire of creation, yet I could feel no heat, just as Bassui promised. I also saw, of course, that just as I, too, am deaf and dumb to the deepest joy of "reality" 99.999999 percent of the time, no one else in the airport seemed aware of the existence of the heaven-on-earth in which, as my father-in-law, Hank, likes to say, we all live and move and have our being. But there I was, feeling fully what it means that we live and move and have our being in the Divine. *Feeling* it.

Just as Hank had been aware of the spirit of Christ walking among his fellow traumatized soldiers that Christmas morning so long ago, I was, at that moment, granted the rapt if temporary awareness of reality as it really is, as spiritual masters have described it to us for millennia, and whose unspeakable glory would be enough to unite humankind forever if only we were to end our waking slumber. Want world peace? Try a little airport enlightenment. It took every ounce of willpower I had not to stand up and scream: "WAKE UP!!!"

"Which was probably a good thing," Tom allowed.

Spiritual gifts are mysteries even to the Masters. Yogananda's autobiography is resplendent with them, and every one comes to him out of the blue. And so it is with beginners. But how I wanted to share this experience with my fellow travelers, whose expressions broadcast nothing but fatigue or boredom or cynicism or a toxic holiday cocktail of all three. "O, come all ye faithless!" I wanted to tell them. "O, the inconvenience of this difficult world," they seemed to say back.

Well, yes, when you're asleep at the cosmic wheel. No wonder the Holy Pig Farmer insists that nothing—*nothing* on earth—is as important as waking up to God. He put it best, I think, when he said, "It's as if we're fish in the ocean asking where the water is. We live in divine energy. The journey back to that awareness takes you, you don't take the journey. Everywhere you are, you are on the God Path. You only have to wake up to the adventure, and say 'Yes!' to everything God throws at you."

39

MIDNIGHT TALKS WITH THE DAUGHTERS OF ISLAM

December 2007

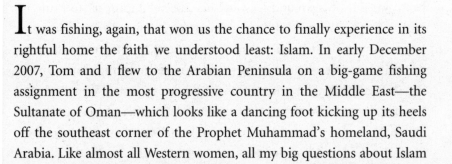

It was fishing, again, that won us the chance to finally experience in its rightful home the faith we understood least: Islam. In early December 2007, Tom and I flew to the Arabian Peninsula on a big-game fishing assignment in the most progressive country in the Middle East—the Sultanate of Oman—which looks like a dancing foot kicking up its heels off the southeast corner of the Prophet Muhammad's homeland, Saudi Arabia. Like almost all Western women, all my big questions about Islam orbited around women's rights. So when I saw a group of elegant abaya-clad women at our hotel I did not hesitate to approach them.

The ladies in black looked for all the world like queens having tea in a courtyard. Winter sunlight splintered off a silver teapot and belly danced on their Prada sunglasses. A camel stork-walked past hotel guests snoozing on the private beach below and twists of frankincense smoke sweetened the air each time someone opened the lobby door of the stately new Shangri-La Barr Al Jissah Hotel. Beyond it all lay the cool, curvy back of the Gulf of Oman, gleaming all the way to Iran. The women insisted I join them and called for another teacup right away. They were, I learned, from Oman's progressive counterpart, Dubai, and they were sisters-in-law, all.

"Oman is so peaceful," offered the beautiful family matriarch, Heyam ali Mustafa. "We drive here just to take a break from Dubai. The traffic at home is terrible, and everyone is so stressed out!"

After a week of running around Muscat, Oman's capital city, this was the first group of women we'd seen gathered together outdoors. Sitting there with them on the horn of the Arabian Peninsula and listening to such chic Muslim women talking about women's rights, fashion, and unescorted road trips to this far outpost of the Middle East, in Oxford English no less, only confirmed Oman's ID as a new Mecca for both high-minded R & R and progressive Islam.

"You must come to my home in Dubai," Heyam insisted, knowing that all flights in and out of Muscat stop in Dubai.

The following week, we did just that. Rather I did, since Heyam's husband was out of town and it would have been "improper" to bring my husband to her home with her husband away. A female driver in a new Mercedes met me at the front door of our hotel, and minutes later I was seated in Heyam's gracious living room surrounded by my hostess and six female family members, three of whom I'd met in Oman. We talked non-stop for the next five hours, nourished by platter after platter of Heyam's marvelous dishes created for her professional catering company, about which I vowed to tell my editors at *Gourmet* magazine. We talked about the things women always talk about—fashion, recipes, aging gracefully, to-botox-or-not-to-botox—and many things women don't talk enough about: politics and religion.

"The sheikh of Dubai and the sultan of Oman, these are the real leaders in the Middle East," Heyam said. "Iran still has problems. And no one knows what to do about Israel!"

"You see," added another woman, "all we want is peace."

"Peace is the true heart of Islam," another added. "We are taught to want only peace."

"And our media," I said, "teaches us the opposite about the Middle East. I'm afraid Americans are kept very ignorant."

The truth was that when we told our friends back home that we were coming here, most of them expressed real concern for our safety. And yet from the moment we set foot in the Dubai airport, and then in Oman, all we felt was the peace my new friends were describing to me. The peace of Arabia, I told them, was the biggest surprise of the trip.

"The peace I feel here is unlike any I've felt anywhere in the world," I said. "It reminds me of the peace I feel in Bhutan, but the peace there is the more sparkly, almost child-like peace of Himalayan Buddhism. The peace of Dubai and Oman is very deep, very dignified, and very grown-up. And it is inseparable from the physical experience of being in this part of the Middle East.

"You feel it everywhere," I told them, "and you know it is the product of millions of prayers. Just as the air in Bhutan is filled with prayer, I think the peace here is the result of so many people praying so often. But tell me," I ventured. "Why is it that the big mosques here have thousands of places for men to pray, and far fewer for women?"

It was a question I'd been burning to ask someone—especially a woman—for weeks.

"Ach!" Heyam replied with a dismissive wave of a hand, "this is because men are lazy! They need to go to pray five times a day. They need that structure, or they wouldn't go at all! We women have the right to go to the mosque to pray any time we want to, but we don't have time to go and pray in public all the time. We're too busy! We just pray at home together when we can."

"And you see that we don't wear the *berqa* in Dubai or Muscat," added another sister-in-law, referring to the black veil, which at the moment seemed at odds with her slim jeans and designer heels, her normal attire at home. "We only wear the *abaya* in public," they explained.

"... And the men wear the *dishdasha*, and we all cover our heads," Heyam added. "This is *cultural*. Everyone in the West thinks we're so oppressed! Not in Dubai and Oman! I have a catering business, she is an engineer, she has her own business, we all went to university in London—this is the New Middle East!"

"Actually, Heyam," added one of the other women, "this is the old Quran." She looked pointedly at me. "You see, Muhammad was the first to give women true equality, especially for the time in which he lived.

He said: 'God offers forgiveness and a great reward for men who surrender to Him, *and* women who surrender to Him, for men who believe *and* for women who believe, for men who obey *and* for women who obey, for men who are modest *and* for women who are modest.' The Quran goes on and on like this."

"Muhammad," added another sister-in-law, "even made it possible for the first time for women to inherit property, and to keep their marriage dowries for themselves."

"And so ..." I ventured carefully, "the truly oppressive practices we hear about back home—women being blamed for rape, for instance (which had just happened in Saudi Arabia and was in all the newspapers), or women treated like property, these ideas were ...?"

"... not Muhammad's!" the women replied almost as a chorus.

"Then the treatment of women by the leaders of Dubai and Oman must be ... closer to the original ideas of Muhammad?" I offered to thunderous approval by my Islamic teachers.

So what, I wondered, did they think of a woman running for president of the United States?

Heyam rolled her eyes.

"A *woman* president? Who would *want* a woman president! She would be far too emotional!"

I think I shocked my new friends with my response, which was that I loved the idea of a woman president, but it had to be the right woman.

"First of all, I wouldn't want a woman president who voted in favor of invading Iraq," I offered. "And I certainly wouldn't want a woman president who had voted to *keep* us in Iraq, which was even crazier, given that as terrible as Saddam Hussein was, he hated Al-Qaeda, and there were no Al-Qaeda in Iraq until we invaded it. Now we've created the Iraqi Al-Qaeda Monster! And you know, don't you, that this entire Afghanistan/Iraq invasion scenario was plotted out by Rumsfeld and Wolfowitz in this weird thing they called Project for the New American Century back in the nineteen-nineties? They actually presented it to President Bill Clinton, who had the brains to treat it like the piece of insanity it was."

Heyam and the other women had gone silent. Had I said too much?

"Oh, no, no," Heyam protested. "It's just that … here in Dubai, we are used to American businessman, mostly oil businessmen—you know Halliburton has moved to Dubai. And we have never heard an American speak so … so intelligently about Iraq. You are very well informed."

"Inshallah," I replied, invoking the charming Arabic phrase for "God willing," which I hoped would amuse my new Muslim girlfriends. Fortunately, it did.

"You know," Heyam offered after the joyful laughter died down, "you have just gone to the heart of Islam with your Inshallah."

I had?

"Yes, you see, we do not follow Muhammad. Americans think Muslims all follow Muhammad. No. We do not. We respect all the prophets—Abraham, Moses, Jesus—and we believe Muhammad was the last prophet, but they are all just prophets, just teachers. In Islam, we follow God. That is all. The very word 'Muslim' means 'one who surrenders.'"

I could hardly believe my ears.

It is so easy to hold unfounded but familiar ideas in our minds and guard them there like faultless truths. It is so easy to cling to them even when new evidence shatters them into a thousand foolish lies. So it is, I think, rare to witness a new idea bloom so brightly in one's mind that the old idea it replaces just tumbles from the vine as naturally as a wilted flower that has had its day and must make way for the beauty of the new. And that is precisely what Heyam's distilled presentation of pure Islam did to my ill-shaped former concept of this foreign faith.

"You just … follow God?" I repeated.

The ladies in black all nodded back at me and we stared at each other for many moments. Finally, a sort of relieved glee swept through my mind.

"Well," I declared with a slap of the knee, "then I must be a Muslim too! A Christian-Buddhist-Hindu-Jewish-Muslim. Because my entire spiritual life has been nothing … *nothing* … but an act of divine guidance every step of the way!"

Heyam called to her daughter and asked the girl something in Arabic, then the smiling teenager scampered upstairs and reemerged with two slim books.

"For you," she said, grinning, and handed me *Islam and Universal Peace,* by Sayed Qutb, and *Fitra, the Islamic Concept of Human Nature,* by Yasien Mohamed. Almost rudely, I read a bit of each while my hostesses waited in silence. One's *fitra,* I learned, is one's "innate spiritual nature" within which "lies the deep, universal moral intuition that human beings are creatures of God to be respected." Sure sounded a lot like the Holy Pig Farmer to me ... not to mention my Buddhist friends in Bhutan. I read out loud: "The Prophet says: 'None of you will be a true believer unless he likes for his brother what he likes for himself.'" Surely another version of Christ's "Do unto others" and the Buddha's call to compassion. I was about to close the book when this caught my eye: "Man has within his reach the ability to contact the eternal source of power, to comprehend the universe and to harmonize himself with it." This was absolute Hindu-Yogananda.

It was past midnight when I finally parted company with my wonderful new friends.

"You know," I said, "the truth is that you are all a prayer answered. On this pathless spiritual path of mine, I have been led to all the world's great faiths ... except Islam. I've been very curious about Islam, but, well, sort of allergic to it too, and I had no idea how to learn about it while honoring the way of this particular journey of mine. I mean, I couldn't just go study Islam with a Muslim teacher—it had to come to me on its own, as ... as God's will. All I could do was ask, which I have ... many times. And finally, here you are!"

"Inshallah," said Heyam, with a demur nod of her head. "And you are a prayer answered for us as well. Your thinking is so refreshing—you have changed our ideas about Americans!"

"Maybe that's because I'm one-eighth Arab!" I replied. "My mother's grandfather came to America directly from Beirut. Of course, he married a red-haired Irish girl ..."

"Ah, this is why you love good food!" Chef Heyam said with happy approval.

"The Lebanese are the cooks in the Middle East!"

"And perhaps," added the quietest sister-in-law of all with a radiant smile and speaking for the first time, "your Arabic blood is the source of your spirituality as well."

Before heading to the airport, we sought out a stylish men's grooming center called 1847, which my editor wanted me to include in my story. Finding it at last hidden beneath the Jumeirah Emirates Towers Hotel, we signed Tom up for 1847's signature shave. I had to do some fast talking to get the barber to allow me—a woman!—into this stronghold of intimate masculinity. As he prepped Tom's face with hot towels and special potions, I documented the complicated process with my camera. When we downloaded the images after we got home, we were astonished to find scrawled on the wall directly behind Tom the large looping signature of another pleased customer: none other than my old lunch buddy Deepak Chopra.

By a quirk of airport scheduling, our flight back to London and on home closed five minutes before Tom and I arrived at Dubai International.

"On Mondays, this flight leaves at eleven-thirty," the pretty clerk informed us gently. "Today is Sunday—today it leaves at ten."

With several apologies, she graciously rebooked us on the next flight ... which left in five hours. Having checked out of our hotel, we decided to tough it out and make camp on a bench by a window.

"It's kind of nice to be in an airport over Christmas without Bing or reindeer," noted Tom.

Not that Dubai's airport needed any added decoration to the Western eye. Set at a literal crossroads of Arabia, India, Asia, and Africa, the place is a thrilling, if befuddling, endless ethnic fashion show. There were women in black abayas without—and with—the berqa, men in white robes with red and white headscarves fastened with black cording, men in pastel robes with hand-embroidered cloth pillbox hats: the traditional costume, we knew, of Oman. There were clutches of giggling girls in hot pink abayas and bright headscarves asparkle with sequins, and Indian women in equally gay saris. There were tall black Africans and short fair-skinned Arabs, all in American jeans, and beautiful slow-moving, hip-swaying coffee-skinned women in the elaborate fabric wraps and headdresses of West Africa. And then there was the occasional American businessman in a suit and tie who seemed awfully dour compared to the graceful fluidity of Arabian men, our favorite of whom sauntered by laughing and pressing a cell phone to his ear while saying what we heard as: "Arabic-Arabic-Arabic-Axis-of-Evil-Arabic-Arabic-Arabic, ha-ha-ha-ha-ha!"

Hour after hour, we watched the people of this part of the world go by. Colorful and not, formal and un-, flowing and buttoned-down, this cavalcade of foreignness kept on passing by, all held with dignity in the broad, sweet peace of the Middle East.

It's hard to say if it was that or the sheer volume of passing humanity . . . or something else. But my just-the-facts, clear-minded, trial attorney husband turned to me and said the last thing on earth I would have guessed he would say at that particular moment.

"It's true," he said, his voice skittering with emotion. "It's true that beneath our clothes and our styles and our ways and our skin color we are . . . we really are . . . one."

Tom had heard people say this his entire life, especially his father, who was given to bouts of authentic spiritual rapture when it came to the holy sanctity of the human community, every member of which he really does consider his brother or sister. And Tom had heard me talk about it and read passages to him about it for years now. But this was the first time he, himself, had experienced it. To say he was moved didn't do it justice. Tom was transformed, which begged the question: what is it about us and airports?

"We're just citizens of the world," Tom concluded.

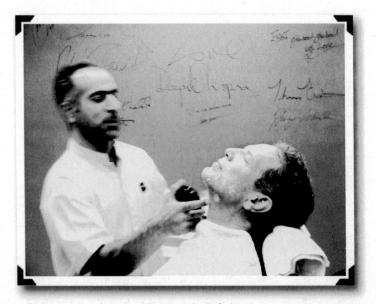

Tom at 1847, Dubai

Deepak Chopra's signature

40

NUNS FOR A WEEK!

March 2008

O h, we'll take the high road, and they'll take the low road, and we'll get to Scotland aforrrrrre ... our luggage!"

I regarded Rande with mirth and pity. She was losing it. We were standing on the ragged hem of western Scotland, having traveled 4,700 miles from the Pacific Northwest to London to Glasgow to the Island of Mull to the Isle of Iona, only to arrive with nothing but the clothes on our backs. Due to a system breakdown at London's Heathrow Airport, our bags were very lost.

"They'll never find us here!" Rande wailed. "We don't even know where we are!"

Iona, in fact, is one of the Scottish Inner Hebrides. These three and a half square miles of rock and heather are also the home of Scotland's early Celtic Christianity. Celtic scholar J. Philip Newell holds annual weeklong retreats on Iona specifically to present the Celts' ancient nature-loving philosophy in its original Scottish setting. I'd met Philip while we were visiting Tom's brother and family in Minneapolis, where Philip happened to be leading a workshop on early Celtic Christianity at Westminster Presbyterian Church where my brother-in-law, Tim Hart-Andersen, serves as minister. Tim graciously agreed to arrange a private meeting, and for one spellbinding hour on a sunny Midwestern spring day, I learned that Rande and I have more in common with the early Celts than either of us could have imagined.

For the record, the Celts were a fiercely talented early Indo-European nation that developed in the Danube, Rhine, and Rhône valleys, then swept across Europe a thousand years before the birth of Christ. They were soon well established from Russia to the British Isles, where they remain concentrated today. Celtic agriculture, medicine (especially surgery), and engineering were all stellar for the time, as was the Celts' love of language and scholarship.

They were also "the most exuberant of the ancient European visual artists," writes Peter Berresford Ellis in *The Celts: A History*, and were especially revered for their metal jewelry, whose complex knotted patterns so many of us love today, including Rande and me. But we knew nothing about their spirituality. I learned from Philip that the Celts believed in the holiness of all of Creation, which is what he called the known universe. From the exploding stars to our very selves, Creation, he told me, "was not made out of nothing by a distant creator as so many churches would have us believe, but is instead a living, holy energy born of the womb of God." We are, therefore, absolutely not "born in sin" but are, in fact, deeply and essentially good. "And the knot at the center of all Celtic art?" Philip concluded. "That represents the profound and joyful holiness that is woven into the heart of all of Creation."

Philip had just recited Rande's and my most closely held beliefs. As serious as we are about the profundity of the spiritual, our own experience of it was a kind of personal euphoria, moments of which we were obliged to grab whenever we could, mostly in our respective morning meditations. I certainly felt it in the old sacred music I'd sung in the church choir I'd belonged to for years, though the woes of the world tended to overshadow most Sunday services. How Rande and I longed for a spiritual model that celebrated the joy of the sacred. Could this longing be in the blood, since both of us share rather concentrated Celtic bloodlines?

"The early Celts were nothing if not joyful," Philip offered. "I think you might feel quite at home with them." I signed us up for his next Iona workshop on the spot. But arriving without our luggage had thrown a bit of a cowl over things, especially for Rande.

"It's a *spiritual* retreat," I reminded her. "We don't need material things."

The truth was, people have been coming to Iona to lighten their psychic load for centuries. Its reputation as "the holy isle" started in AD 563 when a forty-two-year-old Irish monk named Colum Cille—later "St. Columba"—landed in a rowboat full of fellow friars on a half-moon beach now called St. Columba's Bay. The good monk soon founded a monastery, and his legacy was secured a century later when the ninth abbot of Iona published *Life of Columba*, a volume filled with stories of the saint's prophecies and miracles (one monk witnessed Columba "surrounded by adoring angels"). Today, the Iona Abbey glows rosy and robust above the oddly tropical water around Iona, and attracts 140,000 pilgrims every year to this island of only 140 year-round residents.

J. Philip Newell sat at a table at the far side of the St. Columba Hotel dining room surrounded by laughing retreatees. The gentle Scottish-Canadian author, poet, and ordained Presbyterian minister had left the church eight years earlier to spread the word on early Celtic spirituality, and his workshops now fill up a year in advance. At dinner that first night, his ad hoc parishioners were as nourished by his good cheer as they were by the St. Columba's excellent cooking.

"What *is* this?" Rande asked our young red-haired server.

"Tat's the haggis, it t'is," the girl replied.

Rande blanched.

"We make it here fresh. T'is mooch bettah."

It was delicious. As were the free-range Pennyghael Estate venison from Mull, the organic Loch Duart farmed salmon, the bright vegetables from the hotel's organic gardens, and the local Tobermory single malt.

"This whiskey smells soooo good," Rande burbled. "Maybe we could wear it as perfume since ours is in our lost luggage."

"Yoo could at tat," our server agreed.

"Oh, I just LOVE your Scottish accent," Rande told her.

"Tank yoo," the girl replied, "but I'm Irish. Yoo can take yoor whiskey into yoor meetin' wit yoo," she added. "God won't mind."

Once we had gathered for our after-dinner orientation, Philip's purposeful voice brought the group to order—and Rande and me back to sobriety. We would meet there in the hotel's sitting room all week for morning and evening sessions presented by Phillip and Ali, his graceful wife, fellow minister, and retreat partner. The idea was to lead us to the center of Celtic spiritual tradition via historic lecture, chant, song, dance, silent reflection, and prayer, and we would complete our journey with a pilgrimage on foot across the island to St. Columba's Bay.

Philip began by saying that he traces his own Celtic journey back to the four years he served as warden for the Iona Abbey, from 1988 to 1992. Thus his annual Iona retreats are a return to his own Spiritual True North and the island he considers "an extraordinary window into the soul of Creation."

"We are here," he told us, "to assume the posture of listening together to one another and to the earth, which is a deeply held Celtic tradition and dangerously forgotten today."

The early Celts, he said, saw that the heart of all creation was holy and good, and the conviction of Celtic spirituality is that evil behavior springs, therefore, not from the supposedly sinful heart of our being, but from "a deep confusion." Transformation, he insisted, occurs only through love, as was the Celtic way.

"We are here to experience the deep heartbeat of God," Philip concluded. "And when we do, we hear our own name."

"Jess!"

Rande's voice came from her side of our room like the whine of a desperate child.

"I can't sleep!"

"Me either," I replied. As glorious as Iona was, there seemed to be a very fierce creative force just beneath the surface.

"Every time I close my eyes I see all these images," I told Rande.

"You, too? I'm seeing buildings and people and trees and horses, just tumbling and tumbling."

"Me, too! It's all so visual—not like when you can't turn off your thoughts. And it feels like watching a volcano of creativity. Iona is supposed to be so peaceful, but the creative energy here is on spin cycle!"

"Many sensitives can't sleep on Iona at first," Philip confirmed as we all walked to Iona Abbey the next morning. "The energy of Creation here is intense."

It is thought that St. Columba was drawn to Iona for this very reason. During the week, virtually everyone in our group mentioned the island's "enchanting" and "magical" properties. There was, indeed, a luminescence to the landscape of the island, a certain delicious dash to the mineralized sea air and a comfort in the dark cologne of the rock and loam. Even the water around Iona was a saturated South Pacific blue. On the short stroll from the hotel to Iona Abbey where we went to worship morning and night, the Celtic winds seemed to imbue our own energies with fresh charge. That is what sets Iona apart from other pretty British places, and its special electricity was only amplified by its iconic beauty. The endless green fields filled with white spring lambs, the painterly farmhouses against that plane of soaring sky, and even the sweetness of the Abbey's services, so inclusive and free of dogma, all in all a picture-perfect embodiment of Philip's message.

"In the Celtic tradition," he began, "the feminine was holy and the natural was holy. Celtic art and prayer celebrate the Earth and its people as deeply sacred because they come right out of the holy womb of God." Philip opened his book, *Celtic Prayers from Iona*, and read: "You are above me O God, you are beneath, you are in air, you are in earth, you are beside me, you are within ... kindle within me a love for you in all things. May the grace of the love of the stars be mine. May the grace of the love of the winds be mine. May the grace of the love of the waters be mine. In the name of the Word of all life."

"Yes, yes," murmured a man from Texas sitting beside us. "That is what I want to feel. Yes."

Rande and I emerged that first morning feeling restored and found ourselves drawn to the Iona community gift shop across the way. And that's when I saw it.

"Rande, look."

"That's it," she concurred, staring at the beautiful, complex gold Celtic cross in a display case. She knew I had collected little sacred icons from all the world's great faiths but had never found the right cross. Until now. Rande bought one for herself in silver.

"Ah, the nunnery cross," Philip told us before the morning session began. "The design is from a carved stone put there sometime during the last six hundred years."

"Rande!" I said. "I've got it! We're living in one little room with two little beds in a community of spiritual seekers. We all dine together three times a day, we go to worship together morning and night, we wear the same outfit day after day, and our only prized possession is our Celtic cross—we're Nuns for a Week!"

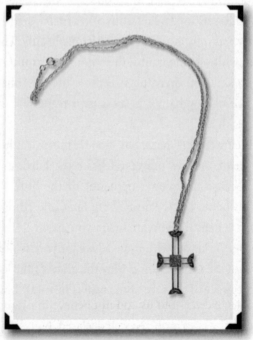

Jessica's Celtic cross from Iona

That morning Philip had us each introduce ourselves to the group in a marvelous way: by the story of our given names. And what stories! Our ages ranged from the early forties to late eighties, and we hailed from as close as Edinburgh and as far away as New Zealand, with most of us being from the States. One was a New Jersey minister who had taken her college-age daughters across France on a Mary Magdalene pilgrimage she'd researched herself. Another had worked for decades with some of the poorest people in West Africa. One sprightly sixty-two-year-old from Berkeley had run a ministry of sacred dance there before she retired; her best friend was at the retreat because all her life she'd done the very Celtic thing of sensing the presence of God in nature, something the church of her youth considered a serious sin.

This radical Celtic understanding of the inherent holiness of the earth and its people was especially apparent on our pilgrimage to St. Columba's Bay. Even the most senior members of our group decided to go, so inspiring was the Celts' call. Rande and I, at least, managed the first part of the journey thanks to borrowed clothes, though we sat out the second half since our hiking boots were in our still-lost bags. The day carried a clean north Atlantic chill. After a long and challenging hike we emerged on St. Columba's beach, where Philip had us choose two rocks: one represented something we wanted to purge from our psyches—we were to throw this one into the sea. We were to take the other one home with us as a reminder of a change we wanted to keep. It turned out that Rande and I both threw away blocks that keep ourselves and others from the joy of the sacred, and we kept symbols of our renewed devotion to our own creativity, which we now saw as "Celtic and holy." At the water's edge we found ourselves standing beside the sixty-two-year-old woman from Berkeley who had always sensed the divine in the natural world. She was sobbing.

"I threw away the shame I've carried my whole life for feeling God in nature," she told us. "And this," she said, holding a smooth circle of Iona's famous green marble in her palm, "represents my transformation."

The early Celts, Newell told us, did not believe in original sin. "Seeing sin in a newborn baby is absurd," Newell declared. Nor did the early Celtic Christians denigrate the feminine. "They worshipped the feminine as a holy source of creativity. And they considered sexuality holy too."

"Well, that's refreshing," Rande whispered.

"Careful," I warned. "We're nuns!"

Everything Newell shared with us perfectly aligned with what the Holy Pig Farmer had been teaching for better than four decades: that we are part of God's holy creation, fully alive to the Spirit, right here on Earth. *Surely,* I thought, *there must be a way to re-enchant the Sunday morning church experience with that! Progressive Christian churches would be filled with young people if we did.*

Soon after we returned to the States, Rande had a vivid and haunting dream two nights in a row. In it she was told that she and I must "drink a vial of sacred liquid from Iona to protect our inner selves." "The dream was so real," she said, "that both times I woke up looking around in a panic for our Sacred Liquid!"

I emailed Philip to see what he thought.

"If you'd been able to take the second half of the Pilgrimage," he wrote back, "you would have come to a sacred spring whose waters are associated with many healings. I never leave Iona without drinking from it."

When I called Rande to tell her, her voice went cold as well.

"So," she said, "if our *luggage* had shown up we would have had our boots and we would have been able to drink the sacred water."

"No, no," I replied. "Don't you see? Losing our luggage was symbolic of losing our baggage! We're not weighed down with all the old ideas anymore and we're not spiritual orphans. We're joyful Celts, and always have been! Your dream was just the creative Celtic power of Iona calling us home."

41

Return of the Two Prophets

April 2008

When I gave Lory my Iona Report, his lake-and-meadow voice took on new urgency.

"Something's happening," he said. "It's nothing I've ever experienced before. People are ready. They are hungry. Hungrier for what I teach than at any time in the last forty years. I think your friend Philip is right that many people are ready for a new kind of church experience."

"Do you have anything in mind?"

"Yes I do," he replied. "And it's so simple. Jesus said, 'When two or more come together in my name,' and that's what people I work with have agreed to do. They meet together with other people—people they didn't know before—and they do the kind of listening I have been instructed to teach them …" Lory's voice trailed off, and I knew he was weeping. "Well," he said, "the healings are profound.

"I've been a mystic all my life," he added without warning, "and I've been ashamed of it all my life. Well, now I'm not. I have accepted my role—it is egocentric not to. I have been given permission to teach what I have been shown."

Meaning that *my* Holy Pig Farmer was finally ready to become everyone's Holy Pig Farmer?

"Yes."

Well, it's not polite to hog the Holy Pig Farmer!

"You can't do it alone," Lory reminded me. "What people need is a spiritual instruction manual. Something that gets them on their own path—which is different from anyone else's path. It could lead them to a Presbyterian church like yours did, or to a mountaintop in Peru, or to a soup kitchen. And being part of one of the groups I help them create gives them the support they need to stay on their own path. Like Weight Watchers, or, more accurately, Light Watchers," he added, cracking himself up.

It was good to hear this painfully humble man enjoy his own joke. He was right. Something is happening. As a double confirmation, on February 2, 2009, only days after Lory's surprising declaration, I received an email from my longtime celebrity journalist pal, Larry Grobel, who, besides being a well-known author and lauded interviewer, happens to be the person who introduced me to the rabbi-like poet-philosopher Noah benShea—and Noah is the person who, along with the Holy Pig Farmer, had prophesied *Roll Around Heaven* more than twenty-five years earlier. And Noah, according to Larry's email, was going to have a one-man Public Broadcasting Service television series! Larry gave me Noah's phone number.

"Well, you know," Noah said in a voice that still sounded like God talking to Charlton Heston, "Einstein said that coincidence is God's way of remaining anonymous.

"In my Jacob the Baker series," he continued, "I wrote that Jacob was a reed, and the breath of God blew through him and made music of him. Well, God chooses God's own violins—sometimes it stuns us. Picasso is a great example: he said, 'There are only two types of women, goddesses and doormats.' What a bastard! But somehow God played through him, made music of him."

Clearly, God was making music of Noah benShea too.

He laughed.

"I take my work seriously. I don't take myself seriously."

But the world sure does. His wise counsel, I learned, has already shown up on thirty million Starbucks cups as "Do not kiss your children so they will kiss you back, but so they will kiss their children and their children will kiss their children."

"Sounds like the Golden Rule to me," I told him.

"The Golden Rule is only golden," he replied, "as long as we're not prepared to treat others with the same disrespect we have for ourselves. Many of us were raised to think that it's an act of character to beat ourselves up. I really do believe that the ability to love others is predicated on our ability to love ourselves."

More echoes of the Holy Pig Farmer! No wonder Noah has been called "a two-thousand-year-old man in a young man's body." But what, I wanted to know, did this widely recognized Oxford University lecturer, think tank consultant, keynote speaker at the Library of Congress, and nominee for the Grawemeyer "Ideas That Improve the World" Award, whose work is now quoted on some 45,000 websites, make of the anti-religion tidal wave that's flooding intellectual thought these days?

"Wisdom is more than intellectual despair," Noah said. "A lot of people think of faith as a pew issue."

"Or a P.U. issue," I just had to add.

Noah laughed his kettledrum laugh. "My feeling is that prayer is a path where there is none."

Is this, I wondered, why a guy born on the Jewish New Year, Rosh Hashanah, never seems to mention that he comes out of the grand rabbinical tradition of storytelling and wisdom?

"People ask me that a lot," Noah replied. "The real reason is that I don't want to spend one more minute of my life being right. People who have to be right are usually wrong. And when I'm in the middle of prayer I never think of what religion the person next to me isn't—you do that and you fall out of prayer."

And there it was. The highest high ground. The clearest sight. The purest of intention. The true Emunah, or Jewish Amen, which means the highest possible spiritual state. Here was yet another teacher of teachers wanting only to see with the eyes of God that forever bore right through the divisions that separate us to touch the holy heart that beats as one within us all.

And there now stood my little story, predicted and protected for a quarter century by the twin Judeo-Christian mountaintops of Noah benShea and the Holy Pig Farmer, brothers of peace and prayer divine, who have devoted their lives to healing the suffering of others and shining light upon the path that prayer reveals so that we might once again find our way home.

So may it be. Amen. Emunah.

EPILOGUE

What on Earth Does All This Mean for You?

Each one of us has the capacity to become a saint.
DESMOND TUTU

Be lamps unto yourselves.
THE BUDDHA

You shall see the most brilliant light;
and you will realize that this light is the root secret of this world.
AMMA SRI KARUNAMAYI

The fact that you are reading *Roll Around Heaven* means that you're already a lot farther down the path than I was when this story began.

Maybe when you started this book you only suspected that reality-as-usual wasn't the whole story and you wanted to know more.

Or maybe you already knew there was more but were afraid to say so. And, as is often the case, perhaps there was no one you felt you could tell anyway. Perhaps this story has provided you with the comfort of confirmation for what might well be the most profound experiences of your life. If so, then please picture me giving you the Ali Baba at-your-service hand spiral.

Perhaps, like me, you now wonder how much spiritual awareness your peabrain is actually capable of, and maybe you want to explore that. Or maybe you just want to find your own version of this mysterious thing we call the "spiritual path," and maybe you even want your own spiritual coach too. Good idea. The reason the Holy Pig Farmer says we can't do it alone is because we can't. And God knows we live in a culture that generally doesn't recognize or encourage, much less celebrate, mystical experiences. In fact, it seems to spend most of its time trying to drag our minds into purgatory—just say no to exploding-car chase scenes!

How to Find Your Spiritual Path

So, how do you find your own spiritual path? Here's my surefire two-step method: 1) Follow Your Heart, and 2) Suit Up and Show Up.

I believe that you already know the general direction of your own Spiritual True North. Maybe you love Thai food and have always been fascinated by the Buddhist altars in Thai restaurants. Maybe you adore stained glass and always make a point of visiting old churches and cathedrals whenever you travel. Maybe you've loved the scent of Indian incense ever since your college boyfriend almost burned down his dorm room with it. And maybe something about all those Indian deities intrigues you no end. Maybe you're like the woman in Minneapolis who wrote about my father-in-law, Hank—the good Jewish girl who loves Christmas carols. Maybe you were raised Louisiana Catholic but you always wanted to live in New York and now you do and all your best buddies are Jewish and you love going to their weddings (few gatherings are more fun than a Jewish wedding!). Or perhaps Celtic art makes your heart race. Or Arabic music. Or Japanese tea ceremonies. Or Plains Indian beadwork. Or the Southern hymns in the movie *O Brother, Where Art Thou?* (Let's *do* go down to the river and pray!) Whatever you're drawn to, if your attraction is strong and consistent over time, that most definitely is your first clue.

You may have long assumed that this sort of interest is only cultural, or that the culture you're drawn to is so foreign that it couldn't possibly hold personal messages for you. But as the Holy Pig Farmer says, there are a million doors to heaven—the trick is finding your door—and all paths, if they are indeed paths of the heart, are valid. The Buddhists would add that your soul has been here before, and you may well have lived lives in places far away from where you live now. Who's to say that the traditions of a previous homeland aren't part of your own unfinished spiritual business this time around? And make no mistake, you might have been raised a Missouri Lutheran, but if you had been born in Bhutan, you'd be a Buddhist. As our Oregonian Christian housepainter buddy, Steve Tate, says: "If you were born over there, you'd think that was normal!"

Yes, you would. And as natural as it is to become ego-identified with your own culture and its predominant faith, or your family's religious tradition, this isn't a football game. When religious scholar, Harvard PhD, Princeton professor, and best-selling author Elaine Pagels was fourteen, she joined an evangelical Christian church. She "craved" the idea of belonging to "the right group" that "alone belonged to God." But she soon learned the cost of exclusivity when her church leaders instructed members not to associate with "outsiders" (except to try to convert them). And when a dear friend died in a car wreck, her church buddies wrote him off as eternally damned anyway because he was Jewish. She soon left that church.

It may be that the spiritual tradition in which you were raised never really spoke to you. Perhaps you didn't care for what this tradition said, as did Rande's and my friend on Iona who was told as a child that experiencing God in nature was "a sin." Or, as noted, if you're like me, you were too clueless for the spiritual to have spoken to you at all ... until now. Maybe the very idea of having your own spiritual path still makes you laugh ... which, of course, I believe would be a crying shame. (Better luck next life!) But, for those with ears to hear, your spiritual future very well may have been whispering sweet somethings to you all along. I'm only suggesting that it might be wise to listen.

Suit Up and Show Up

Once you've determined your own Spiritual True North, then it's time to Suit Up and Show Up. By this I mean don't just sit there, *do* something! A smart first step is to read books about the tradition or traditions to which you find yourself drawn. But sitting in on a service at a church, temple, mosque, synagogue, meeting hall, monastery, longhouse, or ashram will give you a much better sense of the physical expression of any given tradition. Going on a weeklong retreat is even better, and these are usually surprisingly affordable if you can scrape together the money for the airfare to get there.

Your love of Celtic art or stained glass windows may mean that it's time to take one of J. Philip Newell's Celtic Christianity workshops. Or, like President Obama, to make "an unequivocal commitment to a particular community of faith," and simply go to church. Because, I assure you, all-heart progressive Christian houses of worship are still on fire with the same sweet spirit of Jesus that visited me on that freeway long ago and has remained with me ever since. Your attraction to all things Arabic might inspire a serious reading of the Quran, something my honorary nephew, Jackson Kellogg and his wondrous Kyrgyz wife, Ainura, do every evening. Or a visit to a mosque ... or to Oman! Whereas the ecstatic poems of Hafiz could lead you straight into the kindly heart of Sufism, the mystical arm of Islam. Who could resist "All the hemispheres of heaven are sitting around a fire chatting while stitching themselves together into the Great Circle inside of You"? Your fascination with the colorful Buddhist altars in Thai restaurants ought to send you directly to the fine books by the Dalai Lama, as well as lectures by a visiting Tibetan, Bhutanese, Vietnamese, or Thai Buddhist teacher, and I hope to Bhutan for a personal introduction to Himalayan Buddhism at Zhiwaling Hotel (www.zhiwaling.com). However, a preference for the minimalist style of Japanese tea ceremonies might mean that Zen Buddhism is a better match for your sensibilities. If so, I recommend reading the collected talks of Zen master Bassui, *Mud and Water*, and then ... get thee to a (Buddhist) nunnery! At least for a meditation class.

If you're a naturalist and Indian/First Nations traditions call to you the way they do me, then know that the descendents of our original Americans have been bringing their cultures back for decades. A stellar introduction to indian culture is, of course, John Neihardt's 1961 tribute to an Oglala Sioux holy man, *Black Elk Speaks*, a classic that has been in print for half a century.

Surely there is also a pow-wow coming to a fairgrounds/reservation near you. And all tribes have seasonal gatherings that are open to the public.

For the decade I lived in Seattle, every June I would meet my great good friend Terry Williams, the first director of the Environmental Protection Agency's first Office of the American Indian and attend the annual First Salmon Ceremony at the Tulalip Reservation in the town of Marysville. It is held in a traditional wooden longhouse on the very ground where one has stood for thousands of years. There, attendees gather on low indoor bleachers around a central fire pit while tribal elders sing sacred songs that honor their salmon brethren, whose faithful return to their natal streams ensured the survival of Northwest coastal tribes for millennia.

The ceremony is always interrupted by a young "runner" bringing the news that the First Salmon is approaching. Everyone then rises and walks down to the shore of the Tulalip Reservation's beautiful bay to watch the arrival of two dugout canoes. The first holds two young male paddlers and a large glittering Chinook salmon set on cedar branches between them. The second boat is the salmon's escort canoe. The men then bear the First Salmon aloft as the crowd walks it into the longhouse for more ritual celebration, followed by a big salmon dinner, originally designed to give each member of the tribe a bit of the First Salmon as a sort of holy communion with their revered fish.

The longhouse ceremony includes a Blessing of the Fishermen, wherein all fisherpersons are invited to stand in front of an elder who blesses them for the season, sprinkling holy water on their persons with an eagle feather. One year, when I happened to be sitting behind the fishermen, being too shy to stand up with them, a few drops of this blessed water landed on my face. The following month I caught what is still my biggest salmon on record, a Japanese fish print of which graces my writing studio wall. So tribal traditions can have a powerful effect whether you're a member of the tribe or not.

Sensing the divine in nature can sneak up on you. In-the-trenches social activist Barbara Ehrenreich insists that she is "not a religious person," yet while watching "six discrete lightning storms" dance across the horizon beyond her home on a remote Florida isle she felt that she was "being drawn into something" which she came to think of as "the Presence," precisely what Philip Newell and the early Celts call God. The "birds ... and the Milky Way ... the clouds that line up to worship the rising sun" all began to feel, she says, "like a single, living breathing Other." Most assuredly, this landscape is Ms. Ehrenreich's church, and just being there is her practice, defined by her own devotion and vision.

Of course, the range within established spiritual traditions swings wide. If I had to boil everything I've been shown on this journey down to one core principle, it is, without a doubt, the Golden Rule. So any version of a spiritual tradition that preaches discrimination against other groups, insists that its way is the only way, and/or offers fear and guilt to its people instead of love, inclusion, forgiveness, and reverence—well, sorry, but these guys just don't get it, and my advice is to keep looking.

THE MAN

If, like so many of us, the unfortunate tendencies listed above have made you just plain allergic to "organized religion" (though my years as a choir member certainly challenge the definition of "organized"), maybe you need a nondenominational spiritual coach. These are rare and uniquely illuminated human beings who, by virtue of their natural effect on others, wind up in the role of teacher. Some are very well known, such as Southern California–based Deepak Chopra and Eckhart Tolle in Vancouver, British Columbia, both of whom lecture and lead workshops all year long. So do Lory Misel, who lives near Seattle, and Noah benShea, based in Santa Barbara, California. All continue to work with clients privately too. But many fine personal teachers are not destined for the mass market and do their good works quietly and locally, which makes them more coach-like, and also a little tougher to find ... unless, of course, you totally luck out and one finds you, as the Holy Pig Farmer found me. In a way, this happened to my beautiful spiritually minded stepson Eli while he was standing outside the cool vintage Silver Streak trailer he was renovating himself. A lovely older woman approached him. Her office was in the building across the street and she'd been fascinated by Eli's work on his trailer.

She also happened to be a professional spiritual coach! She and Eli talked and talked, and he swiftly became a friend of the woman's entire enlightened family.

Spiritually minded folks do talk. So something as simple as going to a metaphysical bookstore in your area and asking the owner about potential spiritual coaches can work wonders. Don't be surprised if the person standing in line behind you politely eavesdrops on your conversation and invites you to meet his or her own spiritual teacher. This sort of "coincidence" happens all the time once you start seeking in earnest. "God is always geometrizing," reminds my wonderful surrogate fly-fishing father, Roger Bachman, and a better way to explain that bit of cosmic truth I have yet to find.

Rande's husband, Glen Anderson, found his spiritual teacher, John MacPherson, years ago through friends and has studied with him ever since. They are in the process of completing a spiritual retreat and study center called The Lodge in Eastern Washington State. Glen's spiritual group is a "psychokinetic community of friends." They consider themselves "Christian Mystics" but with no specific Christian affiliation. "Our concern," he explains, "is with the spiritual transformation of the individual for themselves and for the good of humanity." Basic information can be found on their website at www.northwestacademy.org.

Tom's and my mystic handyman, Glen Heatherington, found his spiritual coach by accident when he was fifteen years old. Glen was born being able to read auras, and, being shy, he was standing off to the side at a party one night, amusing himself by watching the color fields surrounding everyone else, when he spotted a man with a purple aura. "I'd never seen someone with a purple aura before," Glen says, and he's never seen one since either. "The guy looked right at me across that room full of people and walked up to me ... and I studied with him for the next six years. I called him The Man."

The Man was quite the advanced teacher. Tuned to Glen the way Indian yogis are tuned to their devotees, The Man often called Glen precisely when he needed help with something. "And I mean, I'd be walking by a public phone booth hundreds of miles from my home and the phone in the booth would ring and I'd answer it and it would be The Man with exactly the information I needed to solve my problem. Happened all the time. I never did figure out how he did that." One time after Glen thought he'd figured out how telekinesis (meaning the ability to move objects with one's mind) worked, he spent a good hour telling The Man his theory. When he finished, his coffee cup suddenly began moving across the table toward The Man, who took a sip and set it back down. Then, as the coffee cup made its way back to Glen, The Man said, "Well, that's a good theory, but I just don't know if I believe in all that stuff."

After sharing that story, our normally peaceful handyman looked up, shook a finger at me, and said with surprising ferocity: "And tell your readers to stop giving their power away! They already *know* all the answers! *They're* the mystics!"

HAMMER THROW FROM HEAVEN

You can also ask for signs to confirm the direction of your spiritual path. I happen to be crazy about signs from God because they are so unexpected and playful and dramatic ... and perfect. Who but God would even think to send a frazzled bride-to-be an actual heart-shaped cloud to remind her that He/She/It loves her and all is well? It's like a divine valentine! In fact, that's exactly what it was.

My Canadian friend Susan Barryman gave me a wonderful book titled *Orange Socks: How a Yuppie Goes Yogi* by a spirited Canadian woman named Valerie Simonson. She was a supersuccessful and superunhappy businesswoman who decided to put everything on hold, donned a backpack, and hit the spiritual road in Asia looking for "The Answer." After a brutally austere stint at a Buddhist monastery in the Thai jungle, complete with giant stinging scorpions, she stumbled into a Raja Yoga meditation center in Bali, found her true spiritual calling, and is now a supersuccessful and superhappy Canadian businesswoman ... and a Raja Yoga mediation instructor. And the sign that started it all? Yup, orange socks.

How do you know when God has shown you your spiritual path? Oh, you'll know. Valerie Simonson was drawn to Buddhism, which got her to Asia, and that led her to her future spiritual practice in Bali. (That's why it's called a path.) The heroic thing about Valerie is that she Suited Up and Showed Up and went where she was called. How many of us spend years—decades!—resisting our deepest spiritual callings? In her groundbreaking 1996 book, *Anatomy of the Spirit*, medical intuitive and spiritual coach Caroline Myss tells the story of a client who has recurring dreams about Montana. He asks her what she thinks they mean, and Caroline tells him she thinks they mean he should go to Montana. The young man bravely quits the computer job he hates, moves to Montana, hires on as a ranch hand, and falls in love with and marries the rancher's daughter, and we can assume he's living the life of his dreams. Literally. His dreams were his sign.

My soul brother from church, Lance Deal, has mentioned several times that he's always been drawn to the Himalayas. The Himalayas? That's where Babaji is, the first prince in Yogananda's line of venerable gurus! That's where Bhutan tends the holy flame of Himalayan Buddhism! That's where prayer flags whisper a million prayers a minute all day long! That's as close to heaven-on-earth as any place I know ... besides rolling around heaven with my baby wherever we may be. And if Lance Deal is drawn to the Himalayas, then God only knows what will happen when he gets there, because, as you sports fans no doubt already figured out, Mr. Deal is our four-time Olympian hammer thrower who set and still holds the American hammer throw distance record. Privately, he told me that when he made his record-busting 82.52-meter throw in Milan: "I didn't let go of it until it landed."

He didn't let go of it ... *until* it landed? Do you *think* he gets it? Do you think the Himalayas will get him? Do you think, maybe, he'd better stop turning around in circles like a broken compass needle and get his swirling derriere on a plane to his Spiritual True North? Do you?

The problem is the usual one: far too many of us don't Suit Up and Show Up. And we don't "seek ye first." We forget who we are. We even forget that we know who we are. We get busy with Life, forgetting that Life is Spirit—and ignoring *that* is like missing the tree for the forest.

And of course, once you do find your spiritual way, the key is practice. As religious scholar Karen Armstrong writes in her new book *The Case for God*:

A deliberate and principled reticence about God and/or the sacred was a constant theme ... in Christianity [and] in the other major faith traditions until the rise of modernity in the West. People believed that God exceeded our thoughts and concepts and could only be known by dedicated practice. We have lost sight of this important insight and, I believe, this is one of the reasons why so many Western people find the concept of God so difficult today.

So, practice for the sake of your own progress but also just for the joy of celebrating the Everyday Divine, which, again, is why it's so important to fall in love with The Plateau and enjoy your long quiet years of practice there.

God's Cantaloupe

Another reason to find a group of spiritually oriented people to practice with is that you will need support. And you may not get it from your family or your friends. Once, while I was cod fishing off the Norwegian coast with a bunch of Oslo chefs in an Arctic blizzard, a young guy named Tore Willassen turned to me and said: "I want to know more about the Eastern masters." Between waves of seasickness I replied: "And why did you ask *me* about this?" "I don't know," the young man said. "I've been reading all about these masters and I'm just on fire with them and there is no one to talk to about this!" We talked nonstop for days.

A year later my friend Ugyen Rinzin needed a new chef at his hotel in Bhutan. I emailed Tore about it, who emailed back that a medium had already told him he would receive "a job offer in the East through a friend." Ugyen hired Tore, and Tore adores Bhutan. At Ugyen's request, he even cooked for the coronation of Bhutan's new king in November of 2008. And his study of Himalayan Buddhism shifted into full bloom. When you're on fire with the Spirit, you send out holy smoke signals that fellow pilgrims recognize, and you get—often in the most unlikely of ways—the support you need.

You also learn that while some people equate discussing spirituality with opening birthday presents, others will react like you're talking about dead flies. But, as the English philosopher Bertrand Russell reminds us, "Do not fear to be eccentric in opinion, for every opinion now accepted was once eccentric." And you can remind naysayers who may consider your spiritual search the work of a peabrain that it took scientists a hundred years to believe in the thermometer.

Some people are ready, some aren't, and everyone who progresses spiritually progresses at her or his own rate. Consider my goddaughter's early relationship with cantaloupe. From the time Little Jessica, as we call her, was five until she turned about twelve, she was convinced that she hated cantaloupe. She would not even get near it, much less taste it. No amount of "try it, you'll love it" helped. Then one magical day she decided on her own to nibble some. She absolutely loved it and declared: "I can't believe I missed eating cantaloupe all those years!"

The general historic consensus among spiritual masters is that everyone is heading back to God whether they know it, or want to know it, or don't, in this life or future ones, as the Buddhists and Hindus would say. If so, then in broad strokes, any given soul inhabits a specific body in any given lifetime specifically to accomplish what the Holy Pig Farmer calls a "Life Work," which is to move one's cardinal awareness closer to pure Spirit. Maybe a person's Life Work is an act of everyday service—to raise eleven kids, for instance. (God help them.) Or perhaps it's to really suffer—this is a tough one, I know—so that in their next life they have an acutely developed sense of compassion, and if they're wise, turn fully to the spiritual in this life.

Looking at life on Earth through the eyes of the Buddha sure helps with one of Christianity's stickiest wickets: the riddle of what my father-in-law calls "the unequal distribution of grace," a justice issue that both baffles and bothers him greatly. As the wife of his son Tom, I love the fact that reincarnation is business as usual to Jesus in the Gospel of Thomas, one of the many texts that were "denounced as heresy by orthodox Christians in the middle of the second century," as Elaine Pagels points out in the introduction to her award-winning book *The Gnostic Gospels*. Pagels adds that Harvard professor Helmut Koester further suggests that the Gospel of Thomas, while compiled in c. AD 140, may in fact include material that is even earlier than the gospels of Mark, Matthew, Luke, and John. Also in Thomas, Jesus says: "I have cast fire upon the world, and look, I'm guarding it until it blazes." Talk about Master Bassui's promise that enlightenment feels like a log thrown into a fire. Or Chef Tore's being on fire with the spirit.

Speaking of fire, a person's Life Work could also include being a total flaming narcissist, unable to form "deep and lasting relationships" and destined to end up "marooned on their own island," as the book *The Narcissism Epidemic* predicts, according to a *New York Times* review—though, sadly, not until the narcissist has done substantial damage to those around her or him, as the ego is never happier than when it has successfully plunged everyone in its orbit into painful chaos. Let's hope none of us have to live this kind of miserable life more than once, but, as the Buddhists also say, that's up to us. When our Bhutanese friend Lama Karma was at our home for a dinner party one night in early 2008, a fellow guest jokingly asked him: "So do you think President Bush will come back in his next life as a dung beetle?" And Lama Karma replied quite somberly: "I do not think he is coming back," referring to the Buddhist understanding that each of us is reborn in accordance to our previous actions, and those who have willfully inflicted great harm on others are destined for what is called the Hell Realm, a journey through some 136 "hells" and countless years of great suffering where the anguish is so terrible that even the practice of Dharma (Buddha's teachings) is almost impossible—all of which is designed to teach the offending soul some serious compassion. Just another little incentive to do unto others …

So, given the nature of individual karmic progress, in this life you will find that some people care about spirituality and some don't. It is, of course, completely possible to live an exemplary, high-minded, other-person-oriented life and not give a whit about spirituality. Consider my atheist friend Hazel Wolf in the chapter called Val Speaks, the one whose fundamental kindness bade the Holy Pig Farmer to pronounce her "a holy woman." But then there she was on the night her body died, visiting me in the spiritual form whose existence she completely rejected. Did Hazel need to know about her spiritual nature to have a wonderful life? No. She was one of the happiest people I have ever known. She had no interest in material things, lived very simply, and to my knowledge never owned a house. Her passions were people and the natural world, and that's who and what she served her entire life, and she absolutely loved doing it. Did her conscious and consistent decisions to live a life of cheerful service help create the wonderful life she lived? If you believe the best studies on this subject, absolutely. Did she accrue enough "merit," as Lama Karma calls it, to assure herself an even more wonderful life next time? Buddhists sure would think so. So what did Hazel miss by being a self-proclaimed "atheist humanist"?

She missed God's cantaloupe! She missed the incomparable, astounding, impossibly profound *experience of the divine.*

"What does anything matter so long as you find Him?" Yogananda beseeched his students. "If you could feel even a little bit of the bliss I know, you would understand the magnitude of what you are missing."

Perhaps my wonderful Catholic friend Kathryn Nove put it best: "People who say they don't miss God in their life are like people who have sex but have never had an orgasm, and then say, 'Oh, but I don't miss it!'"

THE GRUMPY GUY IN THE SKY

Let's assume, then, that you've either had it and you want more ... or you haven't had it but you sure as heck don't want to miss it. (For anyone who hasn't had it and doesn't want it, we know a nice monastery we can refer you to, but then you'd really run the risk of experiencing the bliss of God!) So, after you Follow Your Heart, Suit Up and Show Up, receive a few signs of cosmic confirmation, and begin your own brand of regular spiritual practice, then what?

Well, it's simple. You just ask.

Just ask, you ask?

Yes. Just ask.

I know, I know, this is as obvious as a white butterfly in a burned field. But you might be surprised at the number of people whose eyes go blank when I ask if they've asked God (as they understand Her/Him/It) for help with something they're struggling with. Usually they respond one of two ways: Either, "Oh, you don't ask God for help with something that personal/small/unimportant." Or, "Gee, you'd think I would have thought of the obvious, wouldn't you."

Which reinforces the Holy Pig Farmer's basic charge that you are here "to remember that you are God's holy child," and nothing is too small to request of your heavenly parent. Sadly, the old concept of a distant, impersonal, unresponsive creator is still alive and well, just as Philip Newell says He is (yes, that would be the Grumpy Guy in the Sky version of God). And He, of course, is way too busy making, I guess, more beetles and warblers (since He sure must like them, given how many species we've already got) to help measly little us with a trifling thing like paying the mortgage or keeping our kids off meth.

Or healing a paralyzed squirrel?

I mean, there are a bazillion squirrels in the world. And they jump from tree to shining tree all day long. So, by the law of averages, a squirrel is going to miss and fall on its head—or back—roughly every four minutes.

So why in God's name would God care about the one little squirrel that fell onto our patio enough to heal it from complete lethal paralysis and then send seventeen golden eagles—not standard issue bald eagles—to the Holy Pig Farmer's pasture when I called to tell him about healing the squirrel???

Why? Because I asked God to. I asked God (and Jesus and Yogananda and the Buddha and Allah and Moses and Mother Theresa and St. Francis) with all my heart to heal that squirrel. And God and God's buddies said it was good because, as The Mystic Golfer says, we can assert our free will to try to make something happen all we want, but what *does* happen is God's will, too. God just threw in the golden eagles to get your attention when I shared this story with you.

DOWNWIND OF FLOWERS

God's will, if you will, really takes a bow when it comes to healing. This can be one of the most difficult parts of the Mystery to accept, but sometimes one of the most astounding. I stood by my mother's deathbed for weeks on end praying that she would recover and her cancer would vanish. But despite my managing to "drain" the tumors on her neck of truly horrific negative energy, it was time for my mother to go. And go she did. But who doesn't pray for a miracle when someone they love is dying? And why shouldn't we? When I asked that my mother be healed, I knew of two miracle cures firsthand.

My choir pal at Central Presbyterian Linda Cummins, the soprano who had invited me to join the choir in the first place, told me about her mother's miracle recovery from the same disease. Linda was only seven, and her mother had been diagnosed with terminal cancer. Linda heard her mother crying by herself in her bedroom every day. Then one morning Linda heard her talking to someone. Her mother later reported that she was "talking to Jesus," begging Him to spare her life because she had two small children to take care of. She then felt what she described as "a warmth" pass through her body, and her doctor soon confirmed that her wildly metastasized uterine cancer had vanished. "He called it a miracle," Linda says, "officially, in her medical record." Linda's mother lived to be seventy-six.

And a woman who once cleaned house for my mother told me that her husband, a Vietnam vet, had been diagnosed with the death-sentence cancer caused by Agent Orange. Together they prayed and prayed, she said, "begging Jesus for his recovery," but the disease only spread like napalm. "His legs finally turned black," she told me. Then one morning she woke up and saw that his face was black too. Crying hysterically, she screamed at him to go look in the bathroom mirror. He did. And he came back grinning. "That's my beard," he informed his wife, who broke out in hysterical laughter. She knew this meant that his body and his health were coming back. He remains to this day the only known survivor of Agent Orange cancer.

The Reverend Christopher Ian Chenoweth, who publishes the marvelous online service "Positive Daily Inspiration," gave me permission to share this third story of miraculous healing, "Downwind from Flowers."

Several years ago in Seattle, Washington, there lived a 52-year-old Tibetan refugee. "Tenzin," as I will call him, who was diagnosed with one of the more curable forms of lymphoma. He was admitted to the hospital and received his first dose of chemotherapy. But during the treat-

ment, this usually gentle man became extremely angry. The doctors and nurses were baffled. Then Tenzin's wife told them Tenzin had been held as a political prisoner by the Chinese for seventeen years. They killed his first wife and repeatedly tortured him throughout his imprisonment. She told them that the hospital gave Tenzin horrible flashbacks of what he had suffered at the hands of the Chinese.

"I know you mean to help him," she said, "but he feels tortured by your treatments. They are causing him to feel hatred inside—just like he felt toward the Chinese. He would rather die than live with the hatred he is now feeling. And, according to our belief, it is very bad to have hatred in your heart at the time of death. He needs to be able to pray and cleanse his heart."

So the doctors discharged Tenzin and I was the hospice nurse assigned to his care.

He said, "I must learn to love again if I am to heal my soul. Your job is to teach me to love again."

I asked him, "So, how can I help you love again?"

Tenzin immediately replied, "Sit down and drink my tea."

Tibetan tea is strong, laced with yak butter. It isn't easy to drink! But for several weeks, Tenzin, his wife, and I sat together, drinking tea. Each time I arrived, Tenzin was sitting cross-legged on his bed, reciting prayers. As time went on, he and his wife hung more and more colorful Tibetan Buddhist banners on the walls. The room was fast becoming a beautiful shrine.

I asked Tenzin what Tibetans do when they are ill in the spring. He smiled brightly and said, "We sit downwind from flowers." I thought he must be speaking poetically. But Tenzin's words were quite literal. He told me Tibetans sit downwind so they can be dusted with the new blossoms' pollen. They feel this new pollen is strong medicine. One of my friends suggested that Tenzin visit some of the local flower nurseries.

So, the next weekend, I picked up Tenzin and his wife with their provisions for the afternoon: black tea, butter, salt, cups, cookies, prayer beads, and prayer books.

The following weekend, they visited another nursery. The third weekend, they went to yet another. The fourth week, I began to get calls from the nurseries inviting Tenzin and his wife to return.

Later that day, I got a call from the second nursery saying that they had colorful wind socks that would help Tenzin predict where the wind was blowing. Pretty soon, the nurseries were competing for Tenzin's visits.

People began to know and care about the Tibetan couple. The nursery employees started setting out the lawn furniture in the direction of the wind. Others would bring out fresh hot water for their tea. Some of the regular customers would leave their wagons of flowers near the two of them. It seemed that a community was growing around Tenzin and his wife.

At the end of the summer, Tenzin returned to his doctor for another CT scan to determine the extent of the spread of the cancer. But the doctor could find no evidence of cancer at all. He was dumbfounded. He told Tenzin that he just couldn't explain it.

Tenzin lifted his finger and said, "I know why the cancer has gone away. It could no longer live in a body that is filled with love. When I began to feel all the compassion from the hospice people, from the nursery employees, and all those people who wanted to know about me, I started to change inside. Now, I feel fortunate to have had the opportunity to heal in this way. Doctor, please don't think that your medicine is the only cure. Sometimes compassion can cure cancer, as well."

THE ANKLE OF REPOSE

I have also asked for—and received—healings for myself. On one of our upriver weekend visits with my parents, they gave Tom and me their old, but still nice, television. As things tend to do, the television stayed in the back of my car for a while, and finally I decided to haul it into our house myself (Tom was at work). It was heavy and I was wearing wedgie sandals and, you guessed it, I turned my ankle rather badly (but I didn't drop the TV!!).

Ben and Eli came over for dinner that night, and I stoically hobbled around cooking, but by the time we'd finished eating, my ankle was so painful and purple I needed help to walk. Eli, a trained medic, looked at it and shook his head. He'd suffered the same sort of injury playing high school basketball (much more respectable than hurting yourself hauling TVs around). "This will be really sore for weeks," he said, then sweetly put an ice pack on it for me.

But I didn't have weeks! We were heading to Europe on a suite of my travel assignments and were scheduled to cover a lot of ground, including going on a Norwegian moose hunt!, and I had to be able to walk. This dumb ankle injury—I know, I know . . . *I* was the fashionable one wearing the wedgies!—would inconvenience everyone. Before I went to sleep that night I asked for help with my aching ankle, but was awakened in the middle of the night by acute, throbbing pain. That's when I got serious. Placing my own hands around my ankle, I asked Christ, the healer of healers, "with power," as Greg Tatman suggests, to pleeeeeese take care of this injury. And then went back to sleep.

When I woke up the next morning and swung out of bed, I gingerly put a little weight on my hurt ankle . . . and felt nothing. I put a little more on it . . . nothing. I stood up. Nothing! Only the mildest, most distant discomfort. As Tom is my witness, that ankle was healed. The bruise was gone too. Gone.

And by the way, if you still don't believe that God and Jesus and all the saints I called on healed that paralyzed squirrel, then I have a bridge I'd just love to sell you . . . and we'll use the money to open the Brooklyn Bridge Wildlife Rehab Spiritual Healing Center.

WHY BE SHY?

So why be shy about asking God—or any of your favorite saints and sages, or all of them!—for what you need? I'm not talking about "Oh-lord-won't-you-buy-me-a-Mercedes-Benz-my-friends-all-drive-Porsches-I-must-make-amends" kind of asking. I'm talking about asking for what you really *need*, whether you're ready to meet the love of your life or you're just trying to get to a book club meeting and you're late and it's dark and you've lost your way and you don't have the hostess's number with you and your cell phone's battery is dead anyway ... and it's snowing.

Ask to be shown the way.

"Show me the way" is one of the Holy Pig Farmer's favorite prayers. He uses it for everything. Show me the way to get this medicine into the ailing eye of this spooky cow of mine. (The cow instantly went into a sort of trance and held still long enough for Lory to doctor its eye. Then it came to and went nuts-as-usual, but if Lory hadn't had some heavenly help—"heavenly" meaning right here, not up there—that cow would have gone blind.) Or show me the way to help my troubled brother. My friend Angie Altamirano is convinced that prayers said on behalf of others get top priority.

"Show me the way" is also the prayer the Holy Pig Farmer and I suggest you use when you're trying to find your own spiritual path. Show me the way, O God, from where I am right now back to you.

ÉCLAT

For those who like fun reminders, herewith is my own little acronym for a comprehensive spiritual daily practice. It happens to spell a very cool French word (what do you expect from a travel writer!): ÉCLAT ... which, I'm pleased to report, means both "to smash to smithereens" and "brilliant radiance." Could there be a more perfect recipe for smashing your sense of separateness (ego) from the Divine so that your holy radiance can shine forth? Here it is:

1. **E**nter (into communion with the Divine)
2. **C**lear (yourself as deeply as you can of all negativity)
3. **L**ove (the Divine with all your heart—Yogananda reminds us that our love is the only thing God doesn't have and the only thing God wants)
4. **A**sk (for what you and those dear to you genuinely need)
5. **T**hank (the Divine for everything you already have)

Practice **ÉCLAT** every day like brushing your teeth, the more ceremonial the better, and watch your spiritual life bloom with fresh brilliance as your sense of a separate self explodes.

Bend an Ear

I remember reading somewhere that Bertrand Russell once claimed that the universe bends to a strong will. Note that he didn't say God bends to a strong will, but God will bend an ear, and thus do we begin the divine dialogue that can, if we let it, sustain us for the rest of our days.

Not a bad idea. As Bertrand Russell also said: "In the part of this universe that we know there is great injustice, and often the good suffer, and often the wicked prosper, and one hardly knows which of those is the more annoying."

Annoying doesn't begin to cover it. This place can be a nightmare. Who among us hasn't lost someone to cancer? Who hasn't watched a child suffer and felt our heart turn inside out? Who hasn't been so lonely, so terrified, so unsure, so defeated, so damn disappointed that you don't even want to get up in the morning?

The Eastern masters like to remind us that pain is an illusion, to which I always think: "That's easy for you to say, you completely enlightened person, you!" Eckhart Tolle is more practical: your pain, he concedes, is real to you.

Rande has lived with her husband's physical pain for more than twenty years. Glen has fibromyalgia, a mysterious and excruciatingly painful chronic condition that seems to involve severe nerve damage. They have, of course, tried everything. Nothing helps. Glen's pain continues and it is real. And there you have it—a genuinely terrible situation from which there seems to be no relief in sight. Who knows why Glen is suffering like this? But here's what they've done with this awful reality: Glen has turned to the spiritual with a devotion Yogananda would applaud. He has his teacher. He meditates any time he can. His inner vision is blossoming like a cherry tree in spring. He sees light beings now too. He has taken this outrageous karmic card fate has dealt him and is riding it like a missile into the heart of God. And he has confirmed that he never would have done all this if it weren't for the pain. Of course, everyone living with chronic pain will be free of his or her ailing body some day, and the essential spiritual part will move on.

EITHER ORB

How do we know this is true? If you own a digital camera you probably already have all the evidence you need. Go take a look at your photos taken with a flash. See those odd little perfectly round things floating in the air? Those are light beings. Or spirit emanations. The two philosopher-scientists who have studied these light beings most thoroughly, Míceál Ledwith and Klaus Heinemann, simply call them "orbs."

It's true. By some thrilling twist of technology, digital cameras—the cheaper the better—record a broader part of the light spectrum than film cameras ever have. Broader than most of us are able to see because our brains filter out this part of the light spectrum. Some of us see orbs "popping" in our peripheral vision. Others see them all over the place ... because they are.

My other soul brother, Richard A. Herman (note the initials), took a digital picture in our guestroom one night, and a set of seven orbs appeared in the photo, lined up ceiling to floor like a visual representation of the chakras we've all heard about, the energetic centers of the body. On a trip to Washington, D.C., a few years ago, Tom and I visited the Lincoln Memorial one evening only to find Lincoln sitting there in the dark because something was wrong with the lighting. So we were obliged to use a flash. I was amazed to find orbs floating all over my photos, especially a large, bright one sitting on the shoulder of a cute little African American boy who was there with a group of his classmates.

But I've never seen more orbs in one place than in the pictures someone took (with a flash) and sent out over the Internet of Barack Obama and his family at Millennium Park in Chicago on November 4, 2008, the night he was elected forty-fourth president of the United States. Orbs, you see, are drawn to goodness and joy. They especially show up in photographs of people gathered together to celebrate something. Pretty hard evidence of the essential goodness of Creation, don't you think?

Here's another interesting piece of evidence. During her Spirituality 101 series, Oprah aired footage of one of her favorite previous guests, a fellow who had survived a fiery plane crash. While recounting this terrifying experience, he told Oprah, much to her astonishment, that because he was sitting in the back of the plane, and the plane was on fire at its middle, he was obliged to watch his fellow passengers be incinerated before his eyes. But. He also saw what he called "auras" leave the passengers' bodies as they burned—those were orbs. He noted that some were brighter than others. And he understood that this meant that those with the brighter auras/orbs had done more good in their lives than those people with dull auras/orbs. With such vivid evidence right in front of him, the man vowed right then to do everything he could to make his own aura/orb as bright as he possibly could before it was his time to leave his body. Of course, he hasn't been afraid of death since.

FOR GOODNESS SAKE

A word about goodness. In *Mere Christianity*, C. S. Lewis says we are programmed to want goodness. Even the most sadistic among us, who willingly do harm to others, reap good feelings from their misdeeds, not bad. As do the people the Holy Pig Farmer calls crisis addicts, those unfortunate folks who have bought into their ego's game of keeping them upset so their Very Little Self remains on center stage, which gives them the constant drip of drama their egos crave … and it feels *good*. If, Lewis reasons, all of this is so, then does it not follow that the force that created us is also good?

So, one way or the other, we want goodness. Mostly, we want the big things. We want love. We want health. We want purposeful work. What I can say without a doubt is that the more we turn to goodness—true, undistorted goodness—the more goodness arrives. Or, more simply: choose goodness and it will choose you.

How do I know?

Because that's what I did when I had been stripped down to nothing. No love (just the awful bag of hurt that was Harrison), no work (thanks to 9/11), and face-to-face with my big secret terror of being alone. The pain I felt made me, for the first time, understand why people turn to alcohol and drugs. But I made the most important decision of my life, and turned to God instead. God bless the millions of alcoholics who drop the bottle and turn wholeheartedly to AA and other spiritually based recovery programs. They are nothing but heroes.

I know about the power of goodness because when the most fearsome Gray One accosted me in my bedroom, even it was no match for the saints I called upon. "The Lord is even behind the evil," Yogananda told his students, handing them the single most powerful secret weapon any personal war on terror has ever known.

And I know because, as someone who likes results and evidence, I now have a treasure chest of both: the full-force love of a spectacular and devoted husband, an extended family I adore, and even the home of my dreams, and you are reading the purposeful work I have wanted to share with all my heart for many years.

I also know because of something I've been given beyond the comforts of the material world that, in fact, rests like two perfect golden eggs in that sweet, sweet nest: my absolute need for stillness, quiet, and peace, a near-miracle for any former peripatetic world adventurer, and my constant and automatic desire to give to and serve others, which is precisely what the Holy Pig Farmer means when he says we are here to bless the world. This, I believe, is what happens when we are fortunate enough to internalize my father-in-law's truth, hard-won from the belly of war: that we are all literally brothers and sisters. These twin rewards of the spirit are the most valuable and telling of all, because these days spiritual talk is cheap, and actions scream louder than bumper stickers.

To find yourself incapable of anything but being in service is the surest sign of spiritual progress. And I'm not talking about martyrdom; I'm talking about a stream of joyful offerings flowing unfettered from your own heart because you are capable of nothing else. You will find your delight in helping others boundless, whether it's letting someone else have the parking space you wanted or in broader callings, maybe joining the Peace Corps or devoting your life to securing national health care or adopting a special needs child. And, by the way, David Relin will straight up tell you "the people who have devoted themselves to helping others are the happiest people I know."

But mostly I know about the essential power of goodness because I experienced how people reacted to the me-who-wasn't-there that holy day when my Little Mind fell away and the I-who-I-know-as-I was nothing but a human-shaped piece of divine awareness walking through a crowded airport. There wasn't even enough Little Mind left to want goodness for my "self," as the I-who-I-knew-as-I was already adrift in the abject bliss of what already is. Yet every single person at Portland International Airport who noticed this non-me either helped "me" or smiled at "me," and even played heavenly piano music just for "me." And that, I know, is what Yogananda meant when he told his students that they had no idea of the bliss he lived in all the time.

You Cannot Fake This

You cannot decide you will suddenly be holy-holy-holy so you can get people to pay attention to you. Not this kind of attention. They won't. People know. The old tricks of the ego don't work here.

What you can do is what Oprah's guest did as he watched orbs dull and bright leave the bodies going up in holy smoke in front of him. You can indeed decide to side with goodness. And thereby side with God, which is only an "o" away from "good" anyhow. (How many hints do we need?)

From the sweet quietude of that holiest of decisions, if you then ask with all your heart that your spiritual path, your life work, and the answers to your deepest longings to be revealed to you, and agree to "wait patiently for the Lord," you absolutely will be shown the way.

Amen.

BENEDICTION

Go forth into the world in peace; Be of good courage; Hold fast to that which is good; Render to no person evil for evil. Strengthen the faint-hearted; Support the weak; Heal the afflicted. Honor all people, Love and serve the Lord, Rejoicing in the power of the Spirit.

THE REVEREND HENRY W. ANDERSEN

Every saint who has penetrated to the core of Reality has testified that a divine universal plan exists and that it is beautiful and full of joy.

PARAMAHANSA YOGANANDA, *AUTOBIOGRAPHY OF A YOGI*

Spirituality means that no matter what happens to you, you're going to be okay.

OPRAH WINFREY

Acknowledgments

Any story that rolls through nearly two decades had a lot of help along the way. First thanks go to poet-philosopher Noah benShea, a clear reed through whom God made prophetic music with the earliest inkling that *Roll Around Heaven* might be waiting in the cosmic wings, and to our mutual pal Lawrence Grobel, an interviewer's interviewer, who began the dialogue. The story, of course, wouldn't have happened if my cool coffee trader pal Jim Stewart hadn't sent his pig farmer spiritual coach Lory Misel into my fallow clod-filled pasture from which he could catapult me onto much higher ground. One can only blink in wonder at the benevolent force that set these events in motion and that runs through the Holy Pig Farmer like a river of glory. No fence could contain the awe, devotion, and gratitude I have for this true American spiritual master.

It was my eternal soul sister and willing Ethel-to-my-Lucy, Rande Anderson, who confirmed that something was astir: may our split souls ride parallel light waves forever, and may we be able to eat all the French pastries we want next time around.

Chic, Karen, and sweet Julien Streetman, what fun it was to play the sacred messenger in your family trilogy! Edgar Cayce says that when old soul mates meet again they both laugh their heads off and that's exactly what Greg Tatman and I did the night we met, which says it all. Val Brooks

arrived on the scene next, and who could ask for a smarter *and* more talented Marilyn Monroe of an Enlightened Witness? Got questions about
Roll Around Heaven? Go See Val! Go See Val! Go See Val! A golden chalice
of yahoos to our pal Jan Eliot for creating our very own *Stone Soup* comic
strip! Zap! Bam! Wow!! How could the inimitable Deepak Chopra have
known the karmic importance of our divinely appointed lunch date? My
beloved Red Moons rose full and bright later that same year, a merry literary family that sustains me to this day. Add to this embarrassment of literary
riches Book Nest, the No Ink Book Club, and the Bush's Pasture Park Book
Club, and my writing world overfloweth. Our dear friends and fellow choir
members at Central Presbyterian Church in Eugene, Oregon, remain more
important to Tom and me than they know. They turned our inner-choir
courtship into a heavenly romantic comedy with the best sound track ever!

    Girlfriends, of course, are the Superglue of any woman's universe. In
order of appearance: Smartest Apple, how grand to see you again after all
our long monastic lifetimes. Kyoto in Cherry Blossom Time—without
shaved heads—here we come! Extreme applause goes to Nancy Deal-
Whitacre, my always spot-on alto-buddy, and to my honorary niece Sarah
Deal: what divine vegan baking sessions await us! Barb, Shawna, and Molly
McKeown, Mary Beth and Mary Kay Ballantyne, there just aren't enough
style points to do your glamorous clan justice. And who but Barb would
accompany me on both a Norwegian grouse hunt *and* into the Borneo jungle looking like an Anthropologie model the entire time? A Brontë bravo to
Marci Gordon, my own personal hats-and-china sister: hooray! Gayle Landt
(and then dear Ainura) arrived next on a cloud of berry pie and peace:
Mother of God, may we never forget our Galway giggle attacks with our
beloved Alpha Stompers navigating and at the wheel: stay left! With the arrival
of my Sisters of MM, Joan Martinson and JoAnne Kohler, and the surprise
twenty-years-later resurrection of the Buddha Poodles—Martinique, Laurelai,
Angelina, Jannet, and Lucy-poo—my inner goddess circle was complete. May
the force of Amma Sri Karunamayi, Divine Mother reincarnate,
be with us always.

    Soul brothers abound, too, and I am well blessed by my fine fishing
brother, Guido "Green Butt" Rahr (note the first three letters) and the joyful

noise of Walking Man Bruce Stutz, English rose sniffer Terry Hershey, whirling hammer dervish Lance Deal, Techo-Espresso Whiz Marty "Machina" McKeown, New Orleans piano maestro Dr. Martin Jones (followed by dear Jackson!), and, with a motorcycle roar and a choir of adoring angels, my hero and role model, David Oliver Relin. The magical appearance of Richard A. Herman brought me my business partner divine: may our dream of the RAH Foundation live long and prosper and teach thousands of India's children how to read. Let the blessèd vision of Bhutanese Buddhist master Ven. Lama Karma Namgyel lead us on to the Light.

Bhutan remains the center of my holy international community, home of my Bhutanese extended family: Ugyen, Yangzom, and Yuthok Rinzin and Karma Choden. Kadinchey! John Philip and Ali Newell remain squarely in my Celtic heart as two of the finest spiritual teachers Scotland ever produced. Norway would be just another cool destination without the hunters' hilarity of Knut Arne "Gjems Bond," Bertil "Yohn Wayne" Kainulainen, Spirit Brother Tore Willassen, and the Goddess Ingrid Schumway. How can I thank Heyam ali Mustafa and the Daughters of Dubai for welcoming me into their inner sanctuary? May we all take tea together by the Gulf of Oman again soon, Inshallah. Always, I raise a glass of 2005 Domaine Drouhin Pinot Laurène to my petite amie, winemaker Veronique Drouhin, the rose of Bourgogne and the Oregon Wine Country.

On the home front, a lifetime of spiritual vitamin C goes to Carmen, Angie, Marianne and Mary whose laughter fills these rooms with joy. Endless Namastes are due Dr. Laura LaDue for care beyond the house-call of duty. Naturally, everyone we called directed us to Glen Heatherington, America's most mystical handyman: here's to when coffee cups fly! And a special toe wiggle to Ashley Criner, an angel who gives the world's best French pedicures at Bella Vida Day Spa.

On the work front, a bookload of gratitude to Beyond Words publishers Richard Cohn and especially to Cynthia Black, a fearless visionary who sees "new genres" where others see blockades, and to their mighty staff, including Marie Hix, Danielle Marshall, Devon Smith for his handsome, inspired interior design, and to the unsinkable Lindsay Brown, who can track a typo across a crowded manuscript with bloodhound aplomb while coolly juggling the countless other tasks involved in creating books—all publishing houses should have a Lindsay! A heartfelt thank-you to the delightful team at Atria/Simon & Schuster, brilliantly led by publisher Judith Curr, promoted by Kathleen Schmidt, facilitated by Kitt Reckord, and illustrated by Senior Art Director Jeanne Lee, who assigned *Roll Around Heaven* to ace designer Janet Perr, who stepped into the soul of the book and miraculously produced the cover of my dreams. Hallelujah! Untold gratitude goes to my slam-dunk personal publicist, Courtney Dunham, founding owner of Dunham Media, Publicity and Representation, for her purity of heart and absolute devotion to *RAH* and its message. My dear and glorious agent Rita Rosenkranz, how far we've come: from swimming with salmon to flying with pigs! *RAH* simply wouldn't *be* without your steady hand and inspired wisdom. Thank you.

Family support, of course, reigns supreme. It was my beloved parents, Mary and Robert Meeker, who gave me the Little House in the Big Woods when my time came to set out on my own Heroine's Journey, an enchantment that included countless nature spirits and a whole lot of rising trout and diving osprey, powerful energies that anchored me in the holy natural forever. I have no idea how to properly thank them for this and all their other selfless gifts. Does any child, ever? Aunt Katy, you visited us just in time and I know your bright spirit, and Mother's—not to mention my Daddy's!!—are having a great time watching all of this unfold from above. My sisters, Va-Va and Heah-Heah, and their devoted otherhalves, Scott Wilson and John Beal, you are my ever-anchors—Bozorees Unite! Jesse, Amber, Little Jessica, Eli, Ben, Celia, Bronwyn, Maddie, Nate, Isabel, Sarah, Gerry, and Rory, a thousand alabaster jars filled with six million rose petals wouldn't express my love for you all, and you know it. Beau-père and Belle-mère extraordinaire Hank and Mary Andersen, my totally cool sistahs-in-law Jen Andersen-Popp and Barb Chandler, bro-in-law Reverend Tim Hart-Andersen, and the entire Andersen Clan, holy moly, what a powerhouse, what luck, and what fun! And Tom. My miraculous, hilarious husband, perfect Dagwood to my Blondie, and love of my life, no one knows our story better. May we roll around heaven until we fly, fly away into that sweet by-and-by together forever. Amen.

ROLL AROUND HEAVEN
A READERS CLUB GUIDE

This readers club guide for Roll Around Heaven *includes an introduction, discussion questions, ideas for enhancing your book club, and a Q&A with author Jessica Maxwell. The suggested questions are intended to help your reading group find new and interesting angles and topics for your discussion. We hope that these ideas will enrich your conversation and increase your enjoyment of the book.*

INTRODUCTION

When a startling vision of her father's face appears in the sky soon after his death, travel journalist Jessica Maxwell begins questioning her own spirituality. She soon becomes drawn into the bright light of spiritual reality by a "Holy Pig Farmer" she meets through a friend.

Roll Around Heaven chronicles nearly two decades of Maxwell's spiritual adventures, as she travels the globe on her "down-to-earth" magazine-writing assignments only to end up receiving valuable insights into the world's great faiths. Spiced with humor and rich with original flair, Maxwell's adventures will inspire you to embrace the power of the divine in your own life, and the epilogue is designed to help you do just that.

QUESTIONS AND TOPICS FOR DISCUSSION

1. At the beginning of her journey, Jessica Maxwell and her sister see an image of their recently deceased father appear in the sky, despite living a thousand miles apart. What was your initial reaction to this event? How did your reaction to this compare to that of the Holy Pig Farmer, Lory Misel? Of Deepak Chopra? Of the Mystic Golfer?

2. Did your reactions to Maxwell's visions change as the memoir progressed and these supernatural events became more frequent? What qualities did her visions share?

3. Maxwell runs into Deepak Chopra while eating lunch on a business trip. Later, during his talk, Chopra touches on a personal experience of hers she hadn't mentioned to him and she begins to weep. She later sees a black-market copy of his book when she is traveling in Mumbai, India. Do these incidents signal fate to you? Or are they coincidences?

4. On page 51, Maxwell argues that "[i]t didn't take long to realize that it's not only our thoughts that disconnect us from grace. Sometimes it really is the constant messages from our personal environment." Do you agree with her? What do you imagine disconnects or distracts you from spirituality?

5. Describe Maxwell's evolving relationship with church, beginning with the first time she attends with her friend Greg Tatman (see page 83). What made her averse to church as an institution? What ultimately changes her mind?

6. Consider the different versions of the "Golden Rule" on pages 127–128. How does this collection of quotes represent Maxwell's feelings about religion? On Western and Eastern thought? Does the author differentiate between "religiosity" and "spirituality"?

7. Throughout the book, Maxwell's willingness to pursue adventure with an open mind connects her to many people she might not have met otherwise. How much of her journey's success do you attribute to her personality? What personal qualities help her the most?

8. What does Maxwell learn from her romantic relationships? How does her self-awareness and increased spirituality contribute to her relationship with Tom? According to Maxwell, how important is it to have the same spiritual understanding as one's partner?

9. In *Roll Around Heaven,* all of Maxwell's spiritual teachers are male: the Holy Pig Farmer, Yogananda, Greg Tatman, Deepak Chopra. Yet many of the visions, or energies, that Maxwell witnesses in the book have what she describes as feminine qualities. What would you say are "spiritual qualities"? How do spiritual qualities challenge our stereotypical ideas of gender? What do Maxwell's best girlfriends, Rande and Val, provide her with as she lives the story?

10. During Deepak Chopra's talk on page 105 he says, "Detach from the past . . . it's not here." Maxwell considers this idea a "shout-out" to something the Holy Pig Farmer had said in one of their conversations about connecting Western Science with Eastern Wisdom. Did you notice any other connections between Eastern and Western thought or spirituality in the course of her journey?

11. Describe the significance of the book's title. What conceptions of heaven, or hell, did you encounter in the book?

12. What advice did you find the most applicable in this memoir? How did this book inspire you?

A CONVERSATION WITH JESSICA MAXWELL

1. *Do you think that self-discovery requires the insights of others?*

Absolutely! As the Holy Pig Farmer says, "you can't do it alone." Eckhart's log next to a burning log metaphor for the student/ spiritual-teacher relationship itself is about relationship, which is the first step in getting us beyond our sense of a separate self, the first move beyond ego. It's no accident that narcissistic people are incapable of forming deep and lasting relationships with others; they're too obsessed with dogpaddling around inside their own heads!

What do you make of this paradox?

Once you realize that there really is a Little You and a Big You, then you understand that "self-discovery" is actually "Self" discovery, and then the paradox vanishes. One of the big problems of psychological therapy is that it can—done improperly—get people addicted to thinking about their Little Selves, rather than leading them into an ultimately liberating—and healthy! —awareness of the spiritual, or for the more concrete among us, into what modern physics has been trying to teach us for over 100 years!

2. *Throughout the memoir, you include photos and various docu-ments, evidence of the incredible experiences you describe. Why did you choose to include these personal items?*

To help make the experiences credible! I know how wild some of them are—I mean, to have a little puppy bring you a business card when you'd looked everywhere for one? A puppy? It just sounds crazy, but there he was with that beat-up card in his mouth. I thought seeing those little milk-teeth holes in the actual card—which I keep framed on my desk, by the way—would help put the reader right there in my room with me. Absolutely incredulous that yet another astonishing "everyday miracle" was happening again.

This is nonfiction at its most vulnerable, chronicling the ethereal nature of spiritual reality. I can't imagine a better way to concretize the squirrely nature of the spiritual than including the best possible hard "evidence" that these events took place. All of it only underscores the main point of *Roll Around Heaven:* that the spiritual realm is real and it is very wise to do something about this fact. Plus ... it's fun! Who wouldn't want to see Hank's Hat or that box of English soap I bought for Tom before I'd even met him? Everyone loves a scrapbook!

3. *This is your first spiritual memoir. Was it difficult to write about yourself in this way and to include your private, intimate thoughts? How did it differ from your other adventure writing? What did you learn about yourself from writing this memoir?*

I've always been drawn to write about events I've experienced or witnessed myself, as is the tradition of first-person narrative nonfiction. I'm a "put your hand in the hand of the man" type. But it took years to fully own this spiritual adventure of mine. It happened in stages.

First, I just thought it was fun, and I was completely intrigued by the weirdness of it all. It really was, and continues to be, an absolute adventure: You never know what's going to happen next. But it was Rande who helped me begin to take it seriously and who told me that telling this story was my "real work." Still, it took many more years for me to be comfortable with the very subject of spirituality. So I sort of ended up telling people "you gotta hear this one!" in one breath and then apologizing for the spiritual aspects of it all in the next. And I could hardly say the word "Jesus" without sputtering. I still remember the day, sometime in 2004, that I knew I had completely accepted and internalized the spiritual as the bottom line and was 100 percent comfortable saying so. It wasn't all holy-holy-holy or precious or "I've got the answer!" It just simply was. And I knew "it" was utterly integrated into the natural structure of everyday life—no more embarrassment or apologies needed. That was the moment that I knew I was finally fully ready to write *Roll Around Heaven*. It will, of course, be interesting to see how my magazine editors react to the book. Coming out of the spiritual closet like this does run the risk of my never being given another adventure assignment again ... unless it's taking a spaceship to Mars (which I'm far too claustrophobic to do!). Or maybe someone will give me a spiritual adventure column—my dream assignment!

As to how writing *Roll Around Heaven* differed from my other adventure writing, it didn't. I really have told the stories in *Roll Around Heaven* exactly the way I tell any adventure story: just the way they happened. The single disclaimer is the name of Harrison Brandt—that's not his real name for obvious reasons. When I was musing about what to call this guy, the last name "Brandt" came flying into my head, and when I looked up the origin of the name it was absolutely and spookily perfect.

All in all, nothing could have been better training for writing this book than my years as an in-the-field adventure writer. You have to be an ace reporter and as much of a master storyteller as your talent allows—and that takes practice. You also have to be a fearless devotee of the unexpected, which is what adventure writing is all about.

What writing RAH—as family members and friends call *Roll Around Heaven*—ultimately taught me is how genuinely and deeply committed I have become to the spiritual over the years. That transformation, given the screaming deficit with which I started this journey, is the most remarkable "RAH Effect" of all. This is no spiritual one-night stand; it is a profound love match and a lifelong marriage to the spiritual aspects of life, which as physicists and saints well know, are the dancing forces at the holy heart of everything.

4. *What personal qualities have helped you the most on your journey? How much of your success do you attribute to these qualities?*

My lifelong love of treasure hunts! I just love following signs and figuring out where to go next. I suppose that's a form of both fearlessness and faith. It's true that I've never been afraid of the world and, in fact, am deeply in love with it, warts and all. (Though you can hardly get me into an elevator—I do have some fears!!) But a basic attitude of trust really helps. And I came in with this.

Somehow I've always known that God was conspiring in my favor—though I didn't know what "God" was. God, of course, is indeed conspiring in everyone's favor, as hard as that is to believe sometimes, and I can only attribute my knowing this to many lives filled with a lot of spiritual hard labor in monasteries somewhere, because I sure didn't earn my spiritual awareness this time around. I polished it like crazy, but I really did come in with it already in full bloom.

My job in this life was to figure out what the heck spirituality was and then tell you all about it! "Likes to share" would be another helpful trait, along with a rather incorrigible sense of wonder and the classic sense of responsibility of a first-born child. I cannot begin to describe how absolutely responsible I felt about getting this story out there. I carried it on my back for more than ten years and ran into more dead ends than you can shake a giant wooden cross at. Honestly, I didn't relax until RAH was safely with the right publisher at last.

If this was God's little entrance exam for me, well, I sure as heck hope She/He/It is finally convinced of my devotion. So I guess we should add "mosquito-like persistence" to the list.

5. *Was it difficult to capture in words the visions that you saw through-out the course of the book?*

No more than trying to put anything I witness in words. I had to think about it a bit more because I didn't have the usual frames of contemporary reference to draw on—this is new stuff! But that's part of the craft of writing. I don't think describing a light being was any more of a challenge than describing an Amazonian pea-cock bass, a fish so wild looking it inspired me to write that "if an evil wizard turned Cirque du Soleil into a fish, it would look a lot like a peacock bass."

You have to use your noggin. And all your senses. Really, I am very concrete. I like form, color, pattern, scent, and taste, and I'm very sensitive to the relationships among them all. I like variety, therefore, the world's cultures—and faiths—fascinate me to no end. I love people and make friends easily, so "foreigners" never seem foreign. I like things to move—hence my love of travel—and I'm very aware of rhythm—I love to dance! I see humor everywhere al-most to a fault, and like Noah benShea, I take my work, not myself, seriously. Obviously, I love language. You throw in Scottish Second Sight and you've got yourself one natural-born literary, spiritual adventure writer with an eye for the visual, an ear for dialogue, and a weakness for the lighter side who loves a story that moves along at a good clip. *Et voilà!* You're rolling around heaven!!

6. *In your conversation with the daughters of Islam, you were recom-mended some books on Islam so you could better understand their religion. What books would you recommend to someone who has fin-ished your book and is ready to "Suit Up and Show Up" but doesn't know where to start?*

Yogananda's *Autobiography of a Yogi* is a must. Not because he was a Hindu, but because his is the story of an authentic master who wanted nothing but to know God. *Karunamayi: A Biography* is an